Does Religious Education Work?

Also available from Bloomsbury

Transforming Religious Education: Beliefs and Values under Scrutiny, Brian Gates

MasterClass in Religious Education: Transforming Teaching and Learning, Liam Gearon

Is Religious Education Possible?: A Philosophical Investigation, Michael Hand

Teaching Religious Education: Researchers in the Classroom, Julian Stern

Anglican Church School Education: Moving Beyond the First Two Hundred Years, edited by Howard J. Worsley

Does Religious Education Work?

A Multi-dimensional Investigation

James C. Conroy, David Lundie, Robert A. Davis,
Vivienne Baumfield, L. Philip Barnes, Tony Gallagher,
Kevin Lowden, Nicole Bourque and Karen Wenell

Bloomsbury T&T Clark
An Imprint of Bloomsbury Publishing Plc

B L O O M S B U R Y
LONDON • NEW DELHI • NEW YORK • SYDNEY

Bloomsbury T&T Clark
An imprint of Bloomsbury Publishing Plc

Imprint previously known as T&T Clark

50 Bedford Square	1385 Broadway
London	New York
WC1B 3DP	NY 10018
UK	USA

www.bloomsbury.com

BLOOMSBURY, T&T CLARK and the Diana logo are trademarks of Bloomsbury Publishing Plc

First published 2013
Paperback edition published 2015

British Library Cataloguing-in-Publication Data
A catalogue record for this book is available from the British Library.

ISBN: HB: 978-1-441-12799-0
PB: 978-1-474-23465-8
ePDF: 978-1-441-15069-1

Library of Congress Cataloging-in-Publication Data
Conroy, James C.
Does religious education work?: a multi-dimensional investigation/James C. Conroy,
David Lundie, Robert A. Davis, Vivienne Baumfield, L. Philip Barnes,
Tony Gallagher, Kevin Lowden, Nicole Bourque and Karen Wenell.
pages cm
Includes bibliographical references and index.
ISBN 978-1-4411-2799-0 – ISBN 978-1-4411-5069-1 – ISBN 978-1-4411-8038-4
1. Religious education–Great Britain–Philosophy. 2. Religious education–
Great Britain–Methodology. I. Title.
LC410.G7C66 2013
207'.5–dc23
2013016925

Typeset by Newgen Imaging Systems Pvt Ltd, Chennai, India

Contents

Acknowledgements   vi

Introduction   1

Part I   Methodological and Structural Questions

1   Methodological Considerations: Learning from the Inside   9
2   The Strange Position of Education in Religion in
       Contemporary Political Culture   35
3   The Complexities of UK Policy and Practice   63
4   Conceptual Questions, Confusions and Challenges   85

Part II   The Substance of Religious Education

5   Citizenship and Committed Pluralism:
       The Place of the 'Other' in RE's Social and Civic Aims   117
6   Religious Education and the Nature of Texts   141
7   Stories We Tell Ourselves: Making Sense of Religious
       Education in Communities of Practice   169
8   Religious Education and Student Perspectives   189

Conclusions: Imagining and Re-imagining Religious Education   219

Appendices   227
Bibliography   251
Index   265

Acknowledgements

This volume presents some of the findings of and reflections upon a three-year research project funded by the UK Arts and Humanities Research Council and the Economic and Social Research Council as part of their *Religion and Society* programme. The programme director was Professor Linda Woodhead and I should like to pay particular tribute to her inventiveness, graciousness and unfailing generosity of spirit in leading the programme. Together with her administrative team at Lancaster University, Peta Ainsworth and Rebecca Cato, she was always encouraging and constructive, and their collective organization of a wide range of engaging and intellectually stimulating conferences, that offered both professional and public forums for the sharing and interrogation of our work, was enormously helpful in assisting the team in refining our ideas. The work here has been refined and honed (perhaps not sufficiently) through presentations at a large number of national and international conferences, lectures and meetings.

The comments and responses of many colleagues have been enormously helpful. I am particularly grateful to our friend and colleague, Professor Robert Jackson and his team at the *Warwick Religious Education Research Unit*, the Association of University Lecturers in Religious Education, the Philosophy of Education Society of Great Britain, the Association for Moral Education, the International Seminar on Religious Education and Values, British Educational Research Association and the American Educational Research Association. Additionally members of the team have given papers at Oxford University, Fordham University, Utrecht University. Professional presentations have included the National Association of Teachers of Religious Education, the Association of Teachers of Religious Education in Scotland, the John Marcus O'Sullivan Summer School in Ireland, Cornwall Standing Advisory Council for Religious Education, Education Scotland, Victorian Association of Religious Educators. To all those involved in the organizing of these myriad events we are enormously grateful for their questions and challenges, all of which have assisted us in our deliberations. We are indebted to colleagues at the REC, most especially Professor Brian Gates, and colleagues across the United Kingdom who have made comment on our work, including Liam Gearon, Julian Stern, and Mark Chater.

Paul Gilfillan worked for a short time as the RA on the project before taking up a lecturing position at Queen Margaret University. We are grateful to Paul for his assistance in establishing the project. Equally, we would like to thank Christine Reoch, our indefatigable project administrator and Gavin Duffy, who assisted greatly in our work in Northern Ireland. We would have had enormous difficulty in securing the services of the schools without the assistance of Ed Boyle in London and Ruth Leitch in Belfast; we are grateful to both of them.

Above all these we are grateful to the schools, the teachers and the students. It is courageous indeed to subject your school and your practices to such close scrutiny and we do not underestimate the importance of their contributions to our reflections. Not only are they people of courage and generosity, they are professionals who, despite the very real challenges they face on a daily basis, persevere with great fortitude and resilience.

James C. Conroy

2013

Introduction

In 2007 the UK Arts and Humanities Research Council and the Economic and Social Research Council established a major *Religion and Society* research programme, to offer

> a unique opportunity to engage publics, religious groups, policy makers, charities, creative and cultural sectors and others in dialogue about the role of religion in society and it is envisaged that many projects will have outcomes of significance for these groups to explore as part of their Religion and Society programme. (AHRC/ESRC 2007)

The project team for this particular investigation comprised scholars from the University of Glasgow, King's College London and Queen's University Belfast.

This volume is one of the fruits of that endeavour. It is an attempt to excavate what Hopkins would have called the *inscape* of Religious Education as a social and pedagogical practice. Drawing on Duns Scotus, the nineteenth-century poet coined the word 'inscape' in his attempt to point to the *haecceitas* of things: that conjunction of characteristics that marked out and differentiated the particularity and uniqueness of things. Here we deploy and extend the notion of inscape as a heuristic that enabled us to unearth the nooks and crannies of RE. What follows in this study is one attempt to understand how the subject of RE is shaped 'from the inside' – what distinguishes it from other social and pedagogical practices within the school, what its particular characteristics are, and how they come together. There have, over the years, been many studies of religious attitudes and attachments; equally there have been numerous scholarly reflections laying claim to a normative description of how Religious Education should be. This one is somewhat different and, we hope, complementary to these efforts.

If it is somewhat different, it is also a somewhat odd volume, bringing together, as it does, the authorial intentions, impulses and lenses of a broad-based team, drawn from anthropology, education, psychology and theology. It is odd, also, in attempting to bring together a broad spectrum of research methods to understand the *inscape* of a social practice that is striated with contradictions, confusions and conflict; it is odd in its attempt to sew together ethnographic and social description with normative judgements about what constitutes an appropriate pedagogical engagement. Of course, education is ineluctably a normative activity and, as we will demonstrate as we traverse the terrain of the classroom, Religious Education is itself shaped in this normativity. It is conceivable that one might ask purely descriptive questions of its practice. What is not conceivable, however, is that a question such as the one that forms the title, not only of this book, but of the project of which it is a partial record, can be treated in any straightforwardly descriptive manner. To ask, 'does X work?' entails asking what would count as working and, since the thing to which the question addresses itself is a normative practice, the answer can hardly avoid normative considerations. Given the diverse commitments and interests of the research team, it is hard to escape the claims of normativity. But what is interesting is the way in which these claims played off against each other in helping us refine both the interrogation and the analysis.

While resources, photographs, displays, recordings, regulations, contextual data, texts, examinations, focus groups, questionnaires and interviews all play their part in helping us build up a picture of RE as a social practice, the centrepiece of the study here is the ethnography. It is the time spent not only in the classrooms of these 24 schools but in staff rooms and subject bases, in the corridors and over coffee that provide a subtle context for unearthing attachments and dispositions. In analysing these stories we did not impose a pre-formed heuristic on the material, squeezing it into already-determined shapes, but tried to allow the material to speak for itself. The consequence of this was that the shape of the chapters follows, to a large extent, the shape of the material as it presented itself. As we move through our descriptions and analyses we move from policy analysis to thematic description, and from there to certain *aporias* that allow us to question taken-for-granted assumptions and assessments.

While the particular focus of this study was on Year 10 pupils, those who were rising 16-year-olds, the research also took into account the life of the school and Religious Education taught to other year groups. The choice to look at Religious Education at the last stage of compulsory education reflected our concern to have a sense of what the experience might look like as a resource for young people moving into the spaces of adulthood. In order to *write the inscape* of RE we had to interrogate as many sites as possible that had a bearing on the daily practices and experiences in the classroom. Central to this effort was the decision to sew together the complex fabric of policymaking, conceptual framing, resources, teacher normativity and student attitudes and dispositions. In practice, this included (but is not exhausted by) the following engagements and strategies, which range across the descriptive, analytic and normative:

- Exploring current definitions of Religious Education and their contested character;
- Analysing what the many actors involved in Religious Education considered as constituting effectiveness in the domain of Religious Education. This included educational, social, cultural, theological conceptions of effectiveness (and the tensions between these). We also explored the varied ways in which effectiveness has been determined by different interest groups;
- Designing an ethnographic approach that might unearth teachers' and students' beliefs about and experiences of both religion and Religious Education;
- Exploring the experience and effectiveness of Religious Education in varied school settings across the United Kingdom;
- Building capacity in a more nuanced critical assessment of religious beliefs, attachments and education. This capacity building embraces a sustainable network of both academic researchers and teacher practitioners;
- Offering enhanced resources to policy makers and practitioners for the provision of more informed decision-making in relation to educational planning around Religious Education and religious schooling;
- Enhancing the now substantial public conversation on whether religious schools contribute to social cohesion and diversity or are constitutive of social division;
- Analysing the efficacy of prevailing pedagogical practices.

The shape of this text

In sewing together these diverse data, we hope to have provided a substantial picture of this inscape that makes a pioneering contribution not only to the *Religion and Society* programme but also to our understanding of how Religious Education functions – and to contribute to capacity-building in the study of RE. As this volume unfolds, we move from an exercise in understanding *why* the subject is strange, and in its strangeness, unlike other curriculum subjects, to some quantitative reflections on student attitudes and responses. In the course of this unfolding, we suggest that the strangeness of RE is *constitutive* rather than contingent – that is, it is not a strange practice because some teachers and students conduct themselves in odd ways. Rather, as we suggest in Chapter 3, they behave in odd ways because the conditions that shape the subject press themselves on to the individuals and groups *engaged in* the social practice. While legislation across the United Kingdom, governing education as a whole, differs in legislative detail and curriculum shape, it is remarkably similar with respect to desired outcomes. This is not the case for Religious Education, where the imperatives differ somewhat across the United Kingdom and between schools serving different communities. The confusions that emerge in the policy and legislative spaces work their way into the social practices in the classroom. Of course the connections are complex and rhizomatic rather than linear.

Chapter 4 draws a lens on three conceptual confusions and contradictions that emerged in the spaces of the classroom concerning (1) the rationale for Religious Education, (2) the role of the teacher with respect to the shaping of principles and pedagogy and (3) the ways in which truth claims emerge and are handled in the classroom. Of course, the handling of truth claims impacts on how one is to treat the conflicting claims of different traditions and indeed questions about inter and multicultural education are never far from the surface in RE. Hence the next chapter explicitly considers the multiple ways in which multiculturalism configures, and is configured by, the transactions and discursive practices of the classroom. In doing so it highlights moves of pedagogic insight and simultaneously problematizes the ways in which the multicultural imperative emerges and how it reflects certain kinds of epistemic faultlines in the policies and enactments.

Perhaps the next chapter offers the most surprising site for discussion and reflection. Textbooks emerged as a critical actor in the daily activities of the classroom, sometimes shaping practices, sometimes controlling pedagogies, sometimes providing a counterpoint against which the teacher might establish their independence. We were inclined to consider the text as an inanimate object or set of objects to be deployed by the will of the classroom teacher. This turned out not to be the case and here we trace the very complex and active relations between text, teacher, policy and examinations. Complexly interwoven into the actions of the text, formal examinations also proved to be more powerful than perhaps we had anticipated and Chapter 6 offers a somewhat different lens, drilling into the particularities of communities of practice which soon finds that examinations shape activities in quite unexpected and profound ways.

While the student voice surfaces repeatedly in the course of this study, we devote a chapter to a set of nominal and ordinal questions about their experience. Accepting that we have no reason to call into question the overall patterns of reporting recorded here, we nonetheless do find some conflicts between student self-reporting and our other observations of day-to-day engagements. The explanations for these discrepancies probably lie not so much in *mauvaise foi* as in the emergence of a form of discursive hegemony, where certain kinds of expressed attitudes are considered standard. It is nonetheless clear here that RE is perceived by students to be different from other subjects and that this carries both negative and positive readings of the particularity and peculiarity of the subject.

On the basis of the descriptions and analyses of this essay, the closing chapter offers some proposals for a refurbished account of Religious Education. There is today no shortage of claims about how RE should position itself in order to become more relevant, more interesting and so forth. Some of these, including the work of Chater and Erricker (2012), suggest that the way to save Religious Education is to largely abandon religion in favour of a 'personalism' that might be informed by some acquaintance with religious and quasi-religious impulses. In such ways does RE get shaped around the need for the individual to find spiritual fulfilment. While this may indeed offer some educational value, it does rather strike us as the apotheosis of the therapeutic turn in education. (Ecclestone & Hayes 2008). And while we would not wish to underplay the importance of education supporting and nurturing the individual, what we observed in the course of our deliberations was that such education did not self-evidently offer students much real resource for either negotiating their own lives or for engaging with the other.

Shaping the future

During our two-day professional Delphi Seminar (Baumfield et al. 2012), it was noticeable that the invited experts appeared to be more preoccupied by policy matters than research findings. In this it should be remembered that the participants, not the researchers, establish the direction of travel as the discussion proceeds. In the transcript of the proceedings, of some 8,945 words, 3,215 were devoted to policy description and position and some 212 words to research. This concern with policy is hardly surprising, but it is precisely because policy so dominates the concerns of the profession that it is important to develop a robust research base for considering the *shape* of RE. It is our fervent hope that this present work will contribute both methodologically and substantively to furthering the public and academic debate on the role of Religious Education as well as enhancing 'capacity building' within the Religious Education teaching community and its associated scholarly communities. In exposing some of the complex and (occasionally) powerful forces at work in the field, we hope that teachers and researchers will be better equipped to deal with the challenges in everyday practice.

Perhaps more important even than helping teachers fend off some of the vested interests in Religious Education, this work will also help teachers recognize the importance of *language* in the life of the student. As one of our Delphi participants observed,

> When young people are trying to work out for themselves what takes on meaning for them . . . we simply throw an open door and say that all opinions count and all opinions are of equal worth . . . but increasingly that exploring of what has meaning for you has to have some sort of rigour to it, and we need to [help children differentiate] good thinking and something which is flawed.

We recognize all too well the provisionality of our formulations and analyses, and accept that the findings presented here are no more than slices of the data. Indeed, what is on offer is but one refraction of a very full data set; a partial account of the experience of teaching and learning in the classroom and the shape of RE in school and community. We do not claim that the present discussion offers straightforwardly generalizable findings. But we do believe that in offering a range of aporias and vignettes we trouble the current discourse about RE. If this volume then serves to offer some resource to professionals and teachers, to policy makers and legislators, indeed we will have achieved our goal.

Part I

Methodological and Structural Questions

Methodological Considerations: Learning from the Inside

Introduction

This chapter provides a description of, and rationale for, the research methodology used in this study. It also reflects critically on how we selected methods which enabled us to address the various objectives of our research project. The study of Religious Education is, as we have suggested in the Introduction, extraordinarily complex – in part because it is a distinctive social practice within education, which is unlike most other social practices that form and shape the identity of other parts of the curriculum. In order to understand the processes involved and to gain data that reflected this complexity, we conducted ethnographic fieldwork in 24 secondary schools in England, Scotland and Northern Ireland.

The research entailed gathering sufficiently detailed and appropriate data about the role and impact of RE in secondary schooling across the very different religious, cultural and political contexts of England and Wales, Northern Ireland and Scotland. The research required a complex, multimethod approach and involved discourse analysis on policy content, philosophical reflections on the coherence of policy, the analysis of texts and learning resources used in schools, a student survey, practitioner enquiry and, at the core of the study, an ethnographic study of stakeholders' experiences and understandings to explore the various claims made with respect to Religious Education.

Devising an appropriate methodology to address
the research aims and objectives

One of the methodological challenges and defining features of this project is that it is both large in scale while being ethnographic. Much previous research on Religious Education has placed an emphasis on the collection and statistical analysis of large data sets as a means of understanding broad trends in religious belief and adherence among school students. Our project is, in this respect, a marked departure from a large number of quantitative studies drawing upon Likert-type scales and survey-based methods (e.g. Egan 1988; Greer & Francis 1998; Francis 2005). While these studies illuminate certain attitudinal trends, they are methodologically limited in their ability to offer insight into the interior dimensions of the complex social phenomena of religion and education in their enacted interactions. The studies which do manage to illustrate the lived experiences of Religious Education as a social practice in the classroom have tended to be fairly small-scale and focused on very particular transactions (Eke et al. 2005; Hyde 2008), rather than the more comprehensive entailments discussed in this volume. By way of contrast, there are those qualitative projects which explored the pedagogies deployed in Religious Education in order to inform the development of particular Religious Education programmes. A classic example of this in Britain is the Warwick RE Project. This used an interpretive approach to Religious Education pioneered by Jackson and colleagues (1997, 1999) and made use of ethnographic source material to develop resources for use by children in classrooms. The Warwick RE Project also drew on evidence from different religious communities, social science theory, literary criticism, religious studies and other sources (e.g. Barratt 1994 a, b and c; Jackson et al. 1994; Mercier 1996; Wayne et al. 1996, Jackson 1997). Such an approach is, however, unusual in Britain (and other anglophone polities) where the propensity has been to focus on either the philosophical and normative conditions that should govern the practice of Religious Education (Wright 2004; Erricker 2010; Chater & Erricker 2012) or the perceived outcomes of Religious Education on young people's attitudes and dispositions (Francis et al. 2012).

Given the relative dearth of major illuminative studies across the United Kingdom, not enough is known about the factors and processes that are important in promoting effective Religious Education and how students, teachers and other stakeholders perceive and experience Religious Education. Hence, the *Does RE Work* project adopted an in-depth qualitative approach to the study of Religious Education. This included an examination of the processes involved in the teaching of Religious Education and stakeholders' perceptions of it. The experiences of teachers and students were given careful and critical attention over an extended period of investigation across the academic year, which included first-hand observation and a consideration of the practice of Religious Education in the study schools. This required the collection of data and material that was contextualized, and also allowed the identification of key processes and interactions within classrooms, the wider school and local community. Of course, as we discuss below, such close ethnographic work did not preclude other forms of data gathering, but was itself predicated on the emergence of themes and tropes from the ethnography and from our pre-fieldwork enquires.

Refining and framing the research questions and informing the methods

Underpinning the whole project was the repeated desire to get on the inside of what might be referred to as the 'whorléd interior' of Religious Education. The starting point to address this and to inform an initial framework or template for research was an examination of the policy literature and an exploration of professionals who shape policy and practice. The researchers conducted a textual analysis of national policy Standing Advisory Councils for Religious Education (SACREs); the local committees that advise local authorities on matters connected with Religious Education and worship. Using a discourse analysis approach, the team was able to identify discursive similarities between texts to trace the influence of policy on these. As the fieldwork stage got underway, the scrutiny of texts continued as part of the ethnography but this time at school level. This became a major strand in the analysis as the importance of texts was revealed in the shaping of the practice of RE across the schools.

The research objectives, set out previously, necessitated the exploration of the perspectives and positions of key policy actors and experts in the field of Religious Education to help frame and inform specific research questions and instruments. The research team used a modified version of the Delphi Method, originally developed by the Rand Corporation in the 1950s as a forecasting methodology to canvas a reliable consensus of opinion among a group of US Military experts, in order to assess military strategy and the response to risks. Since then the method has become part of a varied family of techniques (Linstone et al. 1975) that can been described as an 'iterative process to collect and distil the anonymous judgments of experts using a series of data collection and analysis techniques interspersed with feedback' (Skulmoski et al. 2007). The approach is not without its critics. A number of social scientists (e.g. Sackman 1974) have cast doubt over the Dephi method's ability to produce reliable results. Sackman (1974) argues that many Delphi-based studies are not conducted within a framework of 'rigorous empirical experimentation' and fail to produce findings based on a real consensus of participants. While such critics are right to stress the need for rigour, it is arguable that the value of the Delphi method is as an iterative qualitative process that goes beyond the focus group in extracting the views of experts by using a systematic process of refinement. Via numerous cycles of feedback and discussion, individuals can revise their judgements on the basis of this feedback. As Conroy and Lundie note 'For us the strength of the method was that it recognises that a constitutive feature of expertise can be its heterogeneity' (2011, 7).

With this in mind, we saw the Delphi method as useful for eliciting professional opinion in order to understand where the key areas of agreement and disagreement arose as to the core entailments of Religious Education across different types of schools and jurisdictions and to assist in the early identification of key nodes of investigation for our subsequent ethnography. We wanted to understand something of how these key professionals mediated policy, whether or not they had the capacity to mediate it, whether or not they spoke with one voice.

The expert panel included prominent figures in the philosophy of Religious Education, policy development, support for the practice of Religious Education in schools through teacher development. Of the 13 participants, eight had involvement in Initial Teacher Education in Religious Education, six had significant research experience in theological focus, five had held policy development roles, five had held leadership roles in related professional organizations and three had published teaching resources in the area. Overall, they were selected to represent professional and religious interests, inspectoral and support interests and, in addition, geographical interests. They included both known advocates and critics of confessional Religious Education in the United Kingdom, drawn from faith school and state school sectors as well as from the Muslim community. A detailed discussion of the place of the Delphi process within the rationale of the project, the emerging themes and some of the issues arising from the use of this approach is provided by Baumfield et al. (2012). For the team of fieldworkers, one of the most significant outcomes of the Delphi process, in line with our aims, was an awareness of the key areas of concern and disagreement with regard to the role and purpose of Religious Education. These informed the project's ethnographic template, overall research methodology and the sensitivity of the fieldworkers.

Following the analysis of the Delphi responses, the research team constructed a conceptual model to guide our understanding of current policy drivers, the variety of understandings of what Religious Education is and what it should achieve, the interrelationship of this with practice in the classroom, and the experiences and perceptions of teachers and students. In order to come to a more complex understanding of the various components in our study, we decided to map them against each other. What emerged was something akin to an hourglass (see Figure 1.1), where we gathered data into the centre, funnelling and focusing it during the ethnographic stage of research so that it would allow us to open up further lines of enquiry and professional engagement. After all, to know may not, in this instance, be enough. Moreover, as intimated in the bottom part of our hourglass, we were keen to subject our own analyses to further interrogation. Consequently, we invited others to reflect on our findings to see how much these resonated with their own experience as students and as educators. In the course of our work, some new lines of enquiry emerged and others were foregrounded. The ethnographic work threw up some unexpected lines of enquiry. Most notably, what emerged from the early engagements in the classroom with regard to the significance of textbooks in the ecology of the Religious Education classroom was much greater than we had anticipated. Consequently we found that the role of textbooks required to be considered in some depth.

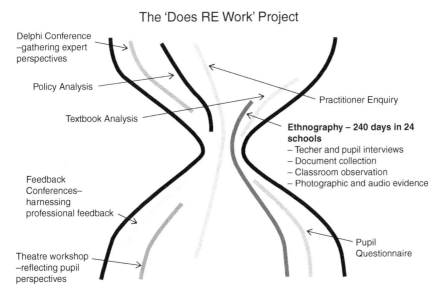

The 'Does RE Work' Project

Delphi Conference –gathering expert perspectives

Policy Analysis

Textbook Analysis

Practitioner Enquiry

Ethnography – 240 days in 24 schools
– Techer and pupil interviews
– Document collection
– Classroom observation
– Photographic and audio evidence

Feedback Conferences– harnessing professional feedback

Pupil Questionnaire

Theatre workshop –reflecting pupil perspectives

Figure 1.1 A methodological hourglass

The final research methods adopted to address the project aims, therefore, comprised a multimodal ethnography, which included an analysis of texts, resources, photographs, interviews, focus group discussions and student questionnaires.

Why ethnography?

As suggested earlier, one of the key aims of this project was to understand, from the point of view of students, teachers and other professional stakeholders, the complexities of the processes of teaching and learning Religious Education and how this is experienced, perceived and constructed. It was very clear from the outset that in order to achieve this we would need to attend to the ordinary everyday experience of the actors and consequently collect in-depth qualitative data over an extended period of time by carrying out first-hand observations in schools.

Ethnographic research methods are a well recognized means of collecting such data. Spradley (1979) describes ethnography as the organized study of groups of people which aims to describe and understand a culture. This includes explaining how the actors involved understand and generate a meaningful reality. Ethnographic studies have their roots in anthropological research and traditionally involved the in-depth, long-term study of one particular site. Today, this approach has become a valuable component of wider modern social research and can address various theoretical perspectives. It is a broad approach that has been used to research social groups and processes within particular settings, which can involve looking at a number of sites. It deploys a range of complementary research methods that usually include participant observation, focus groups, interviews and the collection of documents along with visual records and artefacts which provide further contextual information. Commonly, ethnography is used in conjunction with quantitative methods, such as surveys, in order to allow researchers to gain a more in-depth understanding of the trends they see in the numerical data. In this study, rather than deploying the fieldwork in a secondary (so to speak confirmatory) way, we chose to use the ethnographic records as a source for our subsequent questionnaire. The fieldwork allowed us to create a better-informed questionnaire and to add some figures to the trends we had observed and identified in the field.

A detailed rationale for adopting an ethnographic approach, its strengths and its relationship to phenomenological methods can be found in Conroy and Lundie (2011) and Lundie (2011). Here suffice to observe that it focuses on experiential meanings or the 'life-world' (Findlay 2009). The life-world comprises the 'world of objects around us as we perceive them and our experience of our self, body and relationships' (Brown 2010) and is the locus of interaction between ourselves and our perceptual environments. Ashworth (2003) states that the various interlinked components of the life-world such as a sense of self, embodiment, sociality, spatiality, temporality, project, discourse and mood-as-atmosphere act as a lens through which to view data. Finlay states that phenomenological research seeks to explore the 'structural whole that is socially shared while also experienced in individual and particular ways' (Finlay 2009, 2). Dahlberg et al. (2008, 37) add that such life-world research aims 'to describe and elucidate the lived world in a way that expands our understanding of human being and human experience'. Phenomenological research is also concerned with the subjective interconnection between the researcher and the researched (Findlay 2009) and recognizes the indeterminacy and ambiguity involved in this process.

The ethnographic method is equally concerned with experience and the intersubjective relationship between researcher and researched. However, it strives to go beyond the limits of the phenomenological method by also understanding the wider social context of the various social actors from their own points of view. That is, it seeks to understand the individual in terms of the social constructions and identities he or she makes use of. This approach allowed the research team to more fully understand Religious Education by going to the very source of its practice and construction in the classroom and the school. It permitted the inclusion of various actors' accounts and interactions (including those of non-human institutional and technological actors) along with other contextual material and artefacts to illuminate how Religious Education was composed and, importantly, the extent to which what took place in the classroom reflected broader Religious Education policy and research.

Having an ethnographic approach at the core of the research allowed the collected data and information to 'to speak for itself'. Conroy and Lundie (2011), stress that our research adopted a 'critical ethnographic paradigm', which recognized that 'understanding is intersubjective, not subjective or objective' (Carspecken 1996, 189).

In refining our ethnographic method, the research team moved through the different models of ethnographic encounter as elucidated by Carspecken (1996, 2001) and Hymes (1996) (see Table 1.1).

The research project's ethnography can be seen to move from the comprehensive stage of encounter through to the topic-oriented and finally to

Table 1.1 Types of ethnographic encounter

Ethnographic encounter types	Focus
Comprehensive	The ethnographer approaches a new fieldwork situation with the aim of mapping any significant features of the field
Topic-oriented	The ethnographer focuses on a particular aspect or aspects of the field
Hypothesis-oriented	The ethnographer looks for evidence that proves or disproves a particular relationship hypothesized from previous data

the hypothesis-oriented stage. This is explained in the analysis section of this chapter.

Trying to see and understand social phenomena from the point of view of the subject is not without its challenges. Some of these practical challenges are covered later in this chapter but, of course, a key issue in such endeavours is the possible effects that the participant observer may have on the observed. It would be naïve to claim that our investigation was entirely free from such 'observer effects'. However, spending extended periods of time with those involved in the research schools, building rapport and trust, meant that the behaviours, interactions and accounts of the actors were more 'natural' than might have been the case had the engagement been more perfunctory.

A further issue is that the research team were studying experiences, activities and phenomena that constitutively carry highly charged value attachments where their own biases and values could potentially influence the analysis. However, with a look over our shoulder at Bourdieu and Wacquant (1992), we strove to be reflexively aware of potential biases in the process of gathering and analysing the information. Such sensitivity extended to the potentially sensitive and conflicting issues that were highlighted during the Delphi process.

Sampling the schools involved in ethnographic research

Ethnographic research was carried out in 24 schools: 14 in England, six in Scotland and four in Northern Ireland. Our sample did not include any Welsh schools because, at the time the research was first conceived, Religious Education in Wales was structured and delivered under the same system as that prevailing in England.

In *The God Delusion,* Richard Dawkins (2006) has a tendency, not uncommon among those who harbour strongly negative views about particular social practices, to fix upon examples at the extremities and consider them representative of the practice as a whole. Similarly it is not difficult to find extreme(ly) poor examples of pedagogy and practice throughout education and Religious Education is certainly no exception. There is however an omnipresent temptation to extrapolate from such poor examples and suggest that these are somehow representative or constitutive of the practice as a whole. Given that the focus of our study was, 'Does RE Work?' we wanted to look at schools where Religious Education was perceived to be working well, that is, schools that self-reported as offering high quality Religious Education and where there was some evidence base (examination success, inspectoral reports and reputation) to corroborate such a claim. We also approached many colleagues in the field, such as academics and advisers, to get advice on the identification of Religious Education departments considered to be effective. This was of considerable importance to our study because we wished to see examples of how the best Religious Education departments translated the aims of curriculum designers, policy makers, 'thought leaders' and heads of school into classroom practice, and the constraints and opportunities afforded them in everyday engagement. If Religious Education *worked* in such circumstances then there was no reason to think or suggest that it could not *work* per se. Conversely, had we chosen schools at random or indeed selected schools where Religious Education was deemed to be weak, we might rightly have been deemed to be pathologizing the practice. Moreover, in this way it was also hoped that the team would be able to map diverse models of effectiveness and be transparent about the elective sampling which is inevitable to any long-term ethnographic engagement requiring this intensity of commitment from schools.

Originally we intended focusing on schools in London, Glasgow and Belfast as this would allow us to compare schools within and between these large cities. In total we invited around 280 schools to take part in the study. However, after approaching schools which met our criteria in the three cities, we found that a large number were apprehensive and ultimately unwilling to participate in the project, not infrequently citing their anxieties about the fragility of the subject and their fear that any potential adverse findings would impact negatively on their position in the school and community. While some claimed 'a lack of time', others indicated that they 'were preparing for an inspection', yet others commented that they simply did not want Religious Education put under the microscope. As one, high profile, Head of Department put it in a telephone conversation, 'We would rather not be exposed'. This in itself indicated to us that there was some anxiety about Religious Education as a focus of research even in those schools. A further complicating element was instanced where the Head of Religious Education expressed interest but the wish to participate was overridden by the Head Teacher. In another example of the challenges faced in conducting this kind of research during the course of the study, one school had a change of Head Teacher, who refused to let her students complete the questionnaire towards the end of the data collection on the grounds that examination success took priority over a research study. Despite offering to send a member of the research team to help organize the completion of the online questionnaire and any other necessary support, the rebuff was robust.

The challenge of securing the participation of schools in solely urban settings led to an expansion of the invitation across the whole of Scotland and Northern Ireland, as well as the opening of a fourth field of study in the North East of England. This turned out to offer some benefits as it allowed us to consider whether or not particular or marked differences existed between rural and urban schools and schools outwith the capital cities. As it happened, differences in approach and experience were as likely to occur between schools in the same region or district as between those in urban or rural settings. Of the 14 schools in England, 11 were in the South East and three were in the North-East. These were in inner city, surburban and rural areas and represented a wide ethnic and religious mix among student and staff. For example, we had schools where the majority of staff and students were 'white' and largely non-religious. We also had schools that had a high percentage of students of Asian descent who were Muslim and one school where over half the students were of Afro-Caribbean descent and many were practising Christians. Our English sample also had a variety of non-denominational and denominational schools (Catholic and Anglican). Our six Scottish schools were a mixture of non-denominational and Catholic schools and were spread out across both urban and rural areas, including the highlands. Of our four Northern Irish schools, one was Ecumenical Christian, one was Roman Catholic and the other two were non-denominational.

A further note should be made about the denominational differences between our schools. The major denominational designations included: Anglican, Catholic, Common and Integrated (i.e. a mixture of Catholic and Protestant). We did approach Jewish and Muslim schools, but these all declined and were unwilling to engage in any detailed conversation as to reasons for doing so. As indicated above, we did, however, have non-denominational schools with a high percentage of Asians and Muslims. One of our schools had over 98 per cent

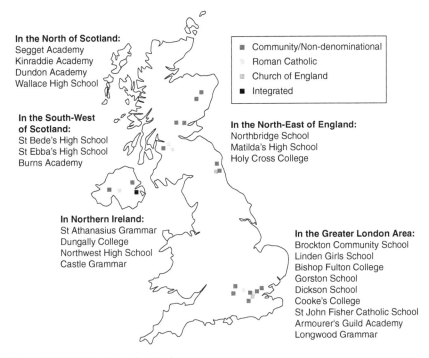

In the North of Scotland:
Segget Academy
Kinraddie Academy
Dundon Academy
Wallace High School

Community/Non-denominational
Roman Catholic
Church of England
Integrated

In the South-West of Scotland:
St Bede's High School
St Ebba's High School
Burns Academy

In the North-East of England:
Northbridge School
Matilda's High School
Holy Cross College

In Northern Ireland:
St Athanasius Grammar
Dungally College
Northwest High School
Castle Grammar

In the Greater London Area:
Brockton Community School
Linden Girls School
Bishop Fulton College
Gorston School
Dickson School
Cooke's College
St John Fisher Catholic School
Armourer's Guild Academy
Longwood Grammar

Figure 1.2 Distribution of schools

Muslim students and another c. 95 per cent Asian students from a variety of religious traditions. The location of our schools is indicated in the map shown in Figure 1.2. All of the names are pseudonyms.

With 24 schools, we cannot claim that our research is a statistically representative sample, which, of course, limits some of the claims that we can make. However, the range of schools involved coupled with the depth of information collected provided much detailed evidence from across a range of school cultures and classroom contexts as well as associated materials and site data, enabling us to generate key insights on the practices, policies and resources of Religious Education in secondary education in Northern Ireland, Scotland and England. The point at stake is not that the observations and conclusions here offer irrefutable evidence about the nature and efficacy of particular practices (pedagogic, social and cultural), but that they indicate the existence and emergence of certain tropes in the practice of Religious Education. Moreover, the data and its analysis also facilitated a greater understanding of the contradictions and confusions present in Religious Education, its successes and limitations and the manner in which policy is, or is not, enacted in the classroom. So, while our sample is not representative, because of the nature of our research methods we can provide substantial insights into what might be deemed the 'ecology' of Religious Education across significantly different kinds of schools across England, Scotland and Northern Ireland. In short, the claim here is that the work is indicative rather than representative. The table in Appendix A gives more details of the location of our schools; their religious affiliation of the schools, and the ethnic, cultural and religious mix of the students.

The ethnographic methods used in the schools

While the bulk of this chapter is devoted to the ethnographic research carried out in schools, other important and valuable methods of data collection and analysis were used by the non-ethnographers on our research team. This included the Delphi event prior to the fieldwork, an online questionnaire distributed to students after the fieldwork and the analysis of textbooks and student work (collected by the ethnographers). We also had a teacher practitioner enquiry element running in some schools. Throughout the research process, we had regular meetings among the ethnographers to compare and learn from our research experiences and regular meetings among the full research team. The data gathering stage of the research was supposed to take only one year, but owing to the challenge of getting an adequate sample and the logistical issues of visiting schools that were distant from each other, the data gathering stage took 18 months. The regular team meetings and other formal and informal communication during the project allowed the various findings from each stand of research to inform each other. During these meetings, in addition to the ethnographers, we subjected the ethnographic data to blind analysis by other members of the team, so as to ensure that individual readings would not distort the overall picture. This proved to be particularly valuable, often with common readings of the data emerging from researchers who enjoyed quite distinctive heuristic perspectives.

What the 'ethnographic' element of the research entailed

Each of the 24 schools was visited by a single ethnographer who carried out 10 days of research per school (i.e. 240 days of ethnography). For the purpose of comparability, we primarily focused on Year 10 in England, Year 11 in Northern Ireland and S4 for Scotland (henceforth referred to as Years 10/11/S4). There were a number of reasons doing so. First, this is the final year for which Religious Education is a common, compulsory subject in all schools. Secondly, the notable growth in Religious Education across all three jurisdictions (see Figures 1.3 and

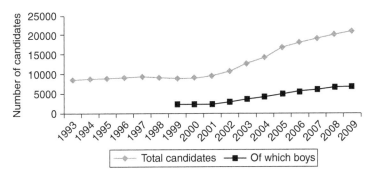

Figure 1.3 Religious Studies A Level 1993–2009 (number of candidates)

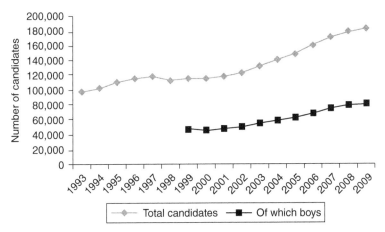

Figure 1.4 Religious Studies GCSE, 1993–2009 (number of candidates)
Source: Joint Council for General Qualifications.

1.4), particularly since 2000, has been quite marked as evidenced in qualification statistics.

In Scotland there was an increase of 1,097 pupils taking RMPS Higher between 2007–8 and 2010–11, representing a 52 per cent increase in uptake over a period of three years (Nixon 2010). Given this increase in Religious Education uptake, it is not unimportant to consider how the subject is treated in the context of a formalized curriculum shaped by public examinations.

We were particularly interested in understanding something about student competence in handling religious *material* at a time when they would be expected to handle complex conceptual and abstract ideas across the curriculum. This last concern was borne out of the important but neglected work of Kerry (1984) who demonstrated that research into the day-to-day transactions of the classroom rarely demonstrated the facility to form and develop conceptual fields and move thinking from the concrete to the abstract. This failure was all the more poignant because of the strong claims that Religious Education was constitutively suited to cultivating these capacities in students. We also considered it important that we were able to place our understanding of what happened in Year 10/S4 Religious Education in a much wider context. Hence we also looked at other Religious Education year groups, other subject areas, other school activities (such as field trips) and the wider context of the community of which the school formed a part (see Appendix B). While not a major feature of the study this was nonetheless important. During the entire process, the researchers felt that it was important to avoid being burdensome to teacher or school and to make our research relevant to the teachers so that they felt included in the process rather than mere subjects. This, we felt, was an important ethical issue. Teachers were invited to comment on our interview and focus group questions and in one final iteration school teachers were invited to assist in the formulation of the questions used in our student questionnaire.

While we originally intended to spend more than ten days per school, given the intensity of the engagement and the varied sources of data wrapped around the ethnography that this period was more than sufficient to enable the team to get an inside view of Religious Education as practiced. Ten days enabled us to get a feel for the nature of the school and the wider community, and for teachers and students to get used to seeing and talking to us. With some of the schools, the ten days of fieldwork occurred over a period of two to three weeks. For most schools, this happened over the course of two to three months. In two of the Scottish schools, the fieldwork extended over a year, which facilitated our seeing the effects of staff change and discussions on how *Curriculum for Excellence* (the refurbished Scottish curriculum) was going to be implemented. In all cases, being in the school for ten days allowed some degree of trust to develop between the researchers and the teachers and students, which lessened the impact of our presence on student and teacher behaviour. It also meant that we got to see good days and bad days. As one teacher said: 'you get to see us warts and flowers and all. We couldn't put up a show for 10 visits'. As a result, we were able to observe the wider context in which Religious Education was taught and see how teachers adapted lesson plans to suit students with different ability levels and learning needs.

While the focus of the ethnography was on the final phase of compulsory RE, the research also took into account the life of the school and Religious Education taught to other year groups. For each school, 'ethnographic' research comprised the following stages and steps.

1. Before going to a school, the ethnographers conducted an initial content analysis by looking at the school's Website and publicly available information such as HMI and Ofsted reports. This offered insights into the stated aims of the school and an overview of provision, special events, information of staff (particularly the Head Teacher), wider community context, and official accounts of school performance, strengths and weaknesses. We continued to examine the overall aims and objectives of the school and how these 'fitted' with the teaching of RE during the course of our fieldwork.

2. Participant observation in Religious Education classes for the year 10/11/S4 students. Depending on the school, and more particularly the teacher, this ranged from simply sitting unobtrusively in the classroom and taking observational notes to actively participating with students in their activities (i.e. group work, invitations to comment on discussions, helping particular students at the teacher's request).

3. Participant observation in Religious Education lessons that our teachers were offering to older and younger age groups. The aim was to be able to compare the teacher's interactions with the year 10/11/S4 students and the content of lesson with their treatment of Religious Education for other age groups. For example, did the requirement to cover content required for examinations or more or less complex content for different age groups alter teachers' pedagogy? More than this we were concerned to unearth the extent to which deep learning was pursued.

4. Shadowing a year 10/11/S4 Religious Education student (chosen by the teacher) to their other lessons for one day. This strategy of 'pupil pursuit' represented one strategy to place Religious Education teaching within the wider context of the school. It enabled us to get a more robust sense of how Religious Education was experienced by the students in relation to the myriad other entailments of the daily life of a student in school. This included a consideration of differences in teaching methods, teaching resources, lesson content and teacher-student interaction in other subjects. It also involved taking notes while observing the lessons. Additionally some teachers were very keen to have us participate in classes (as participant observers). The walk between classes was a valuable opportunity to talk to the student about how these lessons compared to Religious Education. Interestingly, in a minority of cases, the non-Religious Education teachers

we observed were keen to draw our attention to the links between their subject (such as Biology, History and Art) and Religious Education.

5. Participant Observation at key events such as fieldtrips, assemblies, religious services and charity events. This allowed researchers to locate the practices of Religious Education in a somewhat larger understanding of the overall school context and the place of Religious Education, religious observance and how the overall aims of Religious Education teaching might be achieved outside of the classroom. In this vein, we also attended Head Teacher briefings sessions for teachers.

6. Interviews with key staff members such as the Head Teacher, Head of Religious Education, Religious Education teachers and school chaplains (see Appendices C and D).

7. Informal conversations with teachers of other subjects. This was normally done during break time and lunch in the staff common room (it should be noted that all staff members had been informed of the nature of our research).

8. The conduct of focus groups with students. For the sake of comparison, the ethnographers had a core list of questions which had been developed from our key observations as our research progressed with input from the non-ethnographers during our team meetings (see Appendix E). We also took this as an opportunity for teachers to include questions that were of particular interest to them. The results of the focus groups were fed back to the teachers.

9. The collection of samples of pupils' course work, learning and teaching materials, texts, school policy documents and artefacts. While these provided further data for ethnographic scrutiny, the task of offering a somewhat deeper analysis of these documents was passed on to other members of the team who had demonstrable expertise in the analysis of assessment techniques, theological and religious conceits and so forth. So it was that we could look at the logical character of tasks, assignments and questions and whether or not the materials available to, and used in schools were evocations and instantiations of the principled claims of policy documents, professional discourse and educational practice. As a result of these early collaborations, the research team became increasingly conscious of the active role of the textbook; a kind of hidden presence in the classroom, that exercised a considerable, if unacknowledged, influence on Religious Education. The instinct that the nature and influence of the textbook was both substantial and significant received some confirmation as the, then, Department for Children, Schools and Families commissioned the

Warwick Religious Education Research Unit to conduct a substantial review of *Materials used to Teach about World Religions in Schools in England*. Of course, it is one thing to examine, analyse and critique the texts per se, and this can indeed offer important insights into the resources. It is however another to locate them in the actual practices of the classroom. Critical to the nature of Religious Education in a resource intensive world are the multiple interactions between teacher, student and text.

10. An examination of the physical context of the school (classroom layout, staff common rooms and its place within the community). The Religious Education classroom and wider school layout were recorded, using photographs and diagrams to provide contextual information. We were also concerned to understand the level and kinds of resourcing available to Religious Education teachers. While the information was not always transparently available and some schools were reluctant to disaggregate the figures for resources, we were able to glean some insight into the material conditions of Religious Education, which included comparative time allocations.

11. An examination of the cultural and religious context of the school (i.e. ethnic, religious and class background of students and of the wider community). This was based on interviews with Head Teachers and Heads of Religious Education, examining existing school data collected on pupil and staff, religious and ethnic affiliation and community involvement, and on physically walking through and observing the catchment area. Indeed the team collected substantial photographic evidence of the catchment. Of course such records are sensitive and have to be handled with discretion but they were available to the whole team to better understand the community in which Religious Education takes place.

12. At the end of the field data collecting process, and after an initial analysis of the data, an internet student survey was developed and all of the schools invited to have their year 10/11/S4 students participate (see Appendix F). In the end 50 per cent of the schools decided to participate in the questionnaire from which we collected 483 responses. We had hoped for a wider participation and a greater response rate but delays in collecting the ethnographic data (explained above), the timing of the questionnaire (close to exam time) and the reluctance of some schools to facilitate any further research work made this a more limited exercise than we had hoped. Nevertheless, given that the questionnaire was not a free-standing instrument and that the questions were constructed to apply a further lens on to the

existing topography rather than confirming or disconfirming our analyses, the somewhat smaller than hoped for numbers do not undermine its usefulness. Given the level of participation in the questionnaire we cannot use the results to draw direct comparisons between the schools or different populations in our study. However, since our interest was primarily on the social practice that is Religious Education, our inability to draw valid numerical comparisons between schools was not detrimental to our overall analysis.

In addition to the ethnographic work in schools and the collection of data for content analysis, Religious Education teachers were invited at the outset to become involved in a practitioner enquiry. This involved the engagement of Religious Education teachers as partner 'research practitioners' in the evaluation of the effectiveness of their own pedagogical practices through case studies. A total of 16 teachers from different schools chose to undertake some research of their practice. These studies and partial studies of matters of real concern to teachers also played their part in the overall descriptions and analyses.

Analysis of the data and information

A particular strength of the research design was the ability to triangulate different and quite varied types of rich data and evidence from various sources in order that we might pay due attention to the complexity of the social practices that constitute Religious Education in the United Kingdom. However, this presented a challenge for the research team in systematically processing and analysing the enormous volume of complex data and information this produced. In particular, the qualitative material gathered during the ethnographies in the schools, once transcribed, produced a great deal of textual information. The recorded material (ethnographic notes, transcribed interviews and focus groups, programme notes, etc.) is in excess of 3,000,000 words. In addition we had photographic records of the communities where the schools were located, classrooms, displays, field trips and so forth, all of which add to our understanding of the topography of Religious Education. It was important that research team members were able to fully scrutinize the data, adopt a common interpretative framework that addressed the research objectives and questions but also allowed salient yet unforeseen topics to be identified. As suggested above, this was done through members of the team independently reviewing the ethnographic notes and materials, and writing short descriptions of what each considered to be the most salient features of the records together with an interpretation of what meaning or significance might be ascribed to the data record. Subsequently we shared and discussed our analyses. Given that there were a number of ethnographers and others involved, it appeared to the team to be important that we avoided idiosyncratic or disproportionate interpretations. A further interesting and particularly insightful source of corroboration emerged from a decision to present some of the preliminary findings in a conference using the techniques of Forum Theatre (Boal 1979, 2006).

Forum Theatre

Perhaps somewhat unusually, we chose to use the now well-developed Forum Theatre approach of dramatic representation to not only present our findings to a professional audience but also to draw on this and subsequent seminar discussions as part of the corroborative texture of our explorations. Briefly, this entailed a series of seminars with some University of Glasgow drama students who consequently selected particular collections of the raw data to exemplify what they considered to be important tropes in our findings. The group of drama students then worked, with their course leader, to design four short drama vignettes to bring the evidence in the data to life.

Scenario 1. Who wants to understand Religious Education?
Scenario 2. Staff meeting
Scenario 3. Teacher baggage
Scenario 4. Evading questions

These five-minute vignettes were then performed at the project launch of findings conference in March 2011 to an audience of academic, policy and practitioner stakeholders and, importantly, invited groups of Year 10, 16+ students from a range of local secondary schools. These pupils, and their accompanying Religious Education teachers, were invited to comment on the evidence-based scenarios and indicate whether they reflected their own experiences of Religious Education. Overwhelmingly, the dramatized portrayals of key features of our findings resonated not only with the experience of the school pupils and their teachers but also with those other audience members who were Religious Education practitioners. This exercise acted as a validation exercise and stimulated interesting discussion across the whole audience regarding the topic areas. Overall, these drama performances served as yet another part of the iterative research and analysis process and provided affirmation of our findings as well as new insights. The performances were followed by a series of round table discussions, which included members of the research team, policy and practitioner stakeholders, Religious Education teachers and students. These discussions focused on policy and curriculum development; the role of textbooks; school ethos, resources and subject status; the emerging philosophy and ethics model of Religious Education; pedagogy and classroom practice; dealing with controversial topics in the classroom; the practitioner enquiry and the results from the questionnaire and focus groups.

As we have indicated in Table 1.2, we were keen to deploy a range of research methods to address the deceptively simple yet extraordinarily complicated question, 'Does RE Work?' It is indisputable that at the heart of our work sits the ethnographic observations and it is this data that is foregrounded in our observations throughout the remainder of this volume. Yet this core material has been supplemented, refined and modified by other material, reflections and enactments.

Table 1.2 Main Sources of research data and evidence gathered and analysis approach

Types of data/ evidence gathered	Summary of analysis approach
Ethnography in schools	
Observational notes, e.g., narratives of classroom interaction, critical incidents, etc.	Text entered into NVivo software and coded using the analytical framework (see Appendix G). Enabled key themes to be identified across the schools while maintaining context.
Interviews and focus groups inc. school management, teachers involved in teaching and planning RE, other subject teachers, pupils in the selected year group, other relevant staff (e.g. library, support, and resources)	
Photographs and sketches, e.g., room layout, school context, religious artefacts	Photos entered into NVivo software and coded to relevant themes in the analytical framework. These provided particularly useful information on context and layout of RE classrooms.
Samples of anonymized copies of pupils' RE course-work learning and teaching materials, texts, school policy documents, and artefacts collected across the ethnography schools.	Text/document analysis to highlight issues pertinent to the research. Scrutiny of texts highlighted issues such as the importance of text books in influencing what is taught in the schools. The research expanded its focus on RE textbooks as a result.

Continued

Table 1.2 Continued

Types of data/ evidence gathered	Summary of analysis approach
Analysis of pertinent policy documentation at national, local, and school level	Text/document analysis of key policy documents referenced to statements on RE policy and curriculum.
Teacher biographic profile pro forma	Text added to NVivo and analyzed to provide further background and context but also insights on teachers' approaches and actions.

Supporting sources of data/information

Year 10 Pupil survey involving the ethnography schools providing a total of 535 respondents. Focus of survey included views on RE and school.	Statistical analyses producing basic frequencies of pupils' responses and cross tabulations to explore any differences in responses across schools.
Practitioner enquiry – involving engagement of RE teachers across the ethnography schools as partner 'research practitioners' in the evaluation of the effectiveness of their own pedagogical practices through case studies.	Teachers research approach and corresponding analysis varied widely to reflect the focus of their research. The University research team were available to support teachers in the design and analysis of their research.
Participatory research methods with policy representatives and practitioners involved in framing of research questions: • Variation of Delphi approach using an event for key policy and academic experts on Religious Education used at the beginning of the project to explore key informants' views • Presentations of interim findings at seminars in Scotland, Northern Ireland and England • Round table discussion of particular findings at end-of-project conference	Delphi qualitative self-completion proforma and recorded discussions were analyzed using very flexible framework and 'grounded' approach that allowed salient themes to emerge. Feedback and discussion from policy, academic and practitioner recorded and analyzed using project's flexible analytical framework.
Dramatic performance of key findings at the end-of-project conference by the University of Glasgow BEd students specializing in drama. This both promoted findings and allow validation and critique of our findings.	Performance and audience discussion video recorded and analyzed using a 'grounded' qualitative analysis approach.

Developing the analytical framework

Clearly the research objectives and consequent questions provided an initial basis for the analytical framework. Before we could begin to address questions of efficacy or indeed analyse the data we needed to resolve what the various professional and community (religious) groups thought success might look like. As described previously, to help us understand some plausible indicators of effectiveness, we mounted a two-day Delphi workshop that tried to develop more focused questions on effectiveness by drawing on a group of senior professional and academic colleagues from across the United Kingdom. The analysis of the Delphi discussions conversations revealed that there was a lot of agreement about the high level educational concepts that needed to be cultivated. For example, Religious Education should help students develop critical capacities; it should open their imaginations to others and help foster tolerance and community-mindedness. Moreover, there was much agreement about the practices and methods to be adopted in the classroom: enquiry-based; student-centred and active-learning. However, there was far less consensus and clarity about what the high level policy objectives were and what effective Religious Education would look like in practice in various contexts.

The framework was further refined through team discussion. Additionally in 2009, day seminars were held in Northern Ireland, Scotland and England to allow the ethnographers to present their initial observations to practitioners, academics and policymakers and to enable the project team to distil key themes emerging from the pilot phase. This allowed the ethnographers to present and receive feedback on initial observations from this open-ended pilot phase, enabling the project team to distil key themes emerging from the data. This iterative process was central to our research strategy. Just as the Forum Theatre presentations and consequent pupil feedback offered a hermeneutically satisfying corroboration or refutation of our interpretations, so too did our encounters with RE professionals. A set of ten themes (most of which will receive substantial further treatment in this volume) emerged from these processes. Three of these relate to contextual factors and seven address discourse and language:

Contextual themes

1. The role of examinations in setting the aims and content of Religious Education;
2. The fit between teacher, pupil and school values in the Religious Education curriculum, and the relationship of Religious Education to the school ethos;
3. The level of resource and support given to Religious Education.

Language-centred themes

4. The use of ICT in the Religious Education classroom;
5. The language and treatment of immanence and transcendence, touching on pupils' levels of religious experience and religious literacy;
6. The level of intellectual challenge offered by Religious Education, relative to other subjects in the curriculum, with particular reference to differentiation;
7. The frequency and practices of engagement with texts in the Religious Education classroom;
8. The impact of teachers' pedagogical style;
9. The role and approach to multicultural awareness in the RE classroom;
10. The epistemic claims made about truth and plurality in the RE classroom.

This framework, generated during the pilot phase, was then used to generate hypotheses which were investigated in the subsequent ethnography. This can be categorized as a hypothesis-oriented ethnographic encounter or phase of the work.

The ethnographic study had two phases, a pilot, or 'comprehensive' phase (Hymes 1996) comprising 11 schools which sought to distil a list of dominant themes in the discourse of professional practice and brokerage, providing us with a matrix of factors influencing the effectiveness and helping us to answer the question 'why do these particular cultural themes exist' (Carspecken 2001, 22). The second, 'hypothesis-oriented' phase (Hymes 1996), comprising 13 schools, as well as further work in many of the initial 11, helped to focus more narrowly on the particular themes identified. In the early phase of the research (the comprehensive ethnographic encounter model), the ethnographers had a great deal of latitude to gather as broad a contextualized account as possible, guided by an initial observation schedule that facilitated comprehensive note-taking, subsequent categorization and future observations. The imperative to maintain this openness was, as we have iterated time and again in this work, to ensure that our analysis emerged out of the data itself and was not a function of a kind of eisegetical reading of the practices that relied more on our pre-determined dispositions than on how things manifested themselves. The initial schedule focused on the following ten core areas for observation: Spatial/temporal information; documentation collected; non-teaching activities in the classroom; cross-curricular comparisons with Religious Education teaching; involvement of outside partners in the delivery and planning of Religious Education; teacher-student interaction; student-student interaction; relationship between ethnographer, teachers and students; whole-school ethos and influence on relationships; teachers' and students' interactions with curriculum, resources and values.

As the research progressed, and data were scrutinized by the individual researchers and the whole team, the analytical framework emerged and evolved to refine our initial ten themes. (For the final coding and presentation of ethnographers' fieldnotes and collected material see Appendix F). These main themes were: the context of the school and community, the school ethos, the context of Religious Education in the school, the resources allocated to Religious Education teaching and learning, teacher backgrounds, the discourse used in teaching and texts, the role of examinations and the background of students and their experiences of learning Religious Education. The regular research team meetings were important in ensuring that those involved in the analysis were interpreting the material in a consistent way. In addition, the ethnographers coded four coding nodes on one set of field notes, one collated category of data and one transcript, and a meeting to moderate the coding. This demonstrated a high kappa coefficient indicating that there was sufficient consensus to produce a coding comparison within normal parameters and, as we have indicated above, this helped to ensure that idiosyncratic interpolations were largely avoided.

The analysis process

A template was constructed from the emerging themes and categories for the input of ethnographic data into an **NVivo 8** database. Data from multiple sources were entered into the database, including ethnographers' fieldnotes, policy documents, pupils' work, teaching materials and lesson plans, pupils' work, photographic sources, recordings and transcripts of interviews and focus groups and recordings of classroom dialogue. Coding nodes were created in NVivo corresponding to the themes emerging from the comprehensive ethnography, and these were applied both retrospectively to the pilot schools and subsequent observations in the later, hypothesis-oriented phase.

The NVivo qualitative software assisted the analysis process by making the coding and sorting of the information under the framework classifications systematic, and enhancing the ability of the researchers to identify associations between the coded material and generating context-sensitive findings. The process involved the researchers individually and as a team, generating theoretical notes that informed the ongoing analysis, a process first described by Glaser (1978, 83) and endorsed by Wengraf (2001, 209).

The analysis entailed some aspects of the *Grounded Theory* approach developed by Glaser and Strauss (1967), where little is assumed about the research topics and, as part of an *inductive process*, concepts/theory are generated from the data. Indeed, parts of the analytical framework were generated and refined using this process. However, the research also had particular research objectives and foci that the project was seeking to explore and test: a *deductive* process. The initial codes used in the analysis, therefore, reflected the research objectives, questions and related concepts. These were modified, where appropriate, as the team progressed with the analysis.

The qualitative analysis involved working with the coded data to achieve an understanding, explanation and interpretation of the Religious Education experience across the schools that took into account perceptions, interactions, processes, meanings and context. The ethnographers on the project ran a coding comparison, where they blind double-coded 8 nodes of the data, two sections of data from two schools under two themes. There was agreement between them on an average of 85.88 per cent of the coding, producing a median Kappa Coefficient of 0.7, demonstrating significant reliability and comparability between ethnographers' coding approaches.

The teams' interpretations reflected the informants' constructs, views and meanings, and the emerging findings were triangulated with other evidence. Meanwhile we continually maintained an awareness of context to highlight reasons underpinning informants' views, developing a deeper understanding of the nature of Religious Education in the schools, and identifying what factors and processes were important in shaping Religious Education and its ability to impact on young people.

Conclusion

This chapter has detailed the methods of our research and analysis and its underpinning concepts. The scale of the ethnography and depth of the data and analysis means that while we cannot claim that the schools selected were representative in any correspondence sense, our research provides valuable insights into the questions we posed. In particular it provides a nuanced account of how Religious Education is taught in some British schools, where it was identified by the departments themselves as being of high quality, how pupils, teachers and others experience and make sense of it, and what actors are in play. It manages to offer some triangulation with policy, texts, nominal data and professional attitudes. And, while we do not wish to lay claim to have settled the question of efficacy, we have certainly illuminated key issues in the common or garden politics and practices of Religious Education.

2

The Strange Position of Education in Religion in Contemporary Political Culture

Introduction

Know then thyself, presume not god to scan,

The proper study of mankind is man

Plac'd on this isthmus of a middle state,

A being darkly wise, and rudely great.

Pope Epistle 2 Lines 1 to 4

Pope's *Essay on Man* is a stark reminder of the complexity of God talk; indeed, in its echo of the Delphic oracle *gnothi seauton*,[1] it is a reminder of how mysterious even human talk can be. When we attempt to combine God talk and human talk we are apt to end up with something yet more strange than either discourse on its own. When we then add symbolic and organizational language into the mix, matters are unlikely to get much easier. After some years exploring the daily transactions of Religious Education in the various and varied schools across the country it is difficult not to consider it as a strange social and pedagogical practice. It simultaneously assumes the form of the curriculum in general while often being defended by professionals in the field as different and distinctive. Situated at the nexus of a range of competing imperatives that govern social and educational life it appears to inhabit a kind of epistemic and pedagogic twilight zone. So it is that, across Europe, RE takes a variety of forms that, structurally and pedagogically, are positioned variously as church-based, school-based, school-based and denominationally provided, mono-religious state provided, multifaith and critically open, catechetical and so forth. Although the purposes of the endeavour, as articulated by teachers themselves, vary across these very different contexts, three goals consistently dominate the professional articulations of purpose. '[T]eaching in religion, teaching about religion and teaching from religion – are affirmed by most teachers and catechists' (Schweitzer et al. 2009, 246; see also Grimmitt 1987). What is interesting in this broad European space is the elision between what might be considered quite distinctive and, by many, mutually exclusive contexts: the school (teacher) and the religious institution or church (catechist). What is termed Religious Education ends up covering quite different educational intentions from the study of religion at school to nurturing young people within a faith community or in a context designed to support particular faith communities. At its most obvious we can see this slippage in the case of Italy, where there is a legislative requirement to teach Catholic religion across a state that has, like many, witnessed a substantial deterioration of the institutional status of the dominant religion but still has educational roots that lie deep in the power of the Catholic Church. The way of managing the perceived need to retain Catholic Religious Education is to underpin it with an attachment to what is described as 'tradition based openness' (Anthony 2009, 111).

In Britain such elisions are considered by many to be educationally and culturally untenable but, as we saw in both our leading professional conversations and our observations of everyday life, the distinctions are nowhere near as clear cut as is often assumed in formal discussions of such matters. Hence the Heads of Departments of Religious Education in two adjacent state schools, with similar demographic features, managed to articulate and instantiate two quite distinctive and apparently conflicting accounts of the purposes of Religious Education. For one, the educational and cultural problem faced by professionals was religious illiteracy (Wright 2004; Conroy & Davis 2010) with particular regard to Christianity and a consequent desire to present Christianity in a positive light. Practically this concern led to the class teacher (Kinraddie) taking a group of S4 students to the local church in an attempt to combat 'Christian-phobia' and positively expose them to a 'faith tradition and perspective historically indigenous to the area but, [from which students have been] long since alienated'. For the other (Segget) the teacher expresses her dislike of the churches 'weighing in to the RMPS content' and considers talks by local clergy 'at assembly [to be] the worst advert for Christianity'. Moreover, in this school there was a real sense of hostility and intolerance of [the] pupils towards Christianity. It would be a mistake to consider the impulse of some teachers to cultivate a positive response among students towards Christianity as a function of their personal religious affiliations. Across the very different kinds of schools in our study, teacher attitudes towards their local Christian churches and religious communities varied enormously and certainly not in predictable ways. Hence the first teacher, in Kinraddie, was simultaneously concerned to create a more positive impression of the local Christian church than her students ordinarily enjoyed. But, at the same time, she was concerned to pronounce herself a theist but not a Christian. Despite this considered positioning outside official religion, she led the local church youth group! She held this office because her daughter, having been in a Church youth group where they lived previously, wished to join a new one after they moved home. On bringing her child to the group, the Minister discovered that she was a RE teacher and, assuming that she was Christian, asked if she would lead the group. Despite her clarification, the Minister persisted in his invitation, saying that it did not matter that she was not a believer, and she accepted. This elision between school functions and attachments and church functions and attachments is certainly not straightforward and, peculiarly, makes Religious Education vulnerable to the intervention of other kinds of values apart from those directly related to the activity. Arguably the teacher manifests what might be described as a form of *sublimated dissonance*. By this we mean that the teacher is content to live with the epistemic and cultural contradictions that arise where one's personal beliefs and one's institutional position are, if not incompatible, clearly at odds but where she rationalizes the conflict by way of a *via negativa*. In doing so she is able to make sense of her engagement in a social practice at odds with her own beliefs by considering and classifying it as harmless and not doing any damage. More positively she can consider it a good thing as it contributes to common life.

These contradictions offer something of a prelude to our suggestion that Religious Education is indeed a strange social practice and, as we will go on to argue, unlike any other subject in the school curriculum. This strange distinctiveness is evident at a variety of levels. These include the nature of the subject matter, the nature of the language, the nature of the personal involvement and the nature of the social expectations. Let us look at the first of these briefly. Even where other subjects, such as literature and citizenship education deal with metaphysical conceits, they do so in a way that per force must maintain them as *immanent* concerns. So it is that love or passion or justice or truth are formally dealt with as concerns of the material world, epiphenomenal of social and psychological life. In other words, where we are dealing with values and attachments, sense of the other and so on, the metaphysics implied remain firmly rooted in the world of appearance and object. While many pervasive features of religion are indisputably immanent, its claim to a distinctive way of constructing the world relies on claims of *transcendence* (an unknowable God, a non-worldly paradise, blissful enlightenment or whatever). Here, while immanence may indeed be a consitutive feature of religion it is so parasitically. Above and beyond its regulatory social functions and operations, religion refers to or signifies what stands outside the world of everyday experience. The contemporary preference for the present and immanent allows us to indulge an etymologically and epistemologically limited and limiting explication of *religio* (probably from *religiare*) which foregrounds its horizontal or socially binding functions at the expense of its perpendicular or memorial claims. These historic claims to the identity function of religion as the site and vehicle for recognizing and maintaining the relationship between the living and the dead have disappeared as our belief in the efficacy of the dead (i.e. that the dead engage, interfere with and have obligations towards the living) has evaporated. As Geary points out, death is for late modernity the

> ultimate evil, the supreme indictment of our inability to control the universe or even ourselves. Perhaps for that reason we tend to look on the dead as failures in a certain sense, unfortunates to be left behind as we move towards our own goal of avoiding the lapses and failures of diet, character or caution which caused them to falter. (1994, 2)

As we have seen above, and will see elsewhere in this volume, however – and noted in the course of our observations in schools – the transcendent with its attendant talk of the dead is generally elided in the day-to-day transactions of school and classroom. Even in the church schools in our study, religious iconography generally served regulatory functions, exhorting students to moral probity and rectitude. On occasion we witnessed prayers for examination success sitting on wall displays alongside very practical advice on how to secure such success (Conroy et al. 2012). In class discussions attempts by students to ask questions about transcendence were on occasion met with evasion – with, for example, teachers responding to questions about the afterlife by suggesting that should the students return in VI form they would have the opportunity to discuss such interesting but difficult ideas. Sometimes teachers avoided discussions of the transcendent on the grounds that they were just too difficult for many students. So, in one of our schools (Wallace), during a discussion on Buddhism, one of the students was getting distressed. Engaged in a conversation about the concept of impermanence, she gave voice to her distress in the following brief conversation:

> 'I have a soul Mrs McAlpine, my soul is going to go to heaven or hell unless of course I've been killed in a road accident' . . . 'sorry' . . . 'well you know where they leave the flowers at the roadside that's where your soul gets trapped'.

The Head of Department observed subsequently that, '. . . she genuinely thinks there's all these sad souls trapped around the country . . . I think a lot of kids nowadays live in a bubble created by the media and soap operas and they haven't a clue about what the real world is all about'. Both the original anxieties and the response are revealing. While the student may enjoy a very particular theological perspective on the afterlife, it is equally clear that the teacher finds such actual religious investments bizarre. After all, is having one's soul trapped at the site of one's death any more *absurd* than, say, the resurrection of the body – a claim that is absolutely central to the creedal formulations of mainstream Christianity? Despite the insistent claims that the religious represents a distinctive domain, this is an area of significant discomfort for quite a number of the teachers in our study. Steeped, as many appear to be, in the discourse of secular relativism – or perhaps, more accurately, in doctrines of immanence – they are reluctant to accept that students' claims about transcendence have any traction in the discussions about religion. Indeed, the same school's RE webpages indicate clearly, and tellingly, that Religious Education is first about the study of social systems, secondly cultures and lastly faiths. As it is handled in the daily linguistic and symbolic transactions of classroom and school, it is evident that what Voegelin considered as the *immanentization of the transcendent* (Voegelin 1952)[2] is forever present. Perhaps the most common move in this pallid homage to Dewey (1938/1998) is the multiple deployment of the football, or other club, by teachers, unable or apprehensive about placing the epistemic challenges of religious belief directly before their students. So it is, for example, that Mrs Dixon (Dundon Grammar) asks her class, '. . . would you wear anything, like a cross or a kilt, to show your beliefs or a football strip to show pride in what you believe or where you come from?' Interestingly, the question evokes little response from the students. In the ordinary everyday language of the classroom, distinctions between beliefs and attachments often disappear. The model for and the entry point into religious belief is generally something fairly prosaic – as if the problem of religious language could somehow be dealt with without a conversation about the metaphysical and the transcendent. There may indeed be ways in which sport offers analogies to religion – for example, in the ceremonial enactments of mass spectator sport; in the self-denial and asceticism of elite sports people; or, as in the case of the recent London Olympics, as a ground for forgetting distinctions and eliding differences in class and wealth. But these are nowhere in evidence in Mrs Dixon's use of the metaphor, which focuses, somewhat prosaically, on an attenuated analogy with *belonging*. But, as Hervieu-Léger (2000) points out, the analogical relationship between sport and religion fails to move beyond the emotional. In a sense this is how Mrs Dixon uses the sporting analogy and it is a function of how her own inclinations are a particular refraction of, and are galvanized by, the disauthentication and declassification of the transcendent; where the perpendicular reference is subordinated to the horizontal and constantly in search of the immanent.

In other cases, more religiously motivated teachers also fell prey to this move by slipping into the ethical as a substitute for the religious (a slippage often encouraged by official bodies (church and state)). Students commonly expressed the view that Religious Education was rather more concerned with the ethical than the religious. During one focus group conversation students from a church school (St. Ebba's) put it thus:

> Female: Nothing. My mum's side is Catholic, but my dad isn't, so I just don't do anything.
>
> Female: I'm not really sure why I'm at a Catholic school because I'm not brought up to be any religion.
>
> Int: Why do you guys think Religious Education is compulsory for students up to your age? Someone higher up has decided that it's compulsory, so why do you think that might be?
>
> Female: Because it does teach about good morals and stuff and it isn't always about the RE side of it, it's just basics like kindness and all that as well. I think that's quite good.

This relatively benign view of Religious Education, as largely concerned with a somewhat ill-defined moral uplift, reflects a general perception among students that Religious Education was, in the main, vaguely interesting if not very important.

But while lessons were not uniformly concerned with such uplift there was, even in the church schools, a strong tendency to foreground the ethical. In several (not just religiously denominated) sites, where abortion was under consideration, the materials used were often highly charged; in one such lesson a robust account of the wickedness of abortion was accompanied by a graphic image of the remains of a foetus in a pool of blood after suction aspiration; in another, an image of a foetus in a hand was accompanied by explanations that were loaded with emotive language such as 'the foetus is torn limb from limb'. In a further instance, a slide show incorporates a comic 'hoover' replete with accompanying suctions sounds. Despite using the material fairly fulsomely in class, during the subsequent discussion the teacher was keen to disown the resource, claiming that another teacher in another school had created the slides. Perhaps most surprisingly, the teacher observed that 'most doctors won't have any religious perspectives; they are usually atheists. I don't want to stereotype but most won't have any beliefs . . . they have huge egos' (Castle Grammar).

Apart from the particularly jaundiced view of doctors, other things may be at play here. Once again the religious becomes the ethical: the seriousness of one's religious beliefs and attachments are translated into adopting very particular ethical stances. This transformation of the religious into the ethical is not the exclusive prerogative of the postmodern liberal; it is just as likely to appear in the pronouncements of the religious fundamentalist. It was no more probable that students could anticipate a serious discussion of the teleological suspension of the ethical in the church school than in the common school. We shall return to this theme later, but for now it suffices to observe that these examples point towards the oddness of a subject that attempts to simultaneously encapsulate and mediate between these quite distinct worlds.

Too many expectations: Too little resource

The cases discussed above are, in important respects, clear manifestations of those conditions that so concerned Pope – the being stuck in the middle. But the strangeness of RE would appear to reside not only in its enfeebled attempts to bridge the gap between immanence and transcendence – certainly something required of no other subject on the curriculum as a primary entailment – but in the extraordinarily large claims for its educational possibilities and efficacy. Moreover, in the context of Religious Education, over-claiming has a substantial pedigree, with governments and teachers alike offering public approbation of the subject's efficacy as a site, if not *the* key site, for securing the humanizing imperatives of a complex and conflicted late industrial polity. Historically, or should we suggest, *rhetorically*, we have invested Religious Education with a high octane responsibility for making us better citizens – more liberal, more multiculturally aware and so forth. Indeed, in the study which is the focus of this volume, the sheer number of expectations laid at the door of RE by leading professionals, schools senior managers and teachers alike would be daunting for the most accomplished pedagogue! Of course other subject curriculum and guidance can appear to be demanding but few, if any, have anything like the same range (and with so little resource). Symptomatic of the high rhetorical tendency, the opening gambit of the 2010 non-statutory guidance for the subject in England and Wales suggests that Religious Education will:

[develop] an individual's knowledge and understanding of the religions and beliefs which form part of contemporary society.

[provoke] challenging questions about the ultimate meaning and purpose of life, beliefs about God, the self and the nature of reality, issues of right and wrong, and what it means to be human . . .

[develop] pupils' knowledge and understanding of Christianity, of other principal religions, other religious traditions and worldviews that offer answers to questions such as these.

contribute to pupils' personal development and well-being and to community cohesion by promoting mutual respect and tolerance in a diverse society . . .

[make] important contributions to other parts of the school curriculum such as citizenship, personal, social, health and economic education (PSHE education), the humanities, education for sustainable development and others . . .

[offer] opportunities for personal reflection and spiritual development, deepening the understanding of the significance of religion in the lives of others – individually, communally and cross-culturally. (DCSF 2010, 4)

A parallel, though differently (some might argue, more subtly) refracted list appears in the Scottish *Curriculum for Excellence* set of Experiences and Outcomes (Education Scotland n.d.), which evinces a similar list of invocations. Among the most notable, and perhaps most demanding, 'outcomes' is the imperative to 'explore and establish values such as wisdom, justice, compassion and integrity and engage in the development of and reflection upon their own moral values' (Education Scotland). It may indeed be desirable, indeed obvious, in a complex polity that we should nurture wisdom, but should it be the prerogative and obligation of a subject that is, as we shall see throughout this study, frequently marginalized and arguably too often enjoys a less than coherent epistemological, ethical and pedagogical identity? Surely the obligation to cultivate wisdom is a general obligation on education – but there is no evidence that this is stipulated elsewhere in the curriculum documents of any of the other subject areas. In the case of Northern Ireland, the expectations are subtly – but no less for that – focused on cultivating a *Christian* worldview. Hence at Key Stage 4, '[p]upils should develop their ability to think and judge about morality, to relate Christian moral principles to personal and social life, and to identify values and attitudes that influence behaviour' (Department for Education: Northern Ireland n.d.). This offers a very concrete shape to the particular policy moves in Northern Ireland, discussed earlier, which see the main churches have an over-riding interest in the shaping of the curriculum.

Such aims and objects around the personal formation and development embody a formidable set of challenges for both student and teacher, and are not to be found in anything like the same intensity elsewhere. For example, the parallel document within the Scottish *Curriculum for Excellence* corpus on Social Studies (the area of the curriculum students consider to be most akin to religious and moral education) invites students to 'develop their understanding of their own values, beliefs and cultures and those of others'. The distinction between this and the similar proposition in Religious Education is striking. To develop an understanding of something makes no requirement that I own it affectively. However, in Religious Education there is an explicit expectation that the educational process will bring about the express cultivation of certain kinds of virtues; 'establish' is certainly not a neutral conceit – requiring, as it does, actions to secure certain kinds of goods. After all, if one wants to establish geraniums in my garden one has to do something quite specific. Such virtues are, in the way of these things, fairly ill-defined but echo the overtly *moral* imperatives that surface in the curricular guidelines. It is this distinctly moral set of imperatives that distinguishes Religious Education from other areas of the curriculum yet – even if we allow that education in a liberal democratic polity should reasonably cultivate certain moral values – it is unclear from the actual lived experiences in the classroom that Religious Education is as successful as we might hope or expect at doing this.

The complex list of expectations enunciated in official documentation is further supplemented by the less formally grounded but equally salient belief (though more likely, hope) that Religious Education will be the main or supplemental means by which a broad swathe of human (social and psychological) concerns and anxieties will be addressed. The following emerged in the observations and conversations with the protagonists and practitioners who are variously charged with the responsibility for Religious Education:

1. Religious literacy (knowledge and understanding religious ideas and language and their social and cultural impact);
2. Citizenship education;
3. Dealing with truth claims and pluralism;
4. Multicultural awareness;
5. Spiritual and social cohesion –contributing to school ethos;
6. Nurturing pupils in particular communities (including catechesis);
7. Philosophical understanding;
8. Moral development;
9. Very particular 'Socratic dispositions' (virtues);

10. Spiritual life and religious observance;
11. Understanding heritage;
12. Enhancing local demographic considerations (exploring Christian heritage);
13. Sex and relationships education.

Moreover, in many schools, Religious Education appeared to be a locus for a wide range of social imperatives. This manifests itself in RE teachers being frequently called upon (certainly significantly more than other teachers) to lead on, or substantially support, Religious Observance/school charity activities and initiatives connected to community cohesion. They also routinely take on board personal responsibility for inculcating certain kinds of (almost always liberal) virtue – where, for example, the quite reasonable educational concern to promote understanding of multiculturalism is transformed into a much more robust ethical endeavour: actively to combat racism, anti-Islam sentiment and xenophobia. Irrespective of the 1988 Education Act injunction to be attentive to the principal religions of Britain, the decision by many planners to introduce Islam, and the ways in which it is approached in the classroom is often less about communicating the structure and topography of Islamic belief as it is about combating hostile attitudes among students that offend liberal values. As we see below, the teacher's comments in one school (Armourer's School) about introducing Islam earlier in students' studies is a salutary reminder that caution must be taken in considering students' responses to questions of value attachment amid the complexity of really understanding the dynamics of the Religious Education classroom.

> I introduced Islam into Year 8 as opposed to Year 9 because I felt that Islam phobia needs to be tackled far more head on and if you have a look at our schemes of work you'll notice that we do tackle Islam phobia right from the very beginning and if you ask those kids when there isn't a Muslim child actually in the room what they think of when you say Islam they will tell you, 9/11 and 7/7 and that is all you can get and that's all they want to talk about.

A considerable number of teachers in our sample, both in their claims and in the kinds of discursive practices they adopted in their teaching, manifested similar elisions between categories. Hence in another school (Banglatown), Ms Shalima, a Muslim teacher working with a largely Muslim class, discursively slips back and forth between insider and outsider. At one stage, in conversation outside the classroom she declares that she does not share her faith with her students but, de facto, moves almost seamlessly between the world of the insider and the world of the outsider in the teaching mode. PowerPoint slides on the purpose(s) of the lesson (on Zakah) are carefully constructed to offer the appearance of neutral description. The slide reads 'understand the importance of Zakah in the Muslim Community', but the conversation is voiced both in content and tone as an injunction, inviting the students to consider personally 'why it's important for every Muslim to give Zakah'. On another occasion, the lesson objective regarding a phrase from the Qu' ran reads, 'Think about what it is saying about the implications for a Muslim'. The apparent neutrality of the task description on the slide contrasts with Ms Shalima's spoken representation of 'What do you think God is trying to tell us?' Throughout this lesson, and indeed more generally in this context, the teacher(s) have tended to use linguistic forms, tone and images that will help the students to personally place themselves in their own belief system. The point at stake is not whether or not the teacher should or should not adopt a neutral tone, but the way in which teaching about Zakah in this context reflects the strangeness of a Religious Education that vacillates between dispassionate study and subtle forms of nurture. While moves of a liberal professional RE community since the late 1960s/early 1970s, appeared formally to turn away from Religious Education as an expression of Christian nurture[3] (Hull 1984), on the ground that it was not *education*, there appears still to be complex traffic between the two very different conceptions of RE in the public school. What is of interest here is the way in which such elisions are not the preserve of the religiously denominated school but are widespread (though as we have already noted, not universally so) in the discursive practices of a diverse range of schools. There are many who would consider such traffic as little more than an example of poor or misguided practice, and therefore symptomatic of nothing more than an individual predisposition to inappropriately inflect the classroom with personal attachments. Such attempts at personal inflection certainly receive little warrant in contemporary mainstream thinking about what constitutes appropriate pedagogy and purpose in Religious Education (Grimmitt 2000; Erricker 2010). While this may be comforting, we would suggest that more might be afoot here than the mistakes of benighted teachers.

Indeed, in many of our schools we witnessed teachers going to extraordinary lengths to try and meet the copious and conflicting demands with which the subject is freighted. In a number of instances social emergencies such as teenage pregnancy or more interestingly, panics about the internet (Segget and St. John Fisher), led to the introduction of special interventions located specifically in Religious Education. From our observations we consider this not atypical.

RE as constituted in ambiguity

The strangeness of Religious Education is not primarily, we would suggest, a function of arguments about pedagogies. After all, it is common to find education in general subject to quite distinctive claims about what might be the best way to teach x or y – claims that revolve around the relative weight to be placed upon the objective transmission of certain forms of knowledge, and the subjective engagement of the learner in making or contributing to such knowledge. However, as we shall suggest a little later, RE is bedevilled in a quite distinctive way by problems of epistemology that are not easily resolved and certainly not resolved by simply producing more or 'better' materials or pedagogic approaches. Nor does the strangeness of the subject derive from an argument simpliciter about teacher investments, since it is conceivable, for example, that two history teachers (one Irish, one English) could invest the events in the late eighteenth century, which occasioned the rise of the United Irishmen, with quite different meanings. And indeed they may well have quite different emotional and epistemic attachments to those events and their attendant ethical meanings. For the first, the events that led to the loss of an indigenous parliament were signals of oppression and ran counter to the narrative of the Enlightenment; for the second, they were instances of unruly usurpers intent on undermining the moral stability of good governance. Rather, the point here is that, however unpalatable to many, the very conceit of 'learning from' religion is constituted in ambiguity because the 'learning from' is overtly intended to shape the individual's beliefs. And, while 'learning in' religion might appear to be a practice that cries out to be dismissed by liberals as un- or anti-educational (Hand 2011), where it surfaces in the non-religious school, it is not clear that in everyday practice the distinction between 'learning from' and 'learning in' religion is actually or reliably upheld. In some secular schools, it was not uncommon for the RE teacher to run a bible class. Any assumption that students made clear distinctions between their beliefs, their studies, their teachers' beliefs and their engagement with the academic study of religion was repeatedly subject to question.

A further feature which marks the strangeness of Religious Education is the way in which teacher's interpretations of the theological and doctrinal claims of a particular tradition appear sometimes to have little connection to the official explanations of those traditions or indeed to the interpretations and explanations upheld by those communities themselves. Equally, some treatments of religion offered formulaic, superficial and anodyne accounts of a tradition which belied its complex manifestations (theological, political, social and ethical) in the world. Such disjuncts between religion(s) as social practice(s) were common across the range of schools in our study.

Let us briefly look at these two types in turn. The first focuses on a Catholic school (St Athanasius) where the teacher offers a deeply personal and, from an institutional perspective, idiosyncratic interpretation of spirit in that tradition.

Mrs Albarn asks the class:	'What is the Holy Spirit? Or who is the Holy Spirit? Now there's a question for you, who's game?' There follows a long silence.
Jarlath	'Your belief?'
Niamh	'Your faith?'
Jarlath	'A ghost, the ghost of Jesus?'
Mrs A	'What are we proclaiming when we bless ourselves?'
Niamh	'The Trinity'
Mrs A	'My interpretation . . . the spirit, the essence, the presence, Jesus went away, but it's his presence'.

Given the location of the school in the most religiously conservative part of the United Kingdom, what is particularly striking here is the attempt to reshape doctrine in a way that the teacher finds more emotionally appealing. Better by far to turn the notion of spirit into a metaphor than get involved in a difficult theological debate about the Trinity. Similarly in a state school serving a largely Muslim population, the students were very cynical about the theological accuracy of the teachers' explanations and their disassociation from their everyday beliefs. In yet another regular school, one of the teachers (an evangelical Christian) refused to teach about reincarnation or homosexuality on the grounds that they were 'wrong'. While teachers in our study rarely saw the aims and objects of Religious Education in entirely binary terms, in interviews, in their practices, and in their visual representation of religion they tended to foreground particular features and subordinate others depending on their particular attachments. While not common, we did witness examples of teachers and students struggling with complex theological conceits that matched the complexity of the thing being studied. In the 'test' answers in Figure 2.1, the student is responding to an exploration of the Mass in the Catholic tradition.

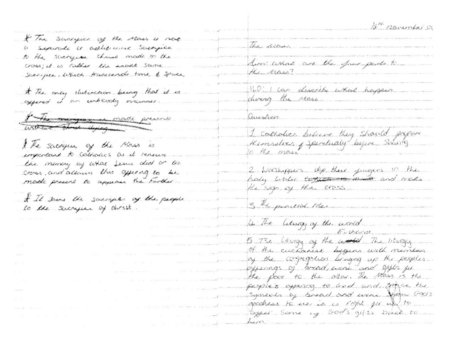

Figure 2.1 Student response – The Mass

Here older, more complex notions of the relationship between God and humanity emerge with the use of the twin conceits of sacrifice and appeasement. The extent to which such responses represent understanding is somewhat imponderable at this altitude, but it does point to the placing of theological language in the classroom and at the disposal of students. It is however interesting here to note the use of the third person. This work was a response to worksheets embedded in a scheme of work on Catholicism in a Catholic school (Bishop Fulton College). Interestingly the scheme was constructed by the Head of Department who, in a marked departure from tradition, was not a Catholic. The very act of replacing a Catholic departmental Head with a non-Catholic on the grounds that the former was a poor educationalist serves to quite precisely heighten the notion that we are dealing with extraordinarily porous categories. Given the normal requirement that RE teachers in Catholic schools are subject to a 'belief' test (legally so in Scotland) this move is particularly interesting.

Finally in these regards, another school in Northern Ireland illustrates the difficulty teachers often have in disaggregating their own beliefs, recognizing their position in relation to doctrinal claims and facilitating the development of the critical faculties of students. Hence one teacher considered critical engagement and reflective thinking to be important, but, in the end, these strategies were harnessed to the process of getting students to confront doubt so that they would emerge with a stronger faith. Of course this does not imply that the teacher wished to determine the content of the students' faith, but she did appear to want them to have a faith. Despite the strong claims made in our professional Delphi Seminar by religious representatives that the cultivation of critical stances was central to the purposes of RE, across all schools it was often highly conditional in practice.

In one of the student vignettes, developed to reflect their reading of some of the ethnographic data, our Forum Theatre Group further exposed the conflicted nature of many RE teachers' engagement with the critical. Using a split scene strategy, two versions of the same substantive lesson were performed in front of an audience comprising sixth form students from four schools that had taken part in the study: one drawing on the co-constructivist tradition, the other on more traditional didactic modes of engagement. Having drawn their material from recordings and field notes, the Theatre Group had imagined that the less didactic approach would be more congenial for the observing students, but this proved not to be the case. In both the immediate responses and in subsequent (recorded) discussion groups, the students made it clear that they frequently wearied of the relentless pursuit of the 'discussion'. Sometimes, they suggested, it was good to be 'told things'. The issue at stake here is constitutive, not because it is a choice between pedagogical preferences per se, but because it intimates a way of looking at RE, which diverts from the engagement with substantive claims to ethical and theological preferences. We are not suggesting that RE is the only site where there is a contest between such pedagogic preferences, but we would point out that it takes a very particular epistemic shape here; a shape that finds the overtly religious – with its claims to truth – simply too discomfiting. One deputy Head Teacher (Wallace) elegantly, if inadvertently, summed up the problem when he opined that he had been brought up a Catholic and considered such RE as indoctrinatory, and that, at the school where he now worked, they were proposing to change the name of the subject to humanities. This change of name would, he considered, change student attitudes. In parenthesis, two questions are worthy of our consideration. First, why, if he was so acutely aware of the indoctrination he received was it so singularly unsuccessful? And secondly, why would excising religion help students understand religion, religions and the religious impulse any better?

Assessment

> I like this part of Buddhism, I quite like this part of Islam . . . you guys change
> my mind a lot through all your discussions and things . . . I find it easier teaching
> you lot not having a particularly strong faith in anything . . . it makes it easier
> for me to understand when I'm not passionate about one thing and we can talk
> about it to each other. (Longwood Grammar)

This observation to her class, by one teacher, highlights the widely held belief that commitment in Religious Education is somehow to be abjured in the teaching of religion – despite the fact that, as we have noted above, the claims for RE conspicuously include one that we will indeed learn *from* religion: ideas that are personally (ethically and spiritually) transformative. This learning *from* religion is differently refracted in different schools, so that in a number of places we witnessed quite overt engagements with the conviction that pupils should be affected by their engagement with religio-ethical ideas. Hence in St. Bede's, the teacher observes that, in addition to learning about religion, '[t]here's the morality as well, what's right, what's wrong, how do you deem what's right and wrong and challenge them to really assess what their position is at the moment, what their standing is and why and pushing them to [say] why do you think I'm looking, not just to give an answer'. In other instances students are invited to articulate their personal responses to particular stimuli, not infrequently 'lights', stars and other (supposedly) *transcendent* stimuli. Or again, they are invited implicitly and explicitly to abjure certain illiberal attitudes and attachments. There were instances (although admittedly rare) where the imperative to foreground the evaluation of one's own attitudes assumed rather strange forms, insofar as the teacher brought deeply personal perspectives to bear, including highly specific views about evil, wicked spirits and so forth.

What these complex instances point to is the 'oddness' of a pedagogical enterprise that marks out its distinctiveness in terms of 'learning from'; an oddness that is manifest most acutely in the domain of *assessment*. As we have already observed, the subject has been shaped in recent years (in Britain at least) by bringing together learning *from* and learning *about* religion as if they were two sides of the same coin, and as if somehow the matter was both decided and unproblematic. But let us ponder this for a moment. The Catholic Church in Scotland (2011) recently developed a new syllabus for Catholic schools entitled *This is Our Faith*, where the learning intentions (the new outcomes) mimic simultaneously the standard performative character of the recently revised curriculum in general (the new Scottish *Curriculum for Excellence*) *and* the grandiloquent claims of *Assessment is For Learning* (AiFL). This confessional mimicry has some very strange consequences, whereby, for example, learning intentions for 15 year olds in Catholic RE now invite the student to personally acknowledge that alongside a new awareness of the incarnation they can assess how this newfound knowledge has enabled them to re-assess their own personal and or faith life.

Such mimicry in its turn throws up some interesting questions. For example, if a student were to observe that she *could not* assess what impact her newly discovered credal knowledge had on her charitable giving, or other tangible expression of her life, would she be deemed to have failed RE? If she understands the proposition but refuses to assent to its changing or shaping of her life, would she equally be deemed to have failed? If, say, she were not religious at all and could not really understand the import of the question, would she also have failed? While it may be seductive to think the problem here is confined to a confusion between, and conflation of, education and catechesis (though undoubtedly that is part of it) in contexts with an explicitly confessional religious character, there is in fact much more at stake. The 'learning from' Religious Education is, in its daily practice and in many diverse environments, rather less straightforward than many of its proponents would suggest.

In his pursuit of the question of self-assessment, Fancourt draws on Black and Wiliam's (2006) work, pointing out that, in schemes of work predicated on the principles of AiFL, a condition of engagement is that the teacher make explicit the feedback cycle for students. In other words, students should be able to assess their own development and progress with respect to the objectives of their learning as well as have an account of the assessment instruments. Fancourt suggests that, as currently constituted, RE entails four levels of self-assessment: self assessment *of* learning about religion; self assessment *for* learning about religion; self assessment *of* learning from religion; self assessment *for* learning from religion. Unsurprisingly, it is the last of these which requires a different kind of engagement, and which could be considered both in documentation and in practice to be somewhat challenging, if not problematic. What we saw in the daily practices of the RE classroom was evidence of the problem identified by Fancourt. The plasticity of the criteria, the constant moving between categories of description and evocation, analysis and involvement, articulated in standard assessment protocols, points to the strangeness of a subject that simultaneously asks students to reflect not only on their knowledge but also on their thinking, and not only on their thinking about their moral, religious or psychological

relationship to the object of study but also on their criticality with respect to it –
an endlessly recursive cycle! The problem posed by the mimicry of the form of
learning intentions in the creation of a modus operandi for self-assessment in the
reflective/affective domain was evident where students themselves considered
that the expectations placed on their study of Christianity tended towards the
theological, while that towards Islam was more descriptive (Linden Girls). The
consequences of this mimetic oddness was compounded by the daily constraints
that saw teachers complain to our ethnographers about the reporting load –
where only two teachers taught every student in the school, and had to report
on each year group. On the day before reports were due, we observed a day of
very unimaginative lessons: an S4 worksheet which the teacher (Segget), in her
own words, 'cobbled together' comprised work to keep her class busy; a double
period taken up watching a film; a lesson spent working from a textbook – so
that teachers could complete these same reports on time.

Policy

We deal more fully in the next chapter with policy across the various jurisdictions
within which the schools were located. But it is worth making a few remarks here
that exemplify the kinds of 'strangeness' that mark out Religious Education. First,
and despite recent attempts to frame a non statutory national framework, the
deep localism manifest in England in the existence of SACREs can be replicated
in no other subject. Here, particular communities get directly to influence
curriculum content and pedagogy in a way that would not be considered
appropriate elsewhere. Church schools have different locally determined
arrangements. Allied to this are the quite different structures in Northern Ireland
and Scotland where, in the case of the former, content in a single 'agreed' syllabus
is expressly shaped by catechetical rather than educational concerns. Indeed,
Religious Education is defined by the Department of Education and the four
main Christian Churches in Northern Ireland, which have a role to play within
the context of the revised curriculum, through 'presenting young people with
chances to develop their personal understanding and enhance their spiritual and
ethical awareness' (Department for Education Northern Ireland 2007). Scotland,
on the other hand, has two state-supported syllabuses – one for common schools
and one for church schools, which, as we have already noted, mimics the form
of the common syllabus but which struggles to provide educationally coherent
outcomes and assessment in the light of this alignment.

Secondly, we see that confusions in the policy domain both reflect and were reflected in the attitudes, dispositions, discourses and cultures of the schools. Recently, the Secretary of State for Education (in England), Michael Gove, decided to withdraw financial aid for students undertaking a Postgraduate Certificate in Education in RE while instating it for Greek and Latin (neither of which is legally mandated), despite more than half those teaching RE in secondary schools having no specialist qualification in the subject. This decision echoed a change of policy direction evident immediately after Gove took up office in May 2010, when he penned a short (though seemingly innocuous) letter to his predecessor Ed Balls, indicating that he proposed downgrading the significance afforded Religious Education in the secondary curriculum. But such a decision sits ill with other parliamentary discussions. Indeed, an idea of what legislators had in mind when legislating for the inspection of pupils' social, moral, cultural and spiritual development can be gained from a debate in the House of Lords in July 1996, wherein '. . . the training of good human beings, purposeful and wise, themselves with a vision of what it is to be human and the kind of society that makes that possible' (Hansard 1996) is made explicit. The ambiguity here mirrors, and is mirrored in, attitudes not infrequently expressed in schools and not infrequently by senior members of staff. These include complaints about the compulsory nature of Religious Education and how organizing resources and timetables would be so much more convenient if the compulsory status of the subject was rescinded. Earlier we observed one deputy head teacher's antipathy to the subject as presently constituted. Here, in more detail, are his full reflections:

> I got brought up a Catholic, so you can imagine what my associations with Religious Education are. It was more indoctrination than education. That was the Catholic Church, so I can understand the kids' reluctance to engage with the label of Religious Education. I know [the Head of Department] wants to call it humanities and I think the name change might change the perspective of it . . . A lot of stuff seems to be moral as opposed to religious, so I'm quite happy with the idea that maybe the religious title is dropped. It will take a few years to work its way through the system but if in 1st and 2nd year they start calling it humanities instead of Religious Education then that might be a nice wee step on the way. Thinking back to what I was like at school I can understand the reluctance of kids to religious . . . There was more important things to worry about than religion when you're a 13, 14, 15-year-old boy.' (Wallace)

While this was not a universal position and senior managers in schools such as Linden, Brockton, Dungally may well have demurred, it remains difficult to think of another subject where someone of this seniority would make such an observation. But, as we witnessed, such sentiments are not unusual in our data in Religious Education. Nor should we consider this antipathy to be isolated. Such opinions were regularly voiced by a range of senior personnel. In another school we observed that students,

> behaviour is of a lower standard than in other classes, and it is one of the few periods in S3 and S4 not taught in classes streamed by ability. Pupils sit a single unit of the Intermediate 2 course (1/3 of an Int 2), and at times do not even sit this. The Head of Department takes each S4 RE class for half of the year, and basically uses the time to teach Psychology and Philosophy, which are his main areas of interest, so that pupils have some experience of these subjects before making their Higher choices. The SMT singled out one Assistant Rector who is a Home Economics specialist to cover some S1 RE on the basis that she is a churchgoer, which caused her some personal difficulties because of the fit between her personal values and those of the RE curriculum in the schools. (Dundon, field notes)

Chater and Erricker (2012) point out that these policy inconsistencies are part of an inexorable decline in the status of Religious Education which, in any event they argue, is a residue of a Christian culture that has not, for some time, had any real purchase on the political and cultural imagination of Britain. They point out that the role of SACREs has not been unproblematic in England, and clearly in Northern Ireland the direct role of the main Christian traditions has continued to have a profound (and they would no doubt argue a nefarious) effect on the shape and content of the curriculum. Not unlike the deputy Head Teacher quoted above, they advocate a reconfiguration of the subject to make it more culturally palatable to a sceptical audience. Such a proposed reconfiguration would subordinate expressly religious language and understanding to a more generalized humanities curriculum, which would in many ways echo the kinds of sentiments evinced in the Toledo Guidelines (ODIHR 2007). The drive, here, is to establish *tolerance* in what is in effect considered to be a post-religious – or perhaps more accurately a 'poly-religious' – culture. While we will return to this issue in our final chapter, suffice to say at this stage that it is at best unclear that the extension of the very thing that has cultivated the conditions about which Chater and Erricker are so vocal is likely to offer any amelioration. The constitutive problems witnessed in these schools tend to arise as a consequence of epistemic muddle and a confusion between the personal, the social and the rational.

Explaining the strangeness

The examples discussed here of the ways in which the strangeness of Religious Education manifests itself in the daily practices of school and classroom needs some kind of explanation. It may of course be possible to construe each particular instance as no more than an isolated and contingent occasion that is representative of nothing but itself. While, as we have suggested earlier, we do not wish to suggest that our study is straightforwardly generalizable, we do nonetheless recognize certain patterns that point us beyond the particular and individual. During the course of this study, we have tried to remain faithful to our desire to allow the conditions of, and attachments to, teaching, learning and organization to surface by themselves. This does not suggest an atheoretical approach but focuses on the emergence of theoretical explanation as a condition of empirical exploration. The condition of strangeness under consideration here itself emerges from considerable constitutive conflict. We observed earlier that the challenge of confusion of purpose was not a consequence of a battle simpliciter between essentialists and constructivists. When we examine discursive practices of professional educational life it is tempting to think of these in binary opposites, traditionalist versus progressives, those who believe in the objectivity of knowledge versus those who think of knowledge in subjective terms, those attached to a transmission model versus those who prefer an experiential model, those who believe in the study of the thing in itself versus those who attach meaning to utility and so forth. Such bifurcations emerged to be rather less seductive in the daily transactions of the classroom hence what surfaces is a more profound epistemic conflict that, itself, goes back to the Middle Ages; the conflict between realists and nominalists, between Aquinas and William of Ockham. This ancient conflict is between those who considered that the world is organized by universal defining categories and those that considered such universals as obscuring the individuality of all things; between those who hold fast to metaphysical shaping and forming essences and those who maintain the singularity of being and event (Eagleton 2012). The first category evokes the principle that description and explanation follow a kind of pre-ordained shape whereas the second holds to the idea that each experience is unique and we build up general cases from reflecting on the overlaps and similarities between individual experiences and occurrences. This conflict was, and, we would suggest, continues to be, worked out in the lived experiences of Religious Education. Once, we considered the world to be the creation of God but this universalist doctrine has gradually morphed into a belief that the world creates God. Consequently, in Religious Education, the study of God as a universal or originary category, shaping the world, has given way to the study of religion as a social and contingent creation. But things are rarely straightforward in this domain since the older notion continues to erupt into the classroom as both a memory and, on occasion, as a desire. While it is possible to see some of the same issues emerge in other spaces in the curriculum – literature and art, for example – the weight of dealing with the clash between universals and particulars is one that RE teachers must confront almost on a daily basis. The religious impulse is meant to simultaneously reflect and offer some universal meaning, some hope or soaring of the soul, but the modes of operation of Religious Education are increasingly tethered to the language of meaning, of social creation and contingent choice which, ironically, ultimately may be *meaningless*. If human beings are no more than flesh and bones, sensations and reactions yet political culture remains attached to a more universalist ethical claim then the challenge for the religious educator, as we witnessed, becomes ever more difficult. In one sense, the daily attempts by RE teachers to offer a space for individual attachment represent the impulse to free up the student from what has come to be considered the tyranny of universals and objective realism in favour of the particularity of opinion. As one group of students in a Catholic school observed,

> They don't force their opinion on you, they let you say yours . . . They say what their opinion is but they still have a discussion, they say 'say what you want' . . . I don't think they really judge you if you do have an opinion that's not theirs either. (St. Bede's)

Here, a Catholic school, notionally committed to the claims of universalism, is perceived by its students to operate within the ambit of the provisional and particular. Indeed the school chaplain at one stage observes that Religious Education is concerned with

> all faiths and all religious experience and human experience within the culture of our country . . . So for example the RE curriculum is not in terms of a strictly speaking pedagogical exercise, it's not exclusively catholic . . . Such moves, common across the schools in our study leave open a key challenge for religious education as a meaningful activity for students.

As Eagleton would have it,

> [b]ecause reality is no longer structured, no longer thickly sedimented with meaningful features and functions, it no longer thwarts our freedom of action as much as it once did; yet by the same token, the more vacuous that freedom now appears. (op cit, 7)

The move to reposition the subject in response to these constitutive problems is noted elsewhere.

This move was regularly made across a number of schools (Northern Ireland being the exception), one of which we discuss in detail in Chapter 4. At this stage, suffice to observe that, in addition to that instance, there was substantial evidence elsewhere of a move away from the explicit study of religion. For example, the Head of Department at Brockton argued that theirs was a philosophical approach concentrating on ethics and philosophy at both GCSE and A Level. Another (Dundon) was in the process of re-positioning himself (after a new course of study) in psychology and philosophy and swapping classes with other teachers so as to encourage further study in philosophy and psychology. Yet a third opined:

> And of course you know that we re-branded it, it's now religious studies. It's interesting because we feel, it might be semantic, but that actually gives a more academic feel. The actual GCSE is called religious studies anyway. RE seems to have a hangover from primary school when we talk about RE and then the other re-branding of names similar to that was A level in philosophy and ethics, so when we had it as religious studies A level we had nobody wanting to do it, but when you call it philosophy and ethics we're [full]. (Gorston)

This epistemological and ethical strangeness of RE is compounded by a further condition of its construction; that it is a social practice and not merely a function of social behaviour. By this we suggest that the meanings with which Religious Education is inscribed emerge within a community that shares certain normative assumptions about what particular actions, activities, interpretations and intentions mean. Those normative assumptions are predicated not only on the disposition to engage with, or share, certain kinds of practices with others operating in the same sphere (social behaviour) but also on the deployment of sanctions in support of the regulation of behaviour. 'For social behaviour, a disposition to at least partial coordination of one's own behaviour with the behaviour of one's fellows is necessary and sufficient' (Esfeld 2003, 12). For social practices, normative reinforcement by way of encouragement and discouragement in the making of commonality is also necessary. The varied and various professional protagonists in our study were influenced by certain powerful incentives to see Religious Education in certain ways, dictated by a number of overlapping conceits. Hence in the Delphi seminar (Baumfield et al. 2012), senior professionals from what might be considered as widely divergent epistemic attachments constantly sought to establish and occupy common ground around certain kinds of perceived liberal values. These values tended to be grounded in the moral superiority of 'otherness', of student voice, of refractions of constructivist pedagogies and of 'relevance'. Such values (even for those who might not have considered themselves liberals) consistently emerged in the ways in which teachers constructed their own professional identity as well as the imperatives of the subject.

But it would be a mistake to conceive of Religious Education as a social practice that was, in its shape and form, confined to the internal dynamics of the classroom or even the school. We would argue that it is a function of a more complex set of forces, confirmations, disconfirmations, encouragements and discouragements, best seen in the way in which religious communities, politicians and other 'interested' parties actively engage in the moulding of the subject. In each of the jurisdictions, as we see in Chapter 3, while the role of churches, religious bodies and so forth differ across the various constituencies of the United Kingdom, they are *all* present in the exercise of shaping RE. From the overt agreement of the main Christian churches in Northern Ireland, to the SACREs in England, the 'communities' have significant influence. The SACREs offer an interesting refraction of this problem given the extraordinary variation in their structure, shape and indeed the advice that they offer the professional groups and the school communities within which they operate. Here indeed we can witness the operation of 'nested identity', reflecting, as it does, the religious demography and disposition of the authority that the SACRE is intended to serve. Hence the St. Helen's SACRE, with the highest recorded population of Christians in the United Kingdom at 86.88 per cent (British Religion in Numbers 2001), is comprised entirely of Christians, while Tower Hamlets, with the lowest Christian population (38.64%), has much greater diversity in its membership[4]. Despite the recommendation of the national Non-Statutory framework (QCA 2004) that Religious Education should address non-religious life stances, Humanists are not permitted to sit, as of Right, on Committee A (although they may be co-opted and sometimes are).

In their particularity and boundedness, religions are themselves social practices and their adherents, both individually and collectively, subject to stratified arrangements of covert and overt epistemic and ethical confirmations and disconfirmations as well as subtle and not so subtle sanctions. Hence the life of the religious person or community, so to say, entails living a life refracted through complex sets of attachments, beliefs and correlated actions. These social practices establish certain forms and patterns of relationship between the individual and/or community and the political, cultural and social life of a polity as a whole. Hence Roman Catholics believe x and wish that this belief be considered (with the expectation of real influence) by legislators in shaping social policy. Given the wide variety of relations within and across religious communities, this inevitably creates a very complex picture of the ways in which influence, policy and practice are transacted and performed in a polity (see, for example, Conroy 1999; Judge 2002). They are not just collections of social behaviours. If we then take this extraordinarily complex social practice, or more correctly social *practices*, and nest them within the similarly complex set of social practices that is education (which is equally shaped by and subjected to a complex set of formal and informal confirmations and disconfirmations) we begin to see why religion might inevitably be somewhat strange (see Figure 2.2).

The particular strangeness here arises because the religious adherent and their community lay claim to a determining influence in shaping the curriculum that would not be considered appropriate by any interest group (say the RSPCA) precisely because we consider them *more than* an interest or pressure group Add to this mix the complex political and legislative environments (as outlined in the next chapter; see also Conroy & Lundie 2013) – as well as the range of expectations, as outlined above – and the picture gets yet more complicated. Here nested identity is no mere metaphor, but a descriptive heuristic that points to this complex relationship between two already complex discursive domains.

Conclusion

In this chapter we have tried to illustrate the myriad ways in which the 'nested' or embedded identity of Religious Education – and the epistemic slips between categories – gives rise to its strangeness. However, it would be a mistake to regard the subject community as an entirely unwitting victim. As we shall see later, in the attempts to respond to the shifting conditions thrown up by a loss of self-confidence and a need to feel relevant, RE teachers appear to partake in a fractured discursive collusion with, for example, exam systems that, at least arguably and as we hope to illustrate later, simultaneously disrupt the fabric of a

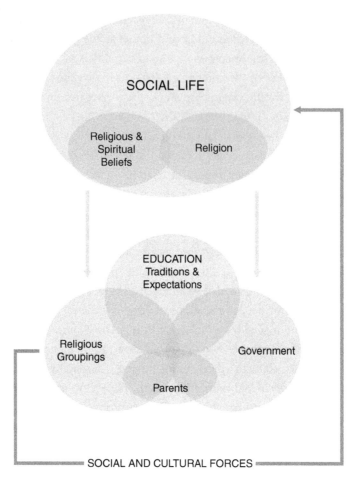

Figure 2.2 Nested Identity

civilized society while claiming to promote the common good. In this sense, the subject of RE represents a very particular refraction of a conflict that continues to mark education more generally. The unintended collusion is clearly seen in this lengthy extract from an interview with one of the teachers in the study.

> Yeah, there's more than a battle, our time is being eroded because of learning for life and work. That's not necessarily a bad thing. I mean I have very good relationship with the co-ordinator for learning for life and work and so therefore the way we are looking at it, is a lot of the things that we teach are quite similar as you said in terms of citizenship and stuff. So we can help the kids and connect the learning, so that maybe within Citizenship or within PD[5] they do certain things and in RE we are developing the side of things. One of the things this year

is kids have a shorter time in 5th year . . . drugs, alcohol, things like that they know they have done all of that in PD and they have done all the things they need to know about the effects of drugs and alcohol; the effects of drugs and alcohol and the society side of things. So I focus on the religious view points. But you have to make sure that they can connect that. You know that in the exam they need to be able to connect those things together. (Northwest)

Recognizing the determined erosion of the subject, the teacher nonetheless embraces the consequent elision of difference between Religious Education and the other 'character forming' entailments in the curriculum. The strangeness of RE is manifest in the ongoing attempts to reposition it with respect to other subjects and entailments in the curriculum. As we proceed the strange character of Religious Education will continue to resurface in myriad ways.

Notes

1 know thyself.
2 While we may not wish to subscribe to Voegelin's theological concerns it does seem that this sense of the immanentization of the transcendent effectively captures a description of the moves that are being made in Religious Education to make truly transcendent claims more acceptable in what is considered to be a post religious culture.
3 A comparison between the ILEA (1968) Agreed syllabus, Learning for Life in 1968 (with quite strong undertones of Christian nurture) and the Birmingham (1975) Agreed syllabus with its emphasis on pluralism points to a decisive rupture in British Religious Education.
4 The St. Helen's SACRE comprises a membership as follows; five Church of England, four Roman Catholics and one representative of the Free churches; whereas Tower Hamlets has seven Muslim representatives, four from the Church of England, three Roman Catholics, one representative of a black-majority Christian church, one Free Churches representative, one Jewish, one Buddhist, one Hindu and one Sikh representative.
5 Personal development.

3

The Complexities of UK Policy and Practice

Evolving Policy and its practical implications in Religious Education in the United Kingdom

While the central resource for this study is ethnographic research, it is important that we do not neglect the policy dimensions of Religious Education across the United Kingdom. Clearly policy and practice are related, and it would be naive to think that practice is either exclusively determined by policy or unrelated to policy; no doubt the truth lies somewhere in between these two poles. As Ball et al. (2011) have pointed out, in a space consistently subjected to policy initiatives, the real challenge is to understand how well policies are enacted, how teachers *act* with respect to policy initiative. Here we attempt to plot the complex policy landscape across the United Kingdom and simultaneously illuminate some of its challenges for everyday practice. Of course central to ascertaining the role and influence of policy on practice in Religious Education, is the most obvious fact that the United Kingdom comprises four different nations – England, Northern Ireland, Scotland and Wales – each with its own distinctive history, constitutional arrangements, traditions and in some cases legislation. This does not mean that there are no shared features, though it does complicate matters. At a formal level common influences can be identified: legislation, non-statutory advice, curriculum bodies, examination boards, professional interest groups and representations from religious communities, for example. Moreover, Religious Education in the different nations is broadly subject to the same social and intellectual influences: the shift to post-industrial societies, the processes of secularization and of globalization, increasing diversity in society and so on. Intellectually, Religious Education has had to respond to these challenges, with English religious educators, for the most part, taking the lead in developing curricular material and pioneering new approaches. In many respects English Religious Education, chiefly because of its size in terms of the number of professional educators and higher-level institutions involved, has dominated intellectual developments in the subject from the 1960s until the present. As a consequence, the tendency in some circles is to equate Religious Education in the United Kingdom with British Religious Education, and then equate British Religious Education with Religious Education in England. There is some logic to these reductions. One can appreciate the reasons for treating England and Wales together, which is the strategy that will be adopted here, for not only are both countries subject to the same social and intellectual influences, both follow the same legislation (though it should be noted that, following the creation of the Welsh Assembly, there are now two different sets of national guidelines to interpret the legislation, see QCA 2004a; DCELLS 2008). Such reductions, common influences apart, however, fail to capture the diversity of arrangements, policies and accommodations that characterize Religious Education in the different parts of the United Kingdom, despite the formal similarities; And yet, as we repeatedly witness in the stories that comprise everyday classroom practice, there remain stark theological and philosophical differences, often occluded by recourse to common language about 'learning from' Religious Education, criticality, experiential learning and so forth. Differences between (nominally) common schools and church schools in Northern Ireland are actually rather less pronounced than differences between common schools across the United Kingdom. In other words, as we have seen already and will note further as we go along, teachers in common schools in the same region often differed markedly with respect to both aims and execution.

The notion of 'policy in religious education' does not admit of a straightforward definition or application. On a narrow interpretation, policy in Religious Education could be confined to the legislative framework pertaining to the practice of Religious Education in schools. Such an approach, while having the advantages of identifying one of the major influences on the nature and practice of Religious Education and of limiting the material for discussion to easily manageable proportions, nevertheless fails to recognize the range of influences that have relevance to policy construction and implementation. By contrast, on a broader interpretation, policy can refer to almost any advice, counsel or factor that influences Religious Education. The disadvantage of this approach is that by ranging too widely it becomes more difficult to distinguish between what is significant in terms of influence from what is incidental or merely local. While there is no fully objective or neutral way of demarcating what constitutes policy in Religious Education, clearly any responsible and realistic interpretation has to identify and consider both the chief influences and the range of influences that determine and condition RE in the different national contexts.

The conjunction of practice with policy in the title of this chapter is meant to indicate that the basic orientation of the analysis is on the ways in which policy is framed and on the influence of policy on the nature and practice of Religious Education in schools and in the classroom. While granting a certain priority to policy over practice, and the assumption that policy 'drives' practice, it is not assumed that there is always a straightforward or necessary derivation of specific classroom practices from some particular policy or policies, or that influence is always unidirectional from policy to practice; rather there is a dialectical relationship between the two, whereby policy influences practice and practice, in turn, influences policy. It is also worth recording that the data generated by the Delphi seminars revealed that many professional religious educators are critical of national policy initiatives, which are regarded as focusing on generic skills and measurable outcomes, while neglecting to appreciate the intrinsic benefits of studying religion and the wider educational aims to which Religious Education contributes. By the same token, there was no universal agreement among such professionals with some considering that there was a need for a common curriculum while others demurred, some believing that it was possible to create expectations that Religious Education could be objectively taught while embodying highly particularistic claims and others claiming that only a policy of substantive neutrality could produce appropriate forms of Religious Education. For some a more felecitious claim was for passionate impartiality, yet even such passionate impartiality is ultimately predicated on the claim to substantive epistemic neutrality.

Policy and practice in England and in Wales

The Education Reform Act of 1988 provides the legal context for the practice of Religious Education in England and Wales. The subject is dealt with in three short paragraphs in Section 8 and in Sections 84–8. For the most part the basic requirements and entitlements of the 1944 Education Act are reiterated: the compulsory nature of Religious Education and the parental right of withdrawal are both reaffirmed, for example, though a number of additional demands are made: (1) that any new Agreed Syllabus 'shall reflect the fact that the religious traditions in Great Britain are in the main Christian whilst taking account of the teaching and practices of the other principal religions represented in Great Britain' (Section 8.3); (2) that RE must be non-denominational in county (now 'community') schools, while making it clear that teaching about denominational differences is permitted, a clause which dates back to the 1870 Education Act; (3) that Standing Advisory Councils for Religious Education (SACREs) must be established and such bodies are granted extended functions, notably to grant determinations (in exceptional cases) to lift the requirement regarding the broadly Christian character of collective worship in schools (to date 230 schools in England have received such determinations) and to require a Local Education Authority (LEA) to set up a statutory Agreed Syllabus Conference to review the Locally Agreed Syllabus every five years and (4) that the Agreed Syllabus Conference, as well as of the SACRE representing denominations other than the Church of England, Committee A, must also reflect the principal non-Christian religious traditions in the area. The Local Authority has a statutory duty to report to the Secretary of State every year on the work of its SACRE. Despite the extensive legislation over time, a cursory glance at the detailed information from a range of local authorities is apt to confuse rather than clarify the status and purposes of the various committees. Consistency of presentation of even the legal position clearly eludes local government. One possible consequence of the evolution of free school legislation is that whatever (modest) force currently underpinning SACREs and Agreed syllabuses is likely to witness significant erosion.

Following the 1918 Act, debate focused on the precise meaning of the different clauses, particularly what it meant to acknowledge that religious traditions in Britain are 'in the main Christian' and what it meant to 'take account' of the 'other principal religions' represented in the country. How many religions were to be studied? What percentage of time was to be allocated to Christianity and what to 'other traditions'? In response to such concerns the Department of Education and Science in January 1989 issued Circular 3/89, which chiefly reiterated the wording of the Act and did little to clarify or explain what precise form of Religious Education was in accord with the new legislation. The position expressed in the Circular was that it was a matter for the LEA to determine whether or not a syllabus produced by its Syllabus Conference conformed to the law. Against this background, John Hull, at the time the editor of the *British Journal of Religious Education*, and one of the most respected voices in the Religious Education professional community, presented his 'considered' interpretation of the Religious Education clauses ('considered' because this interpretation conflicted with his initial interpretation, see Hull 1988, 2). He contended that the requirement for agreed syllabuses to take account of the teaching and practices of the other principal religions represented in Great Britain broke the 'assumed

Christian monopoly' over content that still persisted in some existing syllabuses and gave legal force to multi-faith Religious Education of the form that had been widely practised in Britain 'for the past fifteen years or so'. 'There is absolutely no suggestion', he averred, 'that religious education should be 'Christian-based', 'Christian centred' or should offer an undue emphasis upon Christianity' (Hull 1989, 60) – a curious comment, given that the legislation required syllabuses to 'reflect the fact that the religious traditions in Great Britain are in the main Christian' (perhaps his comment turns on some kind of fine distinction between *in the main* and *undue* emphasis). In his view 'taking account of the teaching and practices of the other principal religions represented in Great Britain' (Section 8.3) means that no Agreed Syllabus meets the requirements of the Act unless it includes the teachings and practices of 'Judaism, Islam, Hinduism, the Sikh faith, and Buddhism' (Hull 1989, 61).

Under the influence of Hull and others (see RE Council 1989), the view that Religious Education in schools should comprise a study of these six religions quickly established itself among religious educators, and received support in 1994 with the publication of Circular 1/94, and of two 'Model' Syllabuses that were intended to exemplify good practice by the School Curriculum and Assessment Authority (SCAA): Model 1, entitled *Living Faiths Today*, was phenomenological; Model 2, entitled *Questions and Teachings* focused on religious practice. This represented a further significant shift in the interpretation of 'local determination', with a nationally determined syllabus, negotiated between bodies representing Religious Education professionals and representatives of the faith communities, promulgated by a national body with responsibility for National Curriculum subjects. These Model Syllabuses have subsequently been superseded by a single Non-Statutory National Framework (QCA 2004a) which, while retaining the emphasis on the study of six major religions, also 'recommends' the study of a range of further traditions 'such as the Bahá'í faith, Jainism and Zoroastrianism', and 'secular philosophies such as humanism' for all pupils (QCA 2004b, 12). This attempt to broaden further the content of Religious Education is a controversial proposal and has met with understandable criticism, even though the Framework has been endorsed by the Religious Education Council of England and Wales and by the main Christian churches. Moreover, as we have seen repeatedly in the schools in this study, expansion and mission creep pose very real practical and epistemic challenges for teachers. Recently, in contradistinction to the advice of the Framework, the 2007 Birmingham Agreed Syllabus for Religious Education has decided not to require six religions to be covered, rather making provision for the study of those religions that are deemed educationally and religiously relevant within the local context; in many cases this will amount to fewer than six religions (see Barnes 2008). The complexity here is, in important respects, an evocation of the strangeness of RE discussed in the previous chapter.

Part of the impetus for the compulsory study of a range of religions comes from the requirement of the 1988 Act that the composition of Committee A on the Agreed Syllabus Conference must reflect the principal non-Christian religious traditions in the area. An examination of the composition of English SACREs in 2008 confirms that this has happened. For example, St Helens SACRE, representing the local authority with the highest population of Christians in the United Kingdom, 86.9 per cent (Office for National Statistics Census 2001), was composed entirely of representatives of the Christian churches, five from the Church of England, four Roman Catholics and one representative of the Free Churches. By contrast, the composition of the Tower Hamlets SACRE, representing the local authority with the largest number of non-Christian religious adherents (ONS Census 2001), was much more religiously diverse: seven Muslim representatives, four from the Church of England, three Roman Catholics, one representative of a black-majority Christian church, one Free Churches representative, one Jewish, one Buddhist, one Hindu and one Sikh representative, a total of 20 members on Committees A and B. In the remaining chapters of this volume the complex relationship between the lived shape of Religious Education and the religious composition of the local community emerges in varied forms. In some of the most interesting examples, the overtly theological[1] claims of religion represented in the community were foregrounded for consideration.

Despite such examples of localism and local determination remaining a legal reality, on a number of practical levels, the influence of the Non-Statutory National Framework (2004) furthers the trend towards central influence and control over the Religious Education curriculum. The National Framework copies the structure and format of the statutory National Curriculum: the Framework includes level descriptors using the National Curriculum eight-level scale, and the Qualifications and Curriculum Development Authority (QCDA) has published exemplification materials which demonstrate how to assess student work using the level descriptors – the exemplification materials cover content drawn only from the National Framework. Some may suggest that, given the indicative non-stautory nature of the exercise and the legislated localism, this was all that might sensibly be done. However, it is equally plausible that a wide range of exemplifications drawn from the many local syllabuses might have offered a stronger sense that the national was in an authentic dialogue with the local. In a number of respects these drives for centralization are the product of professionals who consider that localism has left the subject weak and exposed, And there is little doubt that a series of moves by the current Secretary of State for Education in England (withdrawal of bursary support for those undertaking teaching qualifications in the subject, downgrading its status in a letter to his predecessor, exclusion of examination RE from the English Baccalaureate, disproportionate reductions in the number of available 'training' places despite a huge shortfall of qualified teachers and so forth) reinforces the sense of a subject under siege. Interestingly, however, these moves are not mirrored in the other constituencies – yet as we saw in the previous chapter, many of the identity and practices issues are remarkably similar.

As noted above, the overwhelming trend in Religious Education has been for greater centralization. While there are different manifestations of this in the different constituencies of the United Kingdom the trend is the same. The framework document in England has robust cognates in a Curriculum for Excellence and its predecessor, 5-14, in Scotland and the Core syllabus in Northern Ireland. Advice and guidance from QCA/QCDA are backed up by inspection and examination regimes. The subject appears to be moving ever closer to a position which parallels that of other subjects in the National Curriculum (though see below for qualification). A comparison of Agreed Syllabuses reveals that *most* hold their content in common, despite legal provision for 'local determination'. This centralizing impulse is further advanced by recent draft guidance from the, then, Department for Children, Schools and Families, which explicitly states that 'the Framework and its implementation are the basis of Government policy' (DCSF 2009, 18) and that the Framework should guide Agreed Syllabus Conferences in their production of a local syllabus. The problem is, according to some critics, that the Framework is prescriptive in ways that the legislation is not. On their interpretation, central control over the content of Religious Education is advanced under the pretext of 'raising standards' and local influence is reduced accordingly (Felderhof 2004, 2010). The irony is that in the last years of the Labour Government, that is, 2009–10, it began to scale down its ambition in detailing the content for all other subjects, yet under the influence of QCDA raised this ambition in relation to Religious Education. It is difficult to see this as entirely divorced from the energies and drives of key professional actors who bring to the table normative attachments borne out of particular lenses on both what is perceived to be happening in the classroom and their epistemic and ethical purview (see Chater & Erricker 2012). The closure of the QCDA in March 2012, however, by the Conservative Government, as part of its wider education reforms, has signalled a halt to efforts to determine centrally the curriculum and content of Religious Education. This volte face illustrates the challenge for the teacher in the daily life of the classroom. Under one administration (where there has historically been modest support for the place of Religious Education) they are part of a community seeing its fortunes rise and quite suddenly, under a new government rhetorically attached to the entailments of the subject, their fortunes plummet.

There are also a number of official and semi-official institutions and groups that influence what is taught and practised in Religious Education. Besides the curriculum bodies referred to above, the most significant set of bodies in syllabus creation in the secondary education sector are the examination boards. An increasing number of schools, following the advice of their local Agreed Syllabus, seek to provide their compulsory Religious Education at Key Stage 4 through the medium of a 'short-course' GCSE, comprising 50 per cent of a full GCSE course. The following statement from the Dorset Agreed Syllabus, which places the emphasis on public examinations at Key Stage 4, is typical:

> Whilst there is no legal requirement that students must sit public examinations, students deserve the opportunity to have their learning in religious education accredited. (Dorset Agreed Syllabus 2005)

These examination courses are subject to the commercial pressures of a market in examination board provision. For example, in 2010, three out of five boards offered a GCSE option on Sikhism, one of which was only available when paired with Buddhism, while all five boards offered a course specifically tailored to the requirements of Roman Catholic Religious Education, reflecting the desires of a significant sector of the education 'market'. None of the boards offered courses on any religious traditions other than the six identified by Hull as discussed earlier. While we discuss the nature of examinations and texts in some detail later, it is worth making a couple of points here with regard to the broader policy context. With league tables exerting pressure on schools, teachers and pupils to succeed in examinations, examination board approved textbooks offer teachers a level of certainty in the selection and delivery of learning objectives. A review of textbooks endorsed by the examination boards reveals that these textbooks focus overwhelmingly on either Christianity alone or Christianity and Islam; only one textbook includes four religions: Christianity, Islam, Judaism and Hinduism (for the Edexcel Examinations Board). There are at least five approved textbooks for Catholicism, four for Islam, while the only approved resource for the revised GCSE courses on Buddhism or Sikhism are teacher guides from OCR, leaving teachers who wish to deviate from the market-driven majority reliant on materials which offer much less guarantee of a fit with examination success criteria. It can plausibly be argued that the manner in which the examination system has come to dominate resources and pedagogy at Key Stage 4 constrains the religious curriculum and militates against the contribution of Religious Education to the wider social and moral aims of education in the final years of compulsory education. GCSE Examination syllabi also bear witness to a move towards the increasing popularity of moral philosophy and ethics as a discrete unit within or the totality of a qualification in Religious Studies, though the popularity of this among teachers and pupils is not reflected in the National Framework. In fact in some regards the growth of GCSE options in the philosophy of religion and in philosophical and religious ethics constitute an implicit critique of much post-confessional Religious Education, which until recently at the policy level gave scant attention to truth claims in religion and to religious morality.

A further significant influence on Religious Education in England is the increasing diversity of school provision, with the promotion of 'schools with a religious character', voluntary-aided schools, free schools and academies, which are exempt from the provisions of their Local Authority Agreed Syllabus, but for whom the 2009 DCSF guidance still recommends the Non-Statutory National Framework. The two largest providers of faith schooling in England, the Church of England and the Roman Catholic Church, have adopted the principle of 'additionality' in their syllabus guidelines; that is, they seek to ensure that Religious Education in their schools achieves all of the aims set out in the Non-Statutory National Framework, while incorporating them within a wider Religious Education framework which seeks to develop students' religious learning in line with the faith commitment of the school. The increasing diversity of the state sector, combined with the market forces of Examination Board choice, have tended to create a multiplicity of interpretations of the core guidance and to highlight differences between GCSE examination requirements and those of the National Framework, with regard to attainment objectives, for example. In the meeting of these forces of governmental and parental control, the system established by statute, of Local Authority determination of the Religious Education syllabus, is increasingly elided in practice. However, as our ongoing analysis of the substantial role of textbooks in determining patterns of 'delivery' and engagement demonstrates, such examination-led interventions tend to moderate distinctiveness. Hence, the policy context is one forged by contrary and competing impulses.

The common character of Religious Education in England and Wales changed recently with the decision of the Welsh Assembly Government in 2008 to publish its own National Exemplar Framework for Religious Education. The Welsh Framework enumerates three core skills for Religious Education: engaging with fundamental questions, exploring religious beliefs, teachings and practice(s) and expressing personal responses. While the Welsh Framework refers to 'Christianity and the other principal religions' in each Key Stage, no other religions are specifically named: in this and in other regards it is much less prescriptive that the English Framework. It must be borne in mind, however, that the Welsh Framework emerges out of more than 20 years of common policies and practice with England. More than this, it has been subject to the same ethical and epistemic forces, forces that emerge out of the Lancaster School[2] and which – with their attendant pedagogic practices – continue to be shaped by the Religious Education Council of England and Wales. It may be some time yet before a distinctively Welsh form of Religious Education emerges.

Policy and practice in Northern Ireland

Policy and practice in Religious Education in Northern Ireland take a distinctive form, compared with the rest of the United Kingdom, a form that is in part determined by the very pronounced historical and continuing influence of Christianity. Levels of Christian religious affiliation have historically been and remain high in the province. In the 2001 census, 46 per cent of the population identified themselves as Protestant and 40 per cent identified themselves as Catholic, statistics that are broadly similar to earlier censuses. Recent research reveals that the majority of young people in formal education continue to identify with a religion; for example, a survey of 15–17 year olds in 2003 indicated that 88 per cent regarded themselves as belonging to a religious tradition (see Mitchell 2006, 21–37).

Historically, part of the social significance of a specifically Christian form of religiosity in Northern Ireland is seen in the influence the churches have enjoyed in education, including the legal provisions that pertain to Religious Education. It is unnecessary to rehearse the details of the relevant historical legislation, as it has evolved and developed from the establishment of the state in 1921 to the present (see Barnes 2004; Armstrong 2009), but it is important to grasp the (historical) distinctions between different types of schools, because these have a bearing on the purpose and type of Religious Education that is practised and on the way common legislation is interpreted to yield differences in form and content. Following this we will turn to examine current policy and practice more closely.

Northern Ireland historically has three main legal categories of publicly funded school: controlled, voluntary and integrated (Gallagher & Lundy 2006, 173–5). These legal categories may soon be superseded, with the proposed setting up of a single Education and Skills Authority under new legislation, but their practical educational relevance to educational policy and to the classroom will undoubtedly continue whatever new nomenclature is employed. Controlled schools are wholly owned and run by LEAs (Education and Library Boards), and therefore traditionally comprise the 'state' sector of education, attended chiefly by Protestant pupils. Voluntary schools are publicly funded but are not in the ownership of the state. The majority of these schools continue to be in the ownership and management of the Roman Catholic Church and are attended almost exclusively by Catholic pupils, though there are voluntary grammar schools that are not Catholic. Since 1993 Catholic schools have benefitted from full government funding (provided certain minor conditions were met); thus contrasting with the position of ('voluntary aided') church schools in England and Wales. Integrated schools are a third category of schools that aim to provide a mixed religious environment. They are required by law to achieve a reasonable balance of Catholic and Protestant pupils in the student body; overall just over 6 per cent of pupils attend integrated schools (the first of which was opened in 1981).

Religious Education understandably evolved differently in state schools and in Catholic schools. This reflects the different constituencies that they serve, and the different aims and emphases of the two sectors (or of what used to be called the 'dual system', before the advent of integrated schools). While at one time it may have been appropriate to speak of Religious Education in state schools as providing a form of Christian nurture, this is, with some degree of qualification, not now the case. As society became more secularized in the late 1960s and 1970s, the aims of Religious Education in state schools were modified to fit a less uniformly religious population. In addition, the subject of Religious Education, under the influence of developments in English Religious Education, meditated through teacher training institutions in Northern Ireland, came to justify itself on strictly educational grounds and to pursue educational aims, such as the advancement of religious knowledge and understanding. For many teachers, however, the advancement of knowledge and understanding of religion is compatible with a positive attitude towards Christianity in the classroom and the cultivation of an educational environment where Christian commitment is perceived as good for the individual and for society. By contrast, Religious Education in Catholic schools (where the subject is simply designated 'religion') has remained confessional and concerned with Christian nurture, though this should not be interpreted as incompatible with the aim of achieving academic excellence. Schools regard themselves as faith communities charged by parents and the Church with the responsibility of fostering discipleship and religious commitment to Catholicism, within the context of education and the aims appropriate to education.

Up to the late 1980s, there was little in legislation on the content or form of Religious Education. Voluntary Catholic schools pursued confessional, catechetical Catholic education, which involved sacramental preparation, whereas state schools provided 'undenominational religious instruction based upon the Christian scriptures', as required by the 1947 Education Act in Northern Ireland. At secondary school level biblical instruction was typically supplemented by teaching on contemporary moral issues from a Christian perspective; and in some cases there was additional teaching on religions other than Christianity. This legal 'lightness of touch' approach, which allowed for innovation within limits reflective of evolving social attitudes and beliefs, changed in the late 1980s when the then Conservative government in Westminster, under Mrs Thatcher, indicated that the process of educational reform initiated in England and Wales (which resulted in the 1988 Education Reform Act) would be extended to Northern Ireland. After initial opposition to the proposed reforms, and their revision by the government, the churches supported the introduction of a statutory Northern Ireland curriculum, but only if this could be complemented by a similar statutory programme of study for Religious Education, thus bringing it into line with other 'foundation' subjects. The three main Protestant churches – the Church of Ireland, the Methodist Church and the Presbyterian Church – in conjunction with the Roman Catholic Church – were invited (under the terms of the Education Reform Order (Northern Ireland) of 1989), to draw up a suitable syllabus/ programme for all primary and secondary schools to follow. A Working Group was set up by the churches and its proposed Core Syllabus was given statutory force by Parliamentary Order in 1992 (and published in 1993). The Syllabus focused exclusively on the study of Christianity. The content at all four stages of schooling (i.e. infant, upper primary, lower and upper secondary) was organized under three 'Attainment targets', with the following headings: (1) The Revelation of God; (2) The Christian Church and (3) Morality (see Barnes 1997). The Syllabus essentially provided a list of content that had to be covered as the pupil progressed through the educational system. Importantly, the Syllabus was not intended to provide a complete programme of study. It was a core syllabus that was to be augmented by other material, which reflects the particular aims and aspirations of different types of schools and different approaches to the subject. Thus the Syllabus is intended to facilitate a degree of choice and flexibility at the school and classroom level.

The exclusion of religions other than Christianity from the original Syllabus aroused controversy and debate. Adherents of 'other' faith communities expressed the opinion that some recognition of their existence should have been acknowledged. In defence of the exclusive focus on Christianity, John Frost, one of the co-chairmen of the Drafting Group that drew up the Syllabus, insisted that the aim of education in Northern Ireland was 'to unify the experience of children in terms of Christian education. The issue of other faiths was not a major experience' (*Belfast Telegraph*, 12 May 1992). (Statistically adherents of 'non-Christian' religions represent c. 0.3% of the population). Frost also pointed out that schools were free to complement the core with a study of other religions, if the Board of Governors of individual schools so desired. The exclusion, however, remained controversial; and in February 2002, following a request by Martin McGuinness, then Minister of Education in the devolved government at Stormont, the four Church Leaders established a further Steering Group and Working Party to undertake a review of the Agreed Core Syllabus. As part of the review, the Department of Education (NI) asked the Church Leaders to consider, as an integral part of the Core Syllabus, the inclusion of the study of other world religions (and also the implications of recent equality and human rights legislation). An advisory subgroup on World Faiths was also established. Proposals by the Working Party (which includes the requirement of a short study of Judaism and Islam to be conducted during the first three years of secondary-level education) went to Public Consultation in September 2003; some 400 responses were received, most of which were positive. During this period the Inter-Faith Forum, a group representing a range of inter-faith groups, campaigned in favour of the introduction of a British multi-faith model of Religious Education to schools, on the grounds that the revised Syllabus contravened equality and human rights legislation. The Department of Education received the Churches, final proposals in January 2005 and submitted them to a full Equality Impact Assessment (as required by Section 75(1) of the Northern Ireland Act 1998), the results of which were published in November 2006. Disappointingly for the Inter-Faith Forum, the Equality Assessment upheld the legality of the new revised Syllabus (see Barnes 2002, who discusses the matter in relation to Human Rights legislation). The Department of Education took the necessary steps to give formal effect to the revised Core Syllabus in September

2007. Given the scope within the legislation for supplementing the Core with additional material, however, most state and integrated schools study religions other than Christianity in greater variety and at greater length that that required by the Core Syllabus.

More controversial, from a legal perspective, is that a number of schools, chiefly Catholic but including some state schools, choose English-based examination boards at GCSE level, whose options are incompatible with the statutory Northern Ireland Core Syllabus requirement to study both Catholicism and Protestantism. The motivation for this is more likely to be that of gaining better results than of simply wanting to dispense with studying the 'other' tradition of Christianity; there is a perception among many Northern Irish teachers that standards at the local examination board (CCEA) are more demanding than those elsewhere in the United Kingdom.

But it is undeniable from both the documentary and ethnographic evidence that here too, though differently refracted than in England, the policy and professional spaces are complexly riven with competing impulses (Richardson and Gallagher 2011). It is a measure of the complexity of the policy space that representatives of both Catholic and Common schools could come together to create a joint syllabus and, as we have seen in the previous chapter, both could foreground Christian affiliation in a way not conceivable in the other two jurisdictions looked at here. More than this, it was as common to see a first person ontology (We believe X) in the Common school as it was to witness a third person theological ontology (They believe X) in the Catholic School.

Policy and practice in Scotland

Religious Education in Scotland is, as in so many things, both like England and Wales and unlike them. It is like England and Wales inasmuch as it draws on the same intellectual resources for policy making. This was most especially seen in its inheritance of the Lancaster 'phenomenological' approach and its various refractions. It is unlike them, however, in that it embeds these intellectual and cultural resources in quite different forms. There are a number of ways in which the evolution and conduct of Religious Education has differed markedly from other parts of the United Kingdom. Here we would like to deal briefly with two key historical issues: that of oversight and inspection, and that of the absence of a professional body of specialist teachers of religious educators. The inspection of Religious Education in schools came late to Scottish education, being initiated in 1983. As Darling (1980) has pointed out, the historical absence of any proper or appropriate inspection regime or framework for curriculum development in Religious Education in Scotland relegated the subject to the periphery of the curriculum; for example, a government report in 1972 revealed that 9 per cent and 23 per cent of schools did not even allot an RE period on their school curriculum for 12–13 year olds and 16–17 year olds, respectively (SED 1972). This, of course, is not how the churches perceived matters. Throughout the 1960s and 1970s they remained firmly wedded to the notion of confessional Religious Education, for the most part uninfluenced by wider educational, social and religious developments.

The situation in Religious Education changed, however, with the establishment in 1968, by the then Secretary of State for Scotland, of a committee under the chairmanship of Professor Millar of the University of Aberdeen. The resulting report, entitled *Moral and Religious Education in Scottish Schools*, dealt with the quality of Religious Education in schools and noted the emphasis on bible study and the almost complete absence of specialist teachers (see Laidlaw 1972). The Millar Report aimed to loosen the claims of Presbyterian Christianity on the teaching of Religious Education, but the clear alignment of religious and moral education and the ongoing emphasis on teaching Christianity alongside the prevailing attitudes of politicians and other public figures made this very difficult. While the passage of time has witnessed the diminution of Christianity in the content of Religious Education in schools, strong attachment to a link between religion and morality endures to this day in Scottish curriculum documents.

The second major historical issue in Scotland, and again one ironically related to its strong sense of Presbyterian/Christian identity, was the absence of a professional body of specialist religious educators. Prior to the Millar Report and its subsequently established Committee, The Scottish Central Committee on Religious Education (SCCORE 1978), it was not possible to qualify as a specialist teacher of Religious Education in Scotland (the qualification was only established in 1974). In 1976 there were 'only 149 full-time staff in Scotland with RE as their main teaching subject' (SCCORE 1978, 25). The absence of specialist teachers, however, did not denote a lack of commitment by politicians or official bodies, such as the then Scottish Office, to Religious Education. There was a baseline assumption that the important obligations of the educational community to nurturing religious belief was a sine qua non of the system as a whole and could not be left to a professional subgroup. Moreover, while most commentators recognize the historical importance of Presbyterianism in education, a substantial Roman Catholic constituency has held and retains considerable political influence in education despite the continuous onslaughts on the existence of religious schooling (Conroy 2002; Conroy & McGrath 2007).

The reasons behind the late advent of an inspection regime are complex. Undoubtedly the first was for similar reasons to those adumbrated above with regard to the failure to develop a suitably qualified workforce. A second reason was the durability of a bipartite structure of Scottish public education: denominational (*de facto* Catholic) and non-denominational schools and the concomitant control exerted over the curriculum by church authorities. For many years the Catholic Church jealously guarded its control over the Religious Education curriculum and the approval of teachers, which represented its most significant residual stake in an education system that had been transferred to the State under the conditions of the 1918 Education (Scotland) Act. It was not to be easily dissuaded from maintaining its control over every aspect of Religious Education. But, in 1983, the Catholic Education Service acceded to a request from the then Senior Inspector of Schools to facilitate the inspection of Religious Education in schools. In a relatively small polity such as Scotland, the personal is political and a strong bond between the Senior HMI and the most senior diocesan Religious Education adviser smoothed the path of mandatory inspection of Religious Education in Catholic schools. Interestingly, the inspectoral reports could comment only on issues of pedagogy and not on content. If we consider such reports as actors in the policy and practice communities we can see that they are, to some extent, only able to act at the margins since, as we have noted in the previous chapter, the boundary between pedagogical and substantive attachments is epistemologically porous.

Despite coming late to the realization that education needed a professional infrastructure to thrive, Scotland nevertheless did develop a centralized framework that was more pronounced than that south of the border. In 1992 the Scottish Office Education Department (as it then was) decided to shape the curriculum and teaching and learning around specified forms of experience. This it did by creating the 5–14 Curriculum Guidelines. Of course guidelines, while not legally statutory, nonetheless carry force; and Her Majesty's Inspectorate for Education in Scotland acted on the premise that good Religious Education should follow the Curriculum Guidelines. It would have been a courageous teacher who had the temerity to stand out against the Inspectorate and their doing so would have demanded intellectual argument and resources beyond those embodied in the average teacher. This is not to decry either the intelligence or the capabilities of the average teacher; rather it is to suggest that the force of inspection has been largely irresistible, given that it was, at the time, both the shaper and enforcer of government policy. For example, the first inspector of Religious Education (interestingly an historian, not a Religious Education teacher nor a theological/religious expert) was the central figure in the development of the curriculum in the late 1980s and early 1990s. His successor, Alan Hawke, was effectively the convenor of the 5–14 Working Group on Religious Education, which established the 1992 Guidelines and determined the shape of Religious Education for the next two decades. The development of Religious Education within the curriculum architecture purported to offer Religious Education equal status to the other subject areas (Expressive Arts, Mathematics, English and Environmental Studies). This architecture included a specified time allocation of 10 per cent in primary schools and 5 per cent in early secondary with a substantial 80 hours over two years in the middle of the secondary school and a defined place in the last two years of formal schooling. Rooted in the thrust of the Millar Report, the subject title was to become Religious and Moral Education – itself an interesting alignment of Religious Education and moral education/citizenship/social education, and one which would soon, in the secondary sector experience a further shift towards incorporating philosophical studies, hence the examinations are termed, *Religious, Moral and Philosophical Studies*. Prima facie all these initiatives would suggest that the provision of Religious Education was, in some important respects, and unlike England and Wales, a policy priority in Scotland, but this would somehow belie the all together more patchy reality (Darling 1980; Conroy 2003). One only has to examine HMIE reports to recognize that areas of weakness in Religious Education are not infrequently judged to be a consequence of poor time and resource allocation compared with other subjects. In a 2001 Report it is observed that

> [i]n some schools RME received inadequate attention resulting in pupils displaying a superficial understanding of the issues they were studying. In 30% of departments, pupils followed a course designed by the school, local education authority or the religious authority. The majority of these were judged to be good. Common weaknesses in S3/S4 courses included the following:
>
> - too little support to pupils to see the relevance of the course;
> - too few opportunities for pupils to discuss the essential features of belief and morality associated with different religions and other stances for living; and
> - an over emphasis on worksheets which led to slow progress and lack of interest and challenge. (HMI 2001, 10)

A notable difference between Scotland and the other jurisdictions has been the ambiguous role actually and formally played in Scotland by the major religious groupings; thus while Catholics and Presbyterians, among others, sat on the Government Working Group they were not 'representatives', a scenario quite at odds with the establishment of SACREs in England and Wales and the direct curriculum drafting role of the Christian churches in Northern Ireland. Hence, while the then Scottish Office Education Department may have assumed that having communicant members of the Catholic Church on their committees implied institutional agreement this was not to be the case. Ensuring that those Catholics sitting on the Committee were not acting on behalf of the Church allowed the Catholic Church to walk away from the development of a common document at the eleventh hour, arguing that the aims, pedagogical intent and content were at odds with those of Religious Education in the Catholic tradition. In homage to our observations about the enduring influence of the Catholic Church, despite turning their back on what they considered to be, from their theological and anthropological perspective, a flawed common document, they secured substantial state support to produce their own parallel 5–14 Guidelines, where the relationship of morality to religion was stressed, with the 'two' subjects integrated under the single title, *Religious Education 5-14* (Scottish Office Education Department, 1994; Coll & Davis 2007). This accommodation has been retained in the revisions to the curriculum seen in the development of the *Curriculum for Excellence* (LTS 2010a), with the national curriculum body, Learning and Teaching Scotland materially supporting denominational provision (LTS 2010b). Interestingly, while there is now general acceptance across the denominational/non-denominational divide about the structure, resourcing and objectives of Religious Education, there is no agreement on whether confessional aims are compatible with educational aims (see Baumfield et al. 2011). What is of particular note here is the way in which the syllabus for Catholic schools adopts the form of the state processes and uses the language of *Curriculum for Excellence*, the point of which was ostensibly to free up teacher and student. Thus *This Is our Faith* simultaneously describes itself as guidance and as the exercise of the Bishops' conference 'right and duty to determine the content of the religious education in the Catholic School' (Scottish Catholic Education Service 2012, 3). It is difficult to know how these two claims are actually compatible. But, as we have already seen, and will continue to see, consistency in the policy and practice of Religious Education across the United Kingdom has not, at this stage, been achieved.

Conclusion

The emergence of these quite different policy tropes over the last 40 years contributes to the complexity and strangeness of Religious Education; they bear testimony to the range and variety of factors that condition Religious Education in the four different countries that collectively make up the United Kingdom. While there are common influences, these influences vary in intensity and force in the different national contexts. Moreover, it is clear that the different legislative arrangements both reflect and condition the relative importance of different influences in different contexts. In an important sense context matters: legislation emerges out of different historical, socio-economic, political, religious and demographic factors (this list is not meant to be exhaustive) and in turn legislation conditions the relative importance and curriculum significance of these different influences. An appreciation of the range of influences on education, and on Religious Education in particular, and of the differentiated weightings that these influences enjoy in different settings provides the key to understanding the reasons for the similarities and differences between policy, content and practice in the different national contexts. Yet it is also clear that these differentiated weightings are not explicable in rational terms alone – in some respects pragmatism and satisfying (by gaining the support of) interest groups in a particular educational locality is an important component in producing and winning support for policy decisions and initiatives in Religious Education, and arguably in this instance the influence of interest groups is stronger than on that of policy decisions in other subjects.

A good example of both the differentiated nature of the influences on Religious Education and the extent to which particular influences can shape Religious Education is the role played by religious communities in the different countries. In England and Wales Catholic, Evangelical and Muslim schools (and their respective communities) often bypass local agreed syllabuses and create their own syllabuses and materials, which are complemented by examination boards providing tailored provision, at least for Catholics. This situation is a particular refraction of a historical legacy that sees church schools (and now faith schools) retaining a financial investment and consequent control over aspects of the curriculum. In Northern Ireland the creation of a common syllabus was made possible by the durability of a majority Christian view on not only the purposes of Religious Education but education more generally, and the ability of Christians to translate this broad community agreement into educational policy. Scotland emerges as quite different from both. Catholic schools are wholly owned and managed by the State with only a couple of legal accommodations around staff approval (not appointment) and Religious Education. Here the Catholic Church expects the State to financially support separate syllabus production, materials creation and in-service provision.

All these, and indeed other, interest groups that press for attention and compliance have no parallel in other parts of the curriculum, where the discussion might be around the educational entailments of geography or history as educational practices. In other respects Religious Education in the different countries is, however, broadly similar. For example, the content which began as exclusively Christian and confessional throughout the United Kingdom has expanded, in varying degrees, to accommodate learning about other faiths: each country makes provision for faith schools, and Religious Education in 'common' schools, which is intended to be inclusive of all, is characteristically multi-faith. Yet even here, emphasis needs to be given to the qualifying adjective – broadly. Formal similarities can disguise differences. Faith schools in Northern Ireland and in Scotland, which effectively equate to Catholic schools, are fully funded by the state, but the same type of schools in England and Wales are not. In addition, whereas 'multi-faith' is an appropriate description of Religious Education across the United Kingdom, the denotations of 'multi-faith' vary in the different national contexts: in England until recently, at least six religions were typically studied (though that number is now increasing where schools follow the controversial 'advice' of the Non-Statutory Framework), whereas in Northern Ireland three religions only are studied (formally) and this 'multi-faith' element is confined to one key stage at secondary level. Perhaps most pointedly, in the Delphi seminar, participants from Northern Ireland were more obviously attached to overtly religious (Christian) entailments; in Scotland, while there was a common form of language, the actual gap between substantive aims and intentions was significantly wider than in the other constituencies.

What we have illustrated here are the ways in which the extraordinarily contorted evolution of policy towards Religious Education in these islands is a reflection of our complex relationship with religion itself, wherein we harbour deeply conflicted and contradictory impulses, never quite sure whether religion is a good or a bad thing; never quite sure if we want it; never quite sure what alliances it should cultivate; never quite sure if it is sufficiently educational to be compulsory; never quite sure whether its existence is justified as an instrument of critique or an agent of social conformity; never quite sure whether it should be part of a 'modern' curriculum or cast adrift, as some secularists' counsel. Until some resolution is found to these contradictions Religious Education is likely to remain contested and, in many respects marginal but not entirely abandoned by politicians. Moreover, given that such policy and political complexity emerges out of and gives rise to a range of accommodations it is hardly surprising that such accommodations are accompanied by some contradiction and confusion in the social and pedagogical practices of the subject.

Notes

1 By theological we do not wish to suggest that such community schools evince and promote, as normatively superior, a particularistic account of religious belief or practice. Rather, in some schools serving communities with a substantial religious demography we witnessed considerable attempts to consider seriously the theological claims and explanations of religious attachments.
2 The Lancaster School refers to the approach to teaching RE developed by Ninian smart at Lancaster on behalf of the School's Council in the 1970s.

4

Conceptual Questions, Confusions and Challenges[1]

Introduction

As we have suggested in the previous two chapters, many of the conceptual questions, confusions and challenges to which Religious Education is now felt to be prey are commonly held to be a function of its conflicted location in the school curriculum – standing at the end of a lengthy history of progressive secularization which has seen the subject steadily shorn of its traditional confessional prestige and impelled into uneasy accommodations with other, newer and frequently rival domains of study and learning. Sitting alongside the political maneuvers discussed in the previous chapter are other influential processes, chief among which is the process of democratic modernization in education. This saw the organs of the bureaucratic state eventually displace the older, ecclesial sponsors of popular schooling, and move with some rapidity from a generally benign and respectful disposition towards Religious Education as the chief custodian of national values and moral formation, to a more sceptical and quizzical relationship, in which increasingly complex and wide-ranging demands were made of the subject in order to justify its place in the curriculum (Conroy & Davis 2008, 2010). The culmination of this process is the 'performative' educational culture of the present day, documented throughout this volume and evident in the pervasive sense of technico-rationalist measurement and accountability within which the effectiveness of Religious Education in the delivery of specific social and educational goods is repeatedly vouchsafed. While Religious Education may not be unique in bearing multiple moral, social and curricular burdens of this kind, it is arguably without parallel in the scale and range of these responsibilities and in the combined effect they have had in the past generation in decisively altering the character of the discipline.

It is not surprising then that throughout *Does RE Work?* the conceptual vola-
tility with which the subject is surrounded made itself felt – from the literature
review and Delphi exercise with which the research began (Baumfield et al. 2012),
to the complex mosaic of ethnographic findings yielded by the fieldwork phases
of the investigation. For the purposes of gaining perspective and traction on this
complex interplay of forces, this chapter traces three defined vectors through
specific, localized elements of the data, originating in the Delphi conversations
and worked through in a small number of schools. The sharp focus on a limited
sample of schools does not aspire to positivist replicability, but nor does it seek the
extensive 'thick description' of the case study. The delayering of the experiences
of the selected schools endeavours, rather, to draw out the translocality of the
participant-observed phenomena as it materializes in events, interactions and
interpretations that are embedded *diachronically* in the distinctive histories
and identities of the specific schools, while resonating *synchronically* with the
unsettled hermeneutics of contemporary Religious Education as these are
elsewhere manifest (Maclure 2003). The schools then afford the examination
advanced in this aspect of the research its 'analytic vignettes' (Erickson 1990) out
of which crystallize highly indicative feelings, attitudes, stances and accounts
incrementally consolidating the critical understanding of Religious Education
as a social and cultural practice.

The three themes offered for inspection in this exploration are:

1. The Rationale for Religious Education;
2. The Role of the Teacher: Principles and Pedagogy;
3. Truth Claims in Religious Education.

The excavation of these themes does not pretend to exhaust the available project
data, nor does it seek empirically to cover the full diversity of experiences and
phenomena that might legitimately impinge on the overall thematics of the
study. Instead, the discussion enlists the verticality of the central linguistic
ethnographic methods through which the project fieldwork was undertaken
in order to highlight particular nodes of response, behaviour, interaction,
reflection, cognition and justification which resonate with the conceptual
preoccupations and questions from out of which the projected rationale
originated and from which it then subsequently developed. The mapping of
these iterative patterns of non-deterministic utterance and exchange echoes
Rampton's perception of the anthropological enquiry as 'a site of encounter
where a number of established lines of research interact, pushed together by
circumstance, open to the recognition of new affinities, and sufficiently familiar

with one another to treat differences with equanimity' (2007, 585). The resultant approach is intended not to disparage the established modes of quantitative investigation and qualitative interpretation by which questions of educational purpose and meaning are commonly (and cogently) pursued, but to enrich them by forms of representative 'situated interactionism' (Goodwin & Goodwin 2000) which foreground the selected nodes as discursively illuminating of the frequently obscure or concealed dynamics of power, choice and agency operative across almost all educational settings. The emergent complementarity shares the conviction of the more mainstream methods of educational research that the research participants are dignified social actors functioning within environments where their contextual awareness and commitment may be high, their disciplinary understanding strong and even their professional autonomy relatively flexible. It nevertheless discloses in the unfolding ideological patternings of speech, judgement and disciplinary insight the adjacency of other influences and assumptions, conditioning what Holmes and Stubbe (2003) refer to as the structure/boundary interactions between the controlled and the uncontrolled in any classroom or educational episode. Recognition of these patterns in the evidentiary record argues in favour of depth rather than breadth, close textual reading rather than statistical comparison, allowing us, as Scollon and Scollon suggest '. . . to transport selected and carefully focused slices of life out of the original nexus of activity for collegial, peer-reviewable examination in richer more multimodal formats' (2007, 620). It is these systematic explorations of slices of life that offers the opportunity to draw a telescope on the emergent strangeness discussed in Chapter 2. The three data-vectors with which this present discussion is concerned can then be seen to reinforce – while also further complexifying – sensitive critical interrogation of the principles of effectiveness and coherence in Religious Education as these are shared and negotiated within and beyond the subject's authorized institutional parameters (Erickson 1984).

The Rationale of Religious Education

In key respects, it is entirely unsurprising that the rationale for contemporary Religious Education should have formed a vital workflow in the design and implementation of the project. Much current theorizing on the future of Religious Education – from critical reflection through to policy formation – reprises longstanding concerns around the legitimacy of the subject as a defined mode of learning and a curricular area in the modern school (Freathy 2008; Franken & Loobuyek 2011, 169–77). The contributors to the Delphi phase of *Does RE Work?* went so far as to implicate the project itself in this historic *aporia* in the fortunes of the subject, one participant asking

> Given what we've heard so far, does it make sense as a project? That's the question I begin to ask myself as I look at the questions. How do you isolate your hour a week of RE from the rest of life, you can't do it, it's not feasible in research. (Baumfield et al. 2012, 13)

This issue of the 'mesh' of RE with other aspects of learning and education also obtained, both positively and negatively, in several of the schools. Echoing observations we made in chapter 2, in the vibrant, cosmopolitan atmosphere of a busy London Grammar School, the Head of Department (HOD) of Religious Education viewed these continuities between the subject as currently configured and 'the rest of life' with some ambivalence:

> It's not religious education any more. It's not like when I was at school even. I was doing it 15 years ago and it wasn't anything like that now. It's ethics and philosophy and the GCSE and the A level: their exam is ethics and philosophy because I think religious education has got such connotations with it that it's just not about that. Like today for example we were talking about community. . . . Certainly in previous schools it's like oh RE oh, it's that whole oh it's crap because it's RE and religion is geekie, I can't possibly enjoy it, but like renaming it philosophy and ethics it's like yea that's cool, philosophy yea. It just gives it . . . automatically, they associate geekiness and being quite sad with religion. If you are doing religion and you get ethics and philosophy, so I just think renaming it would give it a different attitude towards it because it's not religious education any more really.

In one respect, the rebranding of the subject as an inflection of the fashionably literate and intellectually respectable 'ethics and philosophy' culture of the twenty-first-century senior school classroom rescues it from the 'geekiness' and obscurantism of 'religion', nonetheless the HOD is experienced and astute enough to suggest that this is 'not Religious Education any more', discontinuous as it is with his personal and professional recollections of a period when the expectation in the Religious Education classroom was that 'At the end of this lesson you will all know what the Ten Commandments are and why you should know them'. This incisive insight into the now problematic place of 'religion' in a Religious Education curriculum that (for good or ill) is in important zones colluding in its own secularization of course ramifies throughout this study. It subtly underlines the impression that the subject is at last succumbing to the internal logic of the classical Enlightenment drivers through which modern mass education was instantiated in the first place and for which religion per se was a superannuated form of thinking for a pre-rational, indeed pre-educational, age. It is also instructive in micro-ethnographic terms that an experienced teacher is prompted by the research to raid his own memories in search of an originating pedigree for the subject alternative to current norms. The pupils in the teacher's school similarly reinforced the added sense of instrumentality by explaining even their enthusiasm for Religious Education in terms of its contribution to ancillary ends:

> It helps you with other subjects as well like History because if you learn about Bible stories it will help you maybe with other things – like if you learn about the Tudors or something it might help you understand why Henry VIII did something like this. It also helps you maybe with Science, understanding an opposition to Science and the Big Bang theory and God and things like that.

In wider conversation with the fieldworker, A-Level pupils in the school went still further in defending the metacognitive benefits of the subject, the fieldnotes recording that,

> RE was seen by pupils as helping to facilitate the process of learning and participating in RE helped build critical skills, evaluation, self-reflection, thinking outside the box, how to work and debate with others.

It is of course perfectly commendable in the era of interdisciplinary learning to see the value of Religious Education reflected in its contribution to the aggregation of knowledge and skills in concentrations relevant both to other areas of the curriculum and to education beyond the school. The use of the verb 'help' is interesting here, however, in its suggestion that one of the chief contributions of the subject on the school timetable is as an 'assist' to other domains of study, whether as backdrop or catalyst. Paul Vermeer (2012) has recently gone so far as to suggest that one of the principal justifications for Religious Education as a continuing area of pupil development in the modern school will be its service to the acquisition of subject-specific meta-concepts and thinking skills such as religious functionalism, the psychology of belief and the social scientific understanding of religious ways of life. The integrity of these and other related defences of Religious Education is not in dispute, but they each do intensify the question of *purpose*: if a vehicle more effective for the realization of these secondary ends could be devised, might it not reasonably replace Religious Education in the teaching of young people?

One Deputy Head Teacher (DHT) in a Scottish non-denominational School also defended the contribution of Religious Education to the promotion of analytical and thinking skills, but sought to contextualize this in terms of older-adolescent socialization and the discovery of the individual's place in the community. His colleague, another DHT responsible for school improvement, echoed the same general sentiments, which were recurrent across the database:

> There's the kind of knowledge and understanding part of it, but there's also the skills part of it that are transferable across other subjects and skills for life, I suppose, and maybe some of the softer skills as well that we're talking about. We're talking about manners and learning to take turns as part of discussion – and so that's in there as well.

For this same DHT, however, recognition of these supplementary enrichments brought to older pupils by the subject called into question one significant feature of the subject's current status in Scotland – its compulsory place in the timetable:

> They're all still doing RE, which is something they are forced to do. They didn't choose to do it and if you put a 13, 14, 15-year-old boy in a classroom and ask him to engage in a discussion over something that may be quite difficult – like it was euthanasia the other day – you can see them switching off and going 'I'll let the other people talk and I'll not get involved'; and some people don't like speaking out in front of others.

The formal opportunity to opt out of Religious Education would appear not to resonate with this teacher or indeed with many others. Bizarrely, the compulsory nature of much of the rest of the curriculum also appeared to have been missed. It is worth observing in this general track through the data from this particular school that the PT of another quite distinct subject felt sufficiently confident to articulate her wholesale opposition to the teaching of religion, defending from her experience of working in French schools the complete separation of religion and education and the outsourcing of all religious enquiry to parents and homes. In engagement with the fieldworker, the S4 and S5 pupils in the school were clearly ambivalent on both the desirability of Religious Education on the timetable and its profile as a potentially 'religious' subject. Citing generally poor experiences of Religious Education in their primary schools, opinions subsequently ranged from 'I'm opposed to RE but I appreciate the need to allow for others' views', to 'You get wider knowledge and understanding that you wouldn't get in other subjects' – this latter comment underlining the general fieldwork impression that older pupils on the whole ratified the settled school management consensus that the subject was 'useful' for citizenship and life skills. Pupils in S4 and older undeniably demonstrated during class discussion and interactions with the ethnographer the generally high levels of critical and analytical thinking favoured by the school leadership. These pupils explained that they enjoyed Religious Education because it stimulated them, challenging their assumptions and making them re-assess the way they saw their world. Those who chose to take Religious Education as a Higher qualification went furthest in their attachment to these academic properties of the subject. They in turn identified a range of professions to which possession of the Higher could contribute – including Law, politics, teaching and management. Religious Education was useful, one pupil commented, in that 'it challenges opinions and views that are built up in the way you are brought up': in other words in its nurture of precisely the same powers of critical reflection championed by the school as a whole. It remained, however, notable that the features of the Religious Education syllabus most prized by pupils for offering these opportunities were those most markedly associated with the examination of moral and ethical dilemmas and the psychology of human behaviour. Indeed, pupils in both S4 and S5 reported to the fieldworker their appetite for *further* discussion of the important moral issues of our time, such as social justice and (pace one DHT!) euthanasia.

Few express criticisms can be levelled at the formulation of a rationale for Religious Education on the secondary school timetable that exploits its continuities with other domains of learning and teaching, or which actively promotes its beneficial influence on the development of the cognitive and reflective capacities of young people as they prepare to move on from school. Nevertheless, uncovering the deposits of meaning and academic investment latent in these semantic clusters around 'critical thinking', 'citizenship', 'moral dilemmas' and 'transferable skills' surely highlights two problems. The first is the at least potential eclipse of the subject by forms of knowledge and styles of enquiry in fact much better aligned with the declared areas and goals of educational interest. The second concern relates to the pervasive and awkward issue of the 'the religious', visible throughout this study. Refracted, however, through the 'deep reading' (Conquergood 1991) of the multi-perspectival yet intermodal ethnographic sources offered here, this problem may be seen to be less about the contraction of religion and religious sensibilities from the heart of the discipline (itself arguably an inflection of wider processes of secularization) and still more troublingly, perhaps, about the management of an educational consensus. Within this manufactured unanimity, the implicit evacuation or declassification of religion typifies the insidious reproduction and authorization of certain licensed and normative forms of knowledge production and moral formation within the boundaries of the school. The deliberate smoothing of the 'angularity' of religion evident here and elsewhere in the programme data can then be seen by this light to raise difficult questions for those strands within religious learning that have, in various forms over the generations, contemplated the subversion or transgression of norms and sought even to test the limits of the rational, autonomous self-cherished in the canons of liberal education (Sharpley & Stone 2011). The loss of such resources from the discipline, indeed, might serve to corroborate Liam Gearon's (2012) profound foreboding that many of the attempted moves in the current institutional revalidation of the place of religion in education at national and transnational levels serve in fact to facilitate the furtherance of an educated 'civil religion' imprinted with precisely the non-religious impulses and values seen in several of the schools in the present study.

It might be thought intuitively that a faith-based school would be the appropriate locus for the demonstration of a more robustly 'religio-centric' vision of Religious Education, more directly attuned to a confessional, evangelical or salvific role for the subject in the lives and affairs of young people (Cooney 2012). In the case of one Scottish Catholic secondary school involved in the study, points of academic and professional departure were certainly distinctive in the approach to these issues – the responses lent added subtlety by the voluntary presence in the school of a notable proportion of pupils from other faiths, including non-Catholic Christians. Proper and inescapable acknowledgement was given by senior staff in the said school to the wider responsibilities of Religious Education seen previously in the non-religious schools highlighted above. Hence the Head Teacher of the school, while explaining the confessional basis of its Catholic Religious Education programme, took pains once again to stress its inclusivity and 'relevance' for all:

> it is a Catholic RE programme, however, there are bits in it where we're talking about life skills, where we're talking about relationships with each other and these are important regardless of religion or lack of religion.

Running through this aspect of the school's rationale was an ideal of *ethos* until comparatively recently seen as possibly the most important signifier of Catholic difference in the Scottish state schooling system (McKinney & Hill 2010). The Head Teacher sought to capture this in an ambitiously comprehensive vision of pluralized Catholic identity and purpose within the school:

> In a Catholic school in particular – maybe somebody from a non-denominational may disagree – it's not just about the two periods of RE. In essence, it's a way of life. What we're about in RE isn't just confined to two periods a week or to the

RE classrooms, but that it's out and about; it's everywhere; the standards we're setting; the behaviours; the expectations of attainment – they all come from our vision of what RE is: a response to the call of God and faith which is what the whole school is about.

One of the school's Religious Education teachers strove, in his comments to the ethnographer, to match this leadership perspective on religion and institutional purpose to the school's grassroots aspirations for the individual learner:

RE is about giving the child a sense of identity: recognition of himself and the role to play within the community . . . in a microcosm of the wider community; starting off in the school, school community; that they are valued, that they are special/unique; really to give them a self-regard for themselves, to give them that recognition and to get them to recognise their importance and with that their responsibilities as well.

The sincerity of these convictions and their attendant hopes for Religious Education is indisputable: staff faithfully pursue a vision of the good life in which Catholic values stamp the corporate, community and individual experiences of the school at as many levels as they can sustain. The values foundation upon which these intentions for the school is raised runs deep into indigenous traditions of Catholic religious practice and educational history in Scotland, as well as into the key educational pronouncements of the post-Vatican II Catholic Church. It is nonetheless at least arguable that in some of the semantic slippages and displacements in the contributions of the staff we can see a sometimes uneasy movement between Catholic identity, Catholic ethos, ecumenical citizenship and the subject of Religious Education which risks presenting the discipline as place-holder for *everything* about its distinctive mission that the school in fact values and wishes to project (Boeve 2012). This may be in part a genuine effort to de-enclavize 'Religious Education' from the narrow confines of the school timetable and to embed it in a wider construction of experiential, pupil-centred learning and teaching. But a Religious Education that is *everything* might also be a Religious Education struggling to define and establish its academic (indeed, in confessional terms, its *theological*) credentials within the curriculum. In this connection, it is interesting to note – as has been observed elsewhere in this volume – that the ethnography of the Scottish Catholic school took place on the eve of a major (and some would argue controversial) reform of the Religious Education curriculum and syllabus across the Catholic sector, inclining it is a more avowedly confessional direction.

The school's Head Teacher in some respects anticipated this misgiving in his bold suggestion that while there was in the school 'the formal RE programme, maybe it is . . . better called Religious Instruction. But then there is the example that we show . . . there's also the religious experience; the religious observance. But they, from our point of view, all come under the banner of RE in the school here.' Although these strong claims do not necessarily assuage the concern that Religious Education is being asked in the school to shoulder an unsustainable burden, in their invocation of the older concept of Religious *Instruction*, they both seek demandingly to ringfence the disciplinary integrity of the subject while reinstating a concept that appears since to have assumed a much greater prominence in the new curriculum for Religious Education in Scotland's Catholic schools. The aims of the Senior Management Team in the school seem clear in this regard: Catholic Religious Education is to combine 'formation . . . [in] the development of Christianity and in particular the Catholic faith . . .' with the opportunity, as one senior pupil presented it, to 'live the gospel values. It's one thing to preach it, but practise what you preach . . . I like the notion of looking at the Bible and things like that and speaking about the life of Jesus and then bringing it into present-day situations . . .' The 'credibility' of Religious Education in the school then derives from the same, parallel enfolding of doctrine within practice: the subject is taught by 'specialists . . . it's got to be done by somebody who firmly believes in what they're saying' (HT) and at the same time it must connect with the complexities and compromises of the variegated contemporary faith community and its extended network of subscribers and users from both the periphery and the pale of the officially Catholic population:

> Even though I said I quite like the traditional aspects of RE, you've got to bring it into present-day context. If the children don't see that, it's just stories that they've just heard time and time again . . . You've got to be able to bring it into the relevance that it has today for the child because things change all the time. (Principal Teacher)[2]

If there is an ambiguity in the generally (and sometimes infectiously) optimistic rationale here, it resides chiefly in the effort to integrate the promotion of a doctrinally orthodox 'immersion' in Catholic Religious Education with a rigorously sensitized attunement to the often conflicted and religiously equivocal conditions in which most pupils live and work. The allusion to 'religious instruction', however indirect, of course prompts the standard battery of scruples that surround the place of faith-based schooling in liberal democratic education systems, but this is not the principal reservation in this context. The discourse of inclusion in the school genuinely presents faith as invitation, and the cadences of leadership-speech suggest a sincere openness to diversity and even the expression of responsible free disengagement on the part of pupils from the dogmatic and fideistic claims of the school. The school seems in this respect to be thoroughgoingly 'liberal'. The tension remains, however, that as well as conscripting the disciplinary characteristics of Religious Education to the broader missionary outreach of the school in ways which extend the jurisdiction of the subject indiscriminately, the school cannot quite unravel the catechetical from the educational in the actual outworking of its philosophy of learning. The confessional school is hence not in any sense automatically released from the paradoxes of Religious Education in a generally post-religious society, though it experiences these paradoxes in distinct and even potentially fruitful ways (Franchi 2011). Sincerely and creatively committed to the instructional and catechetical drivers of faith-based Religious Education (problematic though these may, from external perspectives, be), it is nonetheless driven to many of the same 'therapeutic' compromises with modernity as our other examples – some of these compromises rationalized through the refinement of its own mission; some of them emergent from the inescapable accommodations between 'religion' and 'education' simply demanded by the legislative and demographic imperatives of the dominant educational culture (Leigh 2012).

The role of the teacher: Principles and pedagogy

After more than two decades of international attention on the reform of the curriculum in schools, the return of concentrated scholarly and professional interest in the figure of the teacher (Geerinck et al. 2010; McArdle & Coutts 2010) has impacted on perceptions of educational practice across the spectrum of classroom disciplines. It has long been recognized that the person of the teacher in the pedagogies of Religious Education, and the methodological values to which the teacher is committed, interact in a peculiar chemistry with subject content and values, and that these are directly correlated with the multiple elements of 'effectiveness' with which this overall study is concerned (Jackson 2004, 22–39). Such distinctive characteristics derive in part from the historic responsibilities borne by Religious Education for 'high-status' social and educational outcomes such as the transmission of faith or the preservation of a nation's or community's moral fabric. Even in increasingly secular and sceptical times, however, critical features of this legacy remain alive in the often close affiliations between the personal intellectual and emotional investments of teachers, the perceived subjectivism of much of the experiential content of Religious Education and the liminal questions and issues in which the discipline trades as a determined and imaginative classroom encounter (Bryan & Revell 2011).

Within the Delphi phase of the current project, discussion of the role and character of the teacher inclined to focus on two extremities of a continuum. At one end, the expert participants saw the committed teacher either constrained by inhibiting external restrictions on the flexibility and creativity of her teaching, or else left 'lagging behind' the latest innovations through a confusing lack of status or resource. At the other, participants described an ideal realized in at least some schools of 'passionate impartiality', where the teacher was both a policy actor and an intrepid agent of authentic learning equipped to 'explore' confidently with young people '. . . what makes the difference between something which is good thinking and something which is flawed' (Baumfield et al. 2012, 15–16). This interest in what one Delphi participant referred to as the 'ontology of the person' (16) of course redounds through much of the primary ethnographic data from the school-based stages of the research. Synthesizing the evidence of the fieldnotes and researcher reflections, there are consistent patterns in the lessons agreed by all participants to be 'successful'. These capture a cluster of behaviours around subject commitment, pedagogical repertoire and interactive skills. Three recurrent features seemed especially to impinge on the reactions of pupils: the teacher's possession of confident subject knowledge; the willingness to engage with the situated needs and lifestyles of pupils, and the sensitized promotion of active learning through discussion and debate of those signature features of Religious Education where the personal, the ethical and the 'religious' both meet and diverge. 'I think the teacher is important in that otherwise you might just end up going round in circles' (London School) is a typical expression of this 'pedagogical geometry' in the symbolic spaces of the senior classroom.

In the London Grammar School, seasoned Religious Education staff, and the leadership of the department, clearly foregrounded their philosophy of learning and teaching with a critical-reflective appreciation of the dynamics of teacher-pupil relations accrued as part of the incremental 'guild-wisdom' of the department as it had steadily developed its full curriculum across the year groups. The HOD stated that,

> I think you need [active learning] because especially with our subject: like in
> GCSE we talk about abortion, medical ethics. We talk about those things, but
> I think when you get that relationship and they realise that you're human and

you're not this scary figure. They see you're human and you're normal and they can talk to you and I think you have better lessons.

This emphasis upon the virtues of 'active learning' was of course widespread throughout the schools in the project. The London philosophy was to see this in essentially egalitarian terms, offering it as a means of 'humanizing' the figure of the teacher – presenting the teacher as a co-learner and explorer fully rooted into the discursive culture of the classroom and its paramount stress upon *talk* as the preferred mode of learning and enquiry. This distinctive application of talk to realization of the goals of the subject was further highlighted in the activities of the department in the light of its obvious, if understated, methodological contrast with prevalent norms elsewhere in the school, where traditional, exam-centred and often more didactic strategies were often apparently preferred. Year 10 pupils and older largely endorsed the perspective of senior staff and linked 'talk' directly to two defining features of Religious Education as they had grown in their understanding of it through their school careers – one cognitive and one evaluative. One senior pupil observed that, 'If you talk you kind of pick things up quicker rather than writing it all down. You kind of learn it in your head'; while another claimed that 'I think from Year 7 to Year 11 we just sort of listen, take notes and just take it for granted. But by Year 12 and Year 13 we're questioning everything'.

Following an observed lesson marked by extensive interactive conversation, questioning, PowerPoint presentation, a copious resort to humour and only ten minutes of pupil writing, focus-group pupils from the class subsequently insisted that this was 'an enjoyable and effective way to learn' which 'reduced boredom' and 'encouraged interest' in the topics under investigation. More mature and academically advanced pupils sought to link the collegial atmosphere of interactive dialogue, question-and-answer typical of Religious Education in the upper school with the skills of critical evaluation and individual empowerment that they had come to discern as germane to their wider educational futures:

> I just want to refer back to what we were talking about – evaluation in school. From Year 7 to 11 there's no evaluation to be honest in RE. It's a matter of just regurgitating what the teacher gives, then we just look back for the RE exam. But in Year 12 to 13 that's when we really start to actually evaluate and see what is there, that's when our questioning comes into place. (Year 12 Pupil)

Eliding for a moment the incompatibility of this statement with feedback from the Year 10s (it may be a methodological object of the research, attributable to standard development planning in a progressive and adventurous department), it is clear that the shared preference for speech-centred pedagogies duly privileges a particular kind and style of teaching broadly associated with the rise of democratic classrooms in contemporary liberal education – and firmly oppositional to the performative regulation of examination outcomes and league-table metrics criticized elsewhere in this volume. The HOD presented this stance very much in terms reminiscent of the 'toolkit' recently elaborated for such classrooms by Brookfield and Presskill (2012), with its promotion of what the HOD translated as 'thinking skills and learning styles and trying to make it . . . fun and enjoyable'.

> I'll be honest with you: what I find happens – we will have a starting point over a certain topic and we tend to get sidetracked to be honest in our subject because they are so interested they want to engage with that and I just go with that with them because it just seems to make so much more sense rather than sticking to what is in the book, if that makes sense? It's like for instance yesterday we had a Year 8 group we were looking at how Muslim belief affects their way of life and one of them started talking about the Jews and the various things, so we decided to compare and contrast the two and see what the similarities and what the differences were even though all it was just the Muslim beliefs essentially.

It seems clear that in the setting of bustling, diverse and high-octane classrooms, this approach to the role of the teacher and the pedagogical values he serves can be compelling, especially in the creation of motivation and enthusiasm for a subject competing for its place on the timetable and often impeded by external and internal constraints from which other subjects are largely free. If there is a set of risks attendant upon the account of learning and teaching on offer, then it may well represent particular disciplinary intensifications of vulnerabilities felt generically across many democratic learning initiatives as presently configured. A peril of the otherwise refreshing spontaneity alluded to in the example above lies surely in the populist disposition towards knowledge and understanding in the underlying pupil-centred rationale. There is a danger that the endemic tendency in discursive learning towards the dialectics of 'comparison and contrast' is much less suited to the appreciation of, for example, Judaism and Islam (or the 'differences' between them) than might at first appear, policing conceptual distinctions and imposing upon a promisingly 'religious' topic a predetermined phenomenology of 'comparative structure' ultimately inimical to the goal being pursued. The teacher, of course, may well have at her command a range of interventions to mitigate this and there is no suggestion that the lesson is in itself 'wrong' to move in the direction it does. The integrity of the subject may demand, however, enhanced critical-reflective awareness of all of the forces set loose by the superficially persuasive appeal of talk and interaction as the privileged modes of enquiry in the reportedly democratic classroom (Moulin 2011).

The impression sometimes created, in fact, when Religious Education meets the attractions of this lively, voluble learning environment is that the subject is somehow trying to compensate for its inherited associations with hierarchy, power and sacred authority – influences proverbially linked to the estrangement of most modern young people from the subject (and from religion generally) and difficult to reconcile with the inclusive and participatory logic of much contemporary liberal pedagogy. Although this legacy may be seen to stem from the largely superannuated clericalized affiliations of the Religious Education profession, there may well continue to be defining elements of the study of religion itself which retain this penumbra of hieratic inscrutability – even submission – which the subject today then feels bound to try to remediate or even disown. Once again, the efforts to achieve this often possess an internal consistency and nobility of educational purpose that is thoroughly salutary, but they do give rise to certain conundrums for the destiny of the subject and the methods of teaching supporting it. Perhaps inevitably, in London school the populist instincts of the classroom rationale incline towards the use of mass media texts believed to be attuned to the interests and enthusiasms of young people and deliberately contrasted with the supposed limitations of traditional resources – in the words of the HOD, 'even using films and things like *The Matrix* and all those sorts of things; [in] ways in which it can actually provoke deep philosophical problems . . .'. The reports of pupils confirm this trend, with one senior pupil observing of a Unit Study favoured by herself and her peers:

> I think *Heaven and Hell* were the best because although it was very repetitive – the books and stuff – you got to talk and share ideas between our partners. And then she referred to a video like *The Simpsons*, which you think has nothing to do with RE. But they have produced an episode on Heaven and Hell and Marge and Homer were Adam and Eve and we could understand the story in a picture format rather than reading it out.

In certain regards this quite representative example testifies to the culture of opportunistic 'Associative Indexing' (Chun 2008) now considered a commonplace in Religious Education and which is repeatedly referenced in the lively self-organizing networks of practitioners such as the *RE Online* movement. In a culture mostly indifferent or hostile to the serious educated contemplation of major religious concepts – such as, from Christian belief, for example, eschatology, Sin, Fall – the inspirational teacher looks in a spirit of combinatorial creativity for ingenious vehicles of communication which will authenticate the concepts for younger audiences mostly detached from the doctrinal backdrop which lent these ideas meaning in the first place. The point here is not to repudiate the chosen pedagogy wholesale, but to suggest that its advocates ought to be more alert to some of its unexamined assumptions. In channelling the religious concepts or narratives through a medium that is closely affined to the populist, 'democratic' pedagogical preferences of the progressive classroom, the teacher has to recognize that they may be substantially altered and their merit as a legitimate stimulus to discussion thereby impaired. As is so often the case, the medium, in other words, alters the message, and the allure of a 'relevance' attractive to the media consumption habits of young people risks recreationalizing core concepts upon which successful learning must depend, while hazarding a portrayal of the teacher as an awkward petitioner before the tastes of her pupils, urgently seeking the elusive key to the black box of their understanding and motivation.

The Principal Teacher (Head of Department) in the non-denominational Scottish School actually set out in her individual engagements with the ethnographer to distinguish her credentials from those of her English counterparts, pointing to what she saw as the more exacting and disciplinary-specific academic entry qualifications for the secondary profession in Scotland and the freedom of professional judgement this accorded her.

> Now I think that in itself at a very basic level means that Scottish teachers feel more confident to branch out and I think it goes back right down to that . . . I pick the topic that I know I'm interested in because I always think you teach better what you're interested in and I teach that to the best of my ability. So when I meet up with something I don't know, I go and find some other way of getting it over and you have to think about all the different learning styles of your kids in your class and it's boring for them if they come in week after week and it's just always a text book.

While the Principal Teacher evinces here a welcome scepticism towards the sovereignty of textbooks critiqued elsewhere in this volume, and asserts an autonomy and self-reliance derived from specific national and professional traditions of teacher formation, she places an emphasis similar to that of her English colleague on what the London teacher wistfully articulated as the 'all singing or dancing' expectations laid upon the frontline classroom practitioner.

Whether 'making many units myself', or devising the detailed resources and learning sequences for each lesson, the Scottish PT's sense of professional identity seems predicated on the high-energy exhibition and management of *activity* parallel to her London equivalent, 'because', as she urges, 'modern methodology says if you teach something you're actively involved in it and therefore you learn better'. The pedagogical spotlight on 'actvity' is of course another version of the anti-didactic 'relevance' paradigm, with its tacit understanding of the teacher of Religious Education as a professional who will either implement programmes of work fundamentally aligned to the interests and lifeworlds of pupils or else mediate the apparently less 'relevant' – or unfamiliar or exotic – features of (especially) the 'religious' in Religious Education in forms and events that interface directly with those same educationally prized modes of pupil apprehension (Withey 1975; Egan 2003). This propensity is particularly evident in the context of this specific school (though it is by no means confined to it) in the near-talismanic invocation and embrace of certain multicultural priorities to which Religious Education is expected by school management and Local Authority automatically to respond, from out of the near-universal perception of the subject's obvious intrinsic moral and pedagogical values:

> . . . our . . . material for racism has been moved forward because Guidance suddenly decided to do *Show Racism the Red Card* which we've always done, but suddenly . . . it's all the flavour of the month for them to do that, so we've given them a copy of the unit that we do . . . and we're having on 1st September a *Show Racism the Red Card* day whole school activity . . . and every class that you teach has to have something to do with the racism theme in it. So you're thinking OK great, might do this and might do that.

There is of course nothing essentially untoward in the principled dedication of the school to the tasks of antiracist education; nor is it at all unreasonable to assume that the Religious Education department might have something edifying and enlightening to contribute to it – even when it stems from celebrity-led initiative originally conceived to banish racism from soccer. The London school, given its geographical location and ethnically diverse intake profile, possessed an even more pervasive commitment to antiracism and multicultural education and saw the work of Religious Education as central to the successful discharge of these obligations. The London HOD reflected that:

> We've got kids who come from London and in a London where you've got huge diversity. This whole area is just huge diversity and I think it's more now. It's not so much 'let's sit down, this is what they need to know'.

It's like relating it and how it's relevant.....it's about making the kids well-rounded and understanding one another. Again, like, all my kids were aware who were fasting during Ramadan; all my kids were aware who were celebrating Eid; they're all aware who's going to be celebrating Diwali. It's about creating that . . . let's be honest, I wouldn't be able to do that with those classes if I don't teach them the way I teach them because you couldn't have that discussion.

The lexical moves and shifts within this cache of revealingly autoethnographic professional discourse – from both school contexts – are pregnant with the modulation of treasured, if labile, professional identities and the pragmatics of politically and culturally shaped pedagogical priorities. The speech-records also map multiple sources of ambiguity, with the indexicals and passive deictics of place, time and event spatializing the speaker's locus in a discourse of which she is both the channel and the agent ('suddenly decided . . .'; 'has to have . . .'; 'do this . . . do that'; 'relating it and how it's relevant'; 'aware . . . aware . . . aware') (Ewing 2006). This might be a permanent tension for those occupying appointments of curricular leadership in Religious Education: the pressures of manifold external imperatives and heterogeneous decision-makers laying periodic claim not only to the content and focus of the curriculum but also to the modes of enquiry and communication by which that content and focus is to be mediated and sustained. Multicultural and antiracist education are by no means repudiated in this assessment of their influence, but the assumption that their relationship to Religious Education – and more broadly to *religion* per se – is an educationally straightforward one can be challenged both in terms of their secular superordinate claims on the shape and pattern of the curriculum *and* their contiguity with a highly defined – even inflexible – discursive and pedagogical regime within the classroom itself (Barry 2000; Sikka 2010):

There's a lot of enquiry with the students and I find that particularly in this school because of it being so multi-ethnic. They're just so terribly interested in certain things – and even topics that would be deemed as unacceptable in other subjects. They will enter and engage with it. I'm using the subject like, for instance, circumcision. It's a really weird thing to say, but they have heard of the word; they want to know. But it's also a good way to explain why these things happen and then you can branch out from there and talking about human rights as well because of the gender issues and it's an opportunity.

Once more, although the teacher's planning here is perfectly creative and enterprising, the multicultural driver synthesizes paradigm, pedagogy and ethical principle – propelling the sequence from the regulative social context of the classroom, to ubiquitous relevance-factor and on to the supervening normative order of human rights, where Religious Education becomes tacitly absorbed into the language of Citizenship. It is, in short, unclear if the potent cultural and religious practice of circumcision can actually be comprehended at all in properly religious terms at this juncture. The teleology of classroom learning, here and elsewhere, requires some searching scrutiny if the integrity of Religious Education in an increasingly interdisciplinary curriculum, and an increasingly learner-centred school culture, is to be explained and maintained.

The ethnographer's focus-group fieldnotes and discussions with pupils in the Scottish non-denominational school and the London school certainly demonstrate the full collaboration of young people with the prevailing methods – their contributions frequently stressing to the ethnographer the importance of Religious Education facilitating 'freedom to talk and discuss wider issues and situations' (Scottish School), or commending the subject and its preferred approaches for their contribution to the learners' overall intercultural literacy:

> Yes I think it's knowing about RE. Knowing about other people's religions is just as important as knowing your grammar or knowing science. . . . You'll always have people around you who are different religions and stuff, so it's better to know about other people's religions and lifestyles. I think it stops people's ignorance [which] is what leads to prejudice and if people don't know they're really going to be quite racist. But once you actually start learning about it and you see that everything does have a reason why they do it. . . . (London School)

In simple organizational terms, we see in the granularity of this feedback individualized and collective expressions of an issue documented in many areas of the *Does RE Work?* project: that teachers of Religious Education are asked to do too much and required to inhabit too many overlapping and sometimes conflicting domains of professional responsibility. The sheer expenditure of teacher energy in the close-read examples is daunting, making it no surprise that the DHT in the Scottish non-denominational school should register his admiration for Religious Education teachers with a 'willingness to relinquish a little bit of control in front of the class to get that going . . . that's something that would scare me'. If the subtle present-tense tropes and gerunds in pupil and teacher speech, however, are also reliable in their reification of certain sanctioned forms of 'enquiry', 'knowing', 'learning', 'discussion' and 'relevance', then they also imply a synchronicity between endorsed styles of learning and teaching and the substantial experience of studying and understanding religion which may be, in the last analysis, less reassuring for the subject than at first appears. There is, for example, no self-evident correlation in the literature between 'knowing about' other people's unfamiliar religious beliefs and practices and the embrace of antiracist or multicultural values (Conroy 2009; Bryan 2012). Perhaps, indeed, one form of 'control' has been relinquished in this expository template in favour of another, with neither teachers nor pupils fully discerning it. The impulse running through the responses at the very least raises the spectre that Religious Education and its fashionable pedagogies are held in highest esteem when they in essence serve other ends – and specifically when religion is an exotic point of departure for examinations of life, identity and relationships several removes from the lived experience of religion itself (Swayne 2010).

It may appear transparent that the Scottish Catholic school, articulating (as we have seen) an understanding of the practices of Religious Education from out of a highly specific confessional rationale, will also represent the principles of teaching and pedagogy in very clearly and distinctively defined forms. As Coll (2007) and others (Belmonte & Cranston 2009) have recently documented, the general turn in Catholic education internationally in the last 20 years has been towards an understanding of the Catholic teacher as *witness to faith,* freighted with expectations which intentionally blur the boundaries between professionalism, personal values and the representation of faithful belief and belonging. A plethora of supplementary obligations attaching to the teaching of Religious Education, and the vital expectations surrounding it in Catholic secondary schools, follow from these convictions and it is instructive to note that few of these have been subject to extensive ethnographic examination, particularly from outwith the faith community itself (Convey 2012; Walbank 2012). In committing to the – in many respects – highly commendable aspiration that formal frontline Religious Education be taught by (confessionally committed and approved) subject specialists, the Scottish Catholic school in this section of the study redoubles these burdens – especially in the light of its ambitious, coextensive claim that Religious Education cannot be cordoned within disciplinary or timetabled parameters, but extends beyond the syllabus into the detailed fabric and lifeblood of the school. For some staff, this totalized account of Religious Education takes expressly institutional forms, which might in some sense involve the collaborative *sharing* rather than the *apportioning* of the tasks of the faith community:

> It's the school, it's the parish, it's the home . . . I suppose it's because of the nature
> of this school and its location that actually does exist and the vast majority of

children that I can see do attend Mass or some other religious service supported by the parents. We're really adding to that when they come to school, the RE programmes. (Classroom Teacher of RE)

Pursuit of the assurance that young people are 'being religious' – in a kind of repechage from the ideal of the Catholic Mass to the compensation of 'some other religious service' – is a natural signifier of dispersed accountability. But when we recognize that the said 'RE Programmes' are fundamentally (and increasingly) catechetical, there is a paradox in presenting this as at one and the same time annex and core to pupil learning and development, almost as if the baseline educational aim is to ensure pupils are somehow minimally 'religious' on a ladder that progresses from this stage upwards to faithful assent. 'The full development of the young person's academic [achievement] is important', noted the DHT in the school, 'but so is the social, the emotional, the personal, the spiritual. I think today we've got to watch that we don't lose out on the spiritual dimension.'

Catholic Religious Education appears decentred in such a matrix of seemingly complementary interests and stakeholders, vulnerable to a slippage between multiple, overlapping fields of policy and practice with quite diverse designs on the educational and personal growth of young people from both inside and beyond the believing community. Conjugating the claims of, first, Head Teacher, and then HOD in this refraction of the school's undeniably zealous and well-resourced investment in high-profile Religious Education reveals therefore a much more sedimented understanding of the teacher – and the pedagogical horizons within which the teacher's educational and catechetical tasks are to be completed – than conventional apologetics in the area of faith schooling commonly suggests:

RE may be for some people about the knowledge and understanding: certain facts, figures, the Gospels, whatever it may be. But for me RE is about that experience of seeing that Our Lord came upon the earth to ask of us. And putting that into effect in the day-to-day life of the school. (Head Teacher, Scottish Catholic School)

It's not just a subject because it's a human enrichment process as well. It nourishes children when you give them opportunities to reflect upon their concept of themselves and their place in the world, their responsibility and what they see their role as being – at all time supporting that with the Christian vision of them and their importance and their value, their [in]alienable value . . . to get them to grasp that and to then apply that to see how this is going to affect how you live your life. . . .

Their vision of themselves I think is very much being nourished and enriched by the faith of the school through RE and other aspects of the school. (HOD RE, Scottish Catholic School)

The eloquence of a school leader who has publicly and professionally showcased the faith credentials of his school once more takes us to a plane where religion and education interact to constitute an 'experience'. The involuntary conscription of Religious Education to the reproduction and dissemination of this 'experience' may be perfectly comprehensible and justifiable within the mission of a flourishing Catholic establishment (though lingering doubts may remain in relation to its 'no-hiding-place' applicability to avowedly non-Catholic pupils), but it undoubtedly once again loads the subject area with enormous burdens and blends religion, education and catechesis in a complex cocktail the educational impact of which is decidedly unpredictable. The language of the HOD passionately extends the jurisdictions of all three imperatives so that they meet in a synergy of 'vision', 'value', 'responsibility' nourishment and 'enrichment'. In significant regards, this presentation of confessional Religious Education could only begin to be viably implemented if it has achieved a level of prior corporate ownership almost exactly as its architects desired it – galvanizing partners and stakeholders as comprehensively as multiculturalism and antiracism mobilize secondary schools and sequestrate repeatedly the work of Religious Education in the non-religious sectors. However these movements are finally to be judged, they undeniably condition Religious Education to serve the disciplinary formation of pupil subjectivity in remarkably exhaustive, wrap-around ways and they assuredly alter the shape and character of the formal study of religion (whether 'learning in', 'learning from' or 'learning about') in the modern secondary school wherever it is pursued.

Ethnography and profiling of the nature of learning and teaching within the school largely confirmed the formally 'invitational' character of the confessional syllabus, which was nonetheless sensitized to the realities of a religiously mixed pupil population. This is consistent with the school's rationale for Religious Education explained earlier in this essay. It continues to be troublingly unclear – and endures perhaps as a taxing question for doctrinally assertive faith schools – how can Religious Education in a Catholic school where the subject has been so thoroughly 'universalized' can genuinely maintain its posture of hospitality to those unattached to the faith community? Nevertheless, young people of various backgrounds in the school reported a generally very positive experience in the Religious Education classroom, once more responding to the fieldworker that the subject was 'credible', 'relevant' and palpably enabling of inclusive community values to which all could subscribe – though there persisted a tendency in the upper school to see these values yet again inhering in 'generic' ethical domains such as social justice, care for the disadvantaged and the deliberation of moral dilemmas around 'big ticket' issues such as war and peace. Hence, even the avowedly confessional context of the Catholic school offers no escape hatch from the recuperative tendencies of generic post-enlightenment ethical concerns. Interestingly, the subordination of academic to formational purposes for Religious Education (typical of Scottish Catholic secondary schools and openly amplified by the Church in its new curriculum) appeared not to affect detrimentally its standing in the eyes of pupils. One senior teacher finessed these obvious ambiguities through a kind of dexterous confessional variation on the standard theme of 'pupil experience':

> So, that experience is so important for them – and hopefully they can understand what Our Lord asked of them. It's a day-to-day activity, it's a journey: some young people catch it and others maybe it doesn't really touch on them. . . .

The governing concept of 'experience' exercises a regular pressure over the implied understanding of learning radiating throughout the staff member's comment. 'Understanding' is tied both to the doctrinal ethos of the enveloping environment and also to divine interpellation, the combined influence of which impinges 'hopefully', ungovernably, almost arbitrarily on young people – like a passing angel, or a virus. Not being 'touched' is emphatically *not* construed as personal or academic failure (as it has been portrayed, for example, in some fundamentalist schools (Laats 2010)), but neither, surely, can it be uncritically endorsed as an entirely satisfactory outcome for the workings of the subject.

The Catholic school here represented is in many instances of its moral and religious life radically different from the other schools with which it has been for present purposes ethnographically juxtaposed. The integrity with which it pursues its distinctive objectives commands an intrinsic respect regardless of the passions for and against that faith schools continue to excite among educators and the general public in democratic societies. Yet its configuration of, and orientation towards, Religious Education seems even in its tenacity to take the subject at some critical junctures towards what Britzman's ethnography terms 'the failure of knowledge' (1998, 10): by which he means not the systemic failure of a subject or task to achieve its intended ends or 'learning outcomes' (far from it), but its confrontation with its own limitations in the face of an excess of affect, demand, expectation, hope, resistance, 'experience', which no amount of shared constructivist classification and framing seems able epistemologically to manage or contain (Stern 2007, 98–105). Faith school and non-religious school, striving to articulate a valid, viable practice for contemporary Religious Education, surprisingly often find themselves therefore meeting on the common threshold of a subject brought by their own surplus of intention to the perimeter of its existing possibilities and compelled for an enabling moment quite simply to pause.

Truth claims in Religious Education

Reviewing the ethnography of the selected schools in relation to the perennial issue of truth claims and their place in the sensibilities of contemporary Religious Education constitutes both a coda to the oscillating patterns of meaning and purpose within the schools and a concluding perspective on their respective anthropologies. Throughout the Delphi process, the vexed question of the status of truth claims in the Religious Education of young people provoked non-partisan but widespread anxiety. This concern was parsed evenly across the multiple axes of belief and neutrality present in the seminar by consistent recourse to the language of 'critical realism' – with its now celebrated anti-phenomenological encouragement of a considered, educative encounter through Religious Education with rival religious truth claims, supported by the measured classroom cultivation of autonomous rational reflection and collective deliberation (Wright 2007). 'I think there is a major challenge', noted one of our experts,

> in handling the issue of alternative claims to religious truth, whether one is in a common school or a faith school. I think it's clear that both types of school are acknowledging religious plurality, what isn't clear is whether they are both acknowledging the relative autonomy of other religious conceptions. (Baumfield et al. 2012, 17)

Critical realism as an educational practice in Religious Education teaching – if not as an abstract philosophical position – has been trenchantly interrogated in recent years first by Anna Strhan (2010) and then by David Aldridge (2011), with Strhan in particular proposing that,

> Current models of RE, emphasising the importance of conceptual transparency and the ability to logically evaluate and critique the rival truth claims of religions are already misconstruing the nature of religion. (37)

In place of this predetermination of religious meaning, Strhan and Aldrige, from by no means identical points of departure, each exhort teachers to a recovery in their classrooms of a species of 'textualised hermeneutics', where the vaunted 'openness' of modern progressive, pluralized Religious Education, wherever it is practised, ceases to govern in advance its objects of pedagogical interest (be they 'experiential' or 'transcendent') and opts instead for an authentically deregulated, interruptable learning, 'the subject matter' of which 'must be constituted in the hermeneutic exchange' itself if religion is to be penetrated seriously as a human reality on its own terms (Aldridge 2011, 43). It can also be reasonably inferred from this speculative mapping of a fresh terrain for the conduct of Religious Education, that the forms of post-critical engagement with religion essayed in any such new paradigms for the subject equally incentivize an ongoing institutional *microethnography* of the kind advanced in this chapter and, indeed, in various fashions across this volume: a drill-down into the illocutionary force of text, voice, command and happening across school actors and circumstances, alert to all of the intertextual strata where the production of localized personal and professional speech inadvertently discloses the unspoken costs involved in creating and sustaining a meaningful relationship between Religious Education and the desire for truth.

In the Scottish Catholic school with which we concluded the previous section, it may seem reassuringly obvious that the formulation of truth claims has assumed a relatively seamless dogmatic shape by virtue of the guarantees afforded by credal assent, personal faith commitment and the elective nature of parental choice. The comportment of the Head Teacher offers a beguilingly simple and honest account of this backdrop to the work of Religious Education, couched in the familiar discourse of the Catechism. Indeed, the word 'honest' is a recurrent lexical marker in the school's ethnographic record, sometimes functioning as declaration of intent ('so they honestly believe'), sometimes as conspiratorial admission ('I have to be honest and say . . .'):

> The formation is the first part: you've got to give the youngsters the sense of the last two thousand years and the development of Christianity and in particular the Catholic faith . . . [and] the experience of their faith, so they honestly believe that is where the real growth can come through. There's no point telling them if they can't experience it. So in the day-to-day life of a school how do you experience your faith? Through the love of your neighbour, and through that, the love of God.

The concentric circles of Church, community, Religious Education curriculum and (yet again) '*experience* of faith' secured through the fine-grained textures of school life induce the production of a self-contained (and, in its own terms, completely coherent) yet expansive proclamation of revealed truth. There is sustained throughout the public mission of the school a consistent view that Religious Education can be inherently educational and constitutively evangelical without prejudice to either motivation. Closer inspection does test some of the apparent homologation here by pointing to certain discontinuities in the relations between the various, mutually-validating centres of authority with which the school supposedly articulates. As well as admitting to first-hand acquaintance with 'other' Catholic schools where Religious Education is paid only 'lip service' and treated as a site where 'you can just do your homework', senior managerial and departmental staff are also conscious of unequal distribution of responsibility for catechesis across that community of which they are considered to be a part.

> I have to be honest and say that for a lot of the pupils – and I'm talking here of children who are defined as being Catholics – the school was probably the only place where they were getting any formal regular Catholic education. A lot of them didn't go to Mass. A lot of it was just down to the school. There can be a mindset that says, 'Well I'm sending him to Catholic School, what else do you want me to do?'

This is of course a constant challenge for the Catholic school in modern society, and perhaps explains better than any other cause the recent intensification of catechetical endeavour in Scottish Catholic Religious Education, as the subject absorbs responsibilities previously discharged across a variety of community and parish agencies now figuring much less conspicuously in the lives of the population. The increased influence and, indeed power, accumulated by Religious Education as these historic secularizing processes work their way through the ecclesial system may appear attractive, but they have arguably been purchased at some considerable cost, as the spaces for genuinely 'religious' stimulus, surprise and imagination within the Religious Education curriculum recede before the weighty yet conflicted requirement to form the baseline faith of the next generation.

> As I said high numbers do come to Mass, so if we didn't strike a chord with them then they wouldn't bother; they would just walk out the door and that would be it . . . it is real as well and we are just trying to instil these values within them . . . and they want to be here.

While it would be unreasonable to deny the Religious Education teacher in a thriving Catholic secondary school the basic validity of Mass attendance as a meaningful index of spiritual and religious interest, it remains strikingly unclear where this interest really lies, just as the conflation of 'instilled' values and faithful worship continues to weigh problematically on the core purposes of Religious Education in any school.

For the Scottish non-denominational school, the explicit cultivation in the upper school of the 'individual's understanding of religious beliefs, transcendent issues, and critical and evaluative thinking' (HOD) was motivated idealistically by a radical pluralism which in certain important respects did question the limitations of phenomenological and critical-realist accounts of religious experience. Intriguingly, senior pupils in dialogue with the fieldworker recuperated much of this energy by explaining that the central purpose of their learning in Religious Education was, first, to 'gain awareness of other faiths in order to promote tolerance' and, secondly, 'promoting positive values contributing to citizenship'. This is in no sense a reproach to the HOD or her effectiveness, nor does it minimize the young people's enthusiasm, but it may again underline the internal inertia and vulnerability in the subject that often impedes the committed engagement with religion to which the HOD aspired. Revealingly, some pupils defended their reductive account of the effectiveness of Religious Education by adverting to the scepticism with which significant numbers of their peers – and several of their teachers – viewed the role of the subject in the school timetable. The HOD remained refreshingly unapologetic about her own personal and professional investments and uncertainties, resorting again to the protean indexical of 'honesty' to explain and project them:

> You've also got to be honest enough to say 'No, I don't know the answer to that. I'll find out.' They don't . . . there's no way you *could* know everything about all religions . . . I will say to a class, 'You've taught *me* that. I didn't know that; that's great.' And you can see they go 'Oh, I taught teacher!' It's about . . . knowing yourself and having enough basic knowledge and being supportive.

The discursive patterning of evolving teacher subjectivity – and teacher-pupil intersubjectvity – shifts ironically and revealingly through these sentences and fragments, the texture of speech disclosing interstitially a powerful rapport of professional personality and the idealized representation of the subject matter at its very best. Remarkably, the apodosis of the final statement draws both person and concept back to an abiding insight taken straight from the annals of both faith and philosophy: *know thyself* – not, we might observe, in the Apollonian version of rational self-mastery, but clearly and daringly in the older, archaic, oracular awareness of the liminal, the threshold, the edges of shared meaning-making (Conroy 2004). This is Religious Education become mantic: the teacher glimpsed for a moment as shaman, rather than philosopher. It comes as little surprise, then, that in some of the department's most enthusiastically received lessons – on, for example, the origins of the universe – this same voluble cocktail of intertextual learning across science, myth and faith pushed at precisely the same boundaries of certainty and agnosticism, movingly fluently and imaginatively through a multimedia palimpsest of cosmological theory, creation stories and quiet personal meditation, finding no secure point of conclusion about truth or the claims to it.

It will be obvious that from all three schools the disposition towards the place of truth claims in Religious Education emerges from the complex interplay of the other, multiple forces shaping the internal rationale for the subject and the pedagogies supportive of each rationale. If this was not always as organic a process as the schools wished periodically to suggest, this amounts to no rebuke to staff, students or leadership, but points instead to the internal tensions induced by the various and contradictory appropriations of the subject for which no single school or community is by itself accountable. Truth, indeed, is always represented in this cognitive and affective turbulence as an essence *outside* the patterns of signification to which the subject of Religious Education will somehow 'aspire'. The sympathetic ethnographic profiling of Religious Education in action shows that same truth, however, not to be at all external to its disciplinary signification but to be latent in all of the subject's redoubtable machinery of technique, imitation, repetition, presentation, interaction – which routinely combine to simulate truth. The issue then is not only a particular alignment of truth to signification that Religious Education might somehow seek to safeguard on behalf of any number of candidate (even rival) authorities, but much more subversively the power of signs to *make* realities, to call into existence things that might not be true in the sense that they cannot exist apart from the work of signification that materializes them in classrooms and lessons in the first place.

In the London school, finally, there are two processes of signification that seem to determine the fortunes of Religious Education in the lives of pupils and teachers, and which may point ambivalently to some of the subject's possible futures in the non-religious sector more generally. The first is the representation of *truth as taxonomy*, conditioned by the radical cultural pluralism of the school's social and generational setting. The second is the steady, genealogical emergence of *philosophy as the successor to religion*, with everything this move appears to entail about the so-called progress of reason and the retreat of religion from the regulated zones of pupil learning.

The dual trajectory can be followed at two levels: the increasing prestige of philosophy as the self-proclaimed 'pinnacle' of the Religious Education programme and the developmental understanding of philosophy as a trusted frame of reference to which religious narrative and practices may haltingly lead in the lower school – but only insofar as they fall away from mature educational attention in the upper. 'Increasingly', noted one Religious Education teacher,

> because they find philosophy so fascinating we're getting a larger percentage of students also taking our subject. So we felt that we needed to show them the links that can be made between science and religion to see that really there's not so much of a difference.

> Senior pupils had internalised this prescription as both principle and methodology: The one about life after death in GCSE that was really interesting when you thought about the possibility of an afterlife and near-death experiences and miracles. That was really, really interesting because there's eye-witness stuff then you can start to say whether it's credible or not.

> It's the thinking for yourself. I probably wouldn't just accept someone's opinion now. I would actually say, 'Where is your evidence? Where is evidence that is opposite to your opinion? Let me go through it myself and make up my own mind.'

> [RE] definitely changed what I believe in, in terms of when I was younger I can definitely say that I did believe in quite a few gods and these gods taking a sort of humanly figure . . . now I would say I've a very different view.

As we have suggested, the London School was an establishment that took religion seriously and worked immensely hard to accord recognition to the beliefs and customs of the myriad faith groups within the pupil and local populations. The multicultural credentials of Religious Education were unimpeachable and there is abundant evidence in the ethnographic material of serious sustained attention to cultural and religious difference in the best traditions of comparativism. It may well be, however, that the understandable multicultural elevation within Religious Education of truth as a species of taxonomy – where painstaking, respectful attentiveness to the forms and conduct of religious practice routinely provides the substance of classroom learning – involuntarily strengthens the grasp of deliberative cosmopolitanism on the approaches to religion and religious experience (Carr 2007). Young people in the upper school ('It's quite annoying that primary schools don't place more emphasis on it . . .') appear impatient to advance 'beyond' religion, to a unifying plane of disinterested enquiry which retains due and sincere 'toleration' for all of the outward displays of religious belief while adhering with increasing resolve to the adjudicative capacities of the philosophical method: 'We don't sort of say yes OK, fine, God created the world in seven days and I don't know if many people believe that in Year 11 or Year 10. . . . RE lets you think more freely.' As Lloyd and others have suggested (2007), there may be something highly questionable even in the metaphorization of this concept of developmental progress, in both its underlying description of young people's 'growth in rational understanding' and in its obscured assumption that philosophy offers some kind of external 'view from nowhere' panorama on the nature of religion and the relationship of modern education to it.

Conclusions

The detailed micro-ethnography evident in this discussion has been an considered drilling down into the subtle by-ways of Religious education in three quite different schools. The issues of purpose, teacher self-representation and truth-claiming could hardly be more central to our understanding of the ecology of the subject. This ecology is, in its daily undulations, shaped by the post-enlightenment turn to toleration and the acceptance of difference. It is to questions of tolerance, otherness and citizenship that we now turn.

Notes

1 Different from other chapters in this volume, we decided not to provide attribution for particular field notes, examples and so forth on the grounds that the extensive, detailed and focused discussion here might result in the identification of particular schools. This approach was also adopted in Chapter 7.

2 In this context Principal Teacher' refers to a Head of Department/Faculty.

Part II

The Substance of
Religious Education

Citizenship and Committed Pluralism: The Place of the 'Other' in RE's Social and Civic Aims

Introduction

As we have noted earlier, the latter years of the Labour government in the United Kingdom witnessed a resurgence and renewal of interest in RE teaching in school wherein the social and civic entailments of learning about religions featured prominently. Stephen Lloyd MP, Chair of the All Party Parliamentary Group on Religious Education noted that it is essential for children and young people to be 'taught about different cultures and religions by trained, experienced RE teachers, allowing children to make informed choices' (Burns 2012). This statement succinctly introduces two themes in the civic and social aims of RE – teaching about different cultures and making informed personal choices. These two themes reoccur in proximity throughout much of the policy literature in the domain:

> In my RE lessons I have learnt to become more broadminded, to accept other people's beliefs and faiths and to not let race or religion come in the way of what you see in an individual. (QCA 2004, 6)

> RE is one of my favourite subjects and the reason for that is that most of the time in lessons we discuss issues that make me look inside myself and think very deeply about the world, behaviour, my personality and my beliefs. (DCSF 2010, 32)

Finding some echo in our own study and evident in the later chapter on student responses, these statements set out, in carefully selected examples of student feedback, the two dimensions of Attainment Target 2 of the Non-Statutory National Framework for England – 'learning from religions', which has come to encompass a very broad scope of spiritual, moral, cultural and social entailments within the RE curriculum. This breadth opens up a number of important questions which deserve to be addressed. In particular, what is the correct relationship between learning about and from 'other people's beliefs', 'different cultures', and personal moral and social development? Clearly, within the policy and curriculum guidance there is an implication that learning about others' faiths ought to lead to a greater measure of tolerance and open-mindedness. While there is some dispute about what kinds of educational processes and contact between people of different religio-cultural traditions are most efficacious (Conroy 2008), there is certainly no dispute among politicians and professionals alike as to the desirability of educational interventions leading to such enhanced understanding and engagement. It is unclear, however, whether or not and, if it does, in *what* way this learning contributes to the development of moral capacities for living effectively in a multicultural and pluralistic society. As we have already noted, these patterns of engagement in England are echoed in policy guidance for Wales and Northern Ireland, while Scotland's *Curriculum for Excellence* explicitly separates the elements of 'Christianity', 'world religions' and 'developing beliefs and values' (LTS 2011). Despite some lack of clarity as to how such may be effected, during our two-day Delphi professional seminar the conversation was peppered with attempts (largely unsuccessful) to bring some clarity to what has endured as one of the knottiest problems in Religious Education in the United Kingdom. This chapter explores some of the complexities attending the appropriation of Religious Education in the service of an explicit multicultural citizenship. While we acknowledge that many of the efforts of teachers are compromised by the somewhat larger epistemic and ethical questions dealt with earlier, it is indisputable that, within the ambit of popular professional understandings of pluralist pedagogies, many of the teachers were concerned to see religious education as a positive vehicle for transforming student attitudes towards the other and promoting a singular liberal conception of multicultural tolerance.

Pluralism, multiculturalism and professional perspectives

Other recent explorations of the teaching of RE in England and Wales have pointed to systematic failings to appropriately consider the relationship between learning about others' religions and the nurturing of tolerant and pluralistic dispositions, foregrounding the ways in which content knowledge can be disconnected from personal-reflective activities, at times giving the impression that RE is bifurcated into two separate subjects (Ofsted 2010). It is worth considering if the problem here may not be a systematic but a systemic failure borne out of constitutive challenges in particular readings of Religious Education and leading to many misrepresentations of world religions in curriculum and resources, which can lead to children failing to identify believers as living in the same contemporary world as themselves (Jackson et al. 2010). Considering the problem to be systematic and in an attempt to remedy this situation, some local syllabi have, in recent years, departed from the orthodoxy of presenting six religious traditions in all cases, moving instead to a smaller number, covered in more comprehensive depth (Birmingham ASC 2007; Cornwall SACRE Agreed Syllabus 2011).

During the Delphi discussions a number of participants expressed concerns about a bland, 'civic virtue' approach to religions, in which the purpose of studying other faiths was not to engage seriously with those faith traditions in themselves, their theological and moral content, but rather to foster open-mindedness and tolerance as ends in themselves. The tendency of government guidance, and justifications from professional RE organizations themselves, to promote instrumental rationales for the study of RE, they contended, led to misrepresentations of religion and a bland curriculum for tolerance. Interestingly, of course, many of the participants regularly interact with and are part of the same community that creates syllabuses, offers policy advice and ultimately engages with the legislators in shaping the practices of Religious Education. Of course, while RE is hardly unique in regard to instrumental, 'skills based' curriculum justifications, the subject is particularly vulnerable to such approaches, in that its very essence is threatened by such social and civic aims. Many Delphi participants, for example, stressed the radically counter-cultural nature of much religious and prophetic narrative, and the importance of engaging with difficult and controversial religious teachings. Recognizing that such an approach can be accompanied by something akin to professional embarrassment about the promotion of critical judgement for fear of highlighting differences, many in the group expressed concerns which echo Stern's (2007) critique of a tolerance of 'nice' things: treating all religions as forms of civic order – drawing attention, for example, to the presence of texts approximating to the Golden Rule in all major world faiths, while eliding the very different metaphysical and teleological bases from which they are derived, 'leaving public spaces free of truth but implacably tolerant' (Stern 2007, p. 24).

Members of the seminar expressed concern that this failure to address the metaphysical and teleological substance of religion could hinder the personal search for meaning in religions and thus undermine the very thing so desired by many RE professionals. One Delphi participant noted that:

> [w]hen young people are trying to work out for themselves what takes on meaning for them, where their own agendas are, we simply throw an open door and say that all opinions count and all opinions are of equal worth, and it's just sort-of a sharing of ideas. But increasingly, that exploring of what has meaning for you has to have some sort of rigour to it, and we need to help children to explore what makes the difference between something which is good thinking and something which is flawed.

The expert group all agreed on the importance of subjecting the moral claims of religion to rigorous and open discussion where this was appropriate to the age and interests of the students, in particular with the older (14–17) age group who are the focus of this study. To do this effectively, some experts contended that RE would need to become more controversial, rather than eliding fundamental differences between religious faiths, classroom practices would need to focus more on the subversive and counter-cultural elements of religious narratives. Some participants proposed a pedagogy which re-framed the parameters of the subject through encouraging students to challenge personal and social moralities, pointing to the radical challenge posed by religious teachings:

> I started teaching them St Basil the Great's meditation that the rich man is a thief, and I found that the Business Studies teacher came to my door and told me to stop teaching them that the thing she was teaching was immoral.

> Religious Education was the area [of the school curriculum] where the expressive and the exploratory come out way more than any other subject . . . grasping something beyond the literal.

The possibility of the pedagogical pursuit of personal search for meaning dissociated from the treatment of 'other people's beliefs' as a means to attain the kind of bland tolerance criticized by the panel raises the possibility of an anodyne treatment of the other, which bears no relation to the realities of students' lived experience. As well as being a threat to the personal-reflective dimension of RE, such misrepresentation also risks failing to achieve its own end of multicultural 'tolerance', presenting instead a flimsy account of religious beliefs as concerned with *strange* external practices, disconnected from their theological and spiritual origins, at once making the other appear strange and without understanding the intellectual, cultural and epistemic sources that underpin this strangeness. The resulting caricature of religion is one which can be easily seen through by students. The theme of 'strangeness' is one to which we shall return.

Numerous examples surfaced which suggested that many teachers took this critique seriously, and recognized the need to consider carefully areas of controversy, challenge and ambiguity in religious teachings. Teachers in one school had developed a scheme of work in S1 (age 12) aimed at introducing students to the skills of reading parables and symbolism through stories taken from a range of traditions. Students in another school were encouraged to compare and contrast the biblical definition of love in 1 Corinthians 4 with contemporary secular conceptions of love taken from popular music. Where these exchanges were effective, students were invited into an encounter between the world of their lived experience, and the challenge of reconciling this with faith perspectives, whether their own or those of others.

In the lived experience of many of the classrooms we explored, however, there were examples of precisely the kind of reductive and instrumental approaches to tolerance of which the Delphi participants were so critical. Students in one school were asked to illustrate the Buddhist concept of *dukkha*, suffering caused by impermanence, with examples of disappointing Christmas gifts. In some cases, these somewhat etiolated approaches consisted of the rote learning of simplified 'facts' about others' beliefs, often linked to examination requirements, detached from lived experience. In other cases, religious beliefs and practices were reduced to common denominators, ignoring the profound differences both within and between different faith traditions. The nature of the problem is encapsulated in a conversation between our ethnographer and the head of RE in a secondary school in Northern Ireland, who commented that:

> A lot of our pupils, their home life is very much based around religion, and also it's really good, because lots of parents will say 'well, we understand the importance of my son or daughter's learning of other religions, so that they will respect them'. We did a big thing in Year 7, it used to be RE and you should respect everyone, and now it's RS, respect study, and respect is the core. (Northwest High School)

This impulse to foreground 'respect' as the end of such education dissociates learning about 'other religions' from the search for personal meaning (learning from). It suggests both another refraction of the epistemic confusion regarding propositional claims explored in Chapter 2 and the desire to avoid anything that might look like a comparison between traditions. Frequently in classrooms across quite different schools serving quite distinctive community ecologies, students are introduced to concepts and ideas, practices and claims that are superficially descriptive and offer no particular insight into the theological, philosophical or ethical claims of particular religious traditions. Such approaches undermine the notion of a citizenship for authentic tolerance. Let us consider some instances of the way in which world religions were transacted:

> An S1 lesson in a secondary school in the North of Scotland, a group of students are presenting their group study on Islam. Much of their information has been gathered from internet searches and printed directly onto their poster. One boy stands up, he has a prayer mat, compass, two sets of prayer beads around his hands and is wearing a yarmulke. He explains the compass is so that they 'face North' when praying, and then makes some of the motions of Islamic prayer, without further explanation, 'and the beads are just to help them concentrate, I think.' (Segget)

> As part of a Year 7 lesson of 'Festivals of Light' (a scheme of work which compares Christmas, Hanukkah and Diwali) at a Catholic school in the Greater London area . . . students are writing out a menu for a Hanukkah meal. The teacher reminds them that Jewish people eat fried food on Hanukkah to remind them of the oil that burned in the temple . . . The wall display on 'Festivals of Light' already includes a Christmas tree . . . and Menorah . . . and will be completed with a large Diwa lamp. (St. John Fisher)

> A student in a secondary school in the West of Scotland is interviewed about what they have gained from their RE lessons, she tells the ethnographer that she doesn't know any Jews in her home town, but if she met one, she would know what to feed them. (Gorston)

> A Year 9 class in a Catholic grammar school in Northern Ireland makes use of a textbook prepared for Catholic schools and bearing the *Imprimatur* of one of the Irish bishops. There is a section on Islam, which covers Islamic dress – the woman pictured in the textbook is wearing a burqa and niqab . . . Toward the end of the lesson, the teacher asks what lessons on modesty 'we' can draw as Catholics from learning about Islam. (St. Athanasius)

> In one very quick-fire S4 revision lesson in a secondary school in the North of Scotland, 23 new terms relating to Buddhism, are introduced by the teacher – 12 in English, a further 11 in Pali. In total the terms appear 84 times, spoken or in writing, where an average of 2.6 sentences are deployed to explain each term. Only 11 examples are given to illustrate the term, only one of which comes from Buddhist tradition. On 8 occasions a metaphor is used to explain the term, only once are pupils invited to answer questions. (Segget)

A Year 10 focus group in the North East of England express their disaffection with RE – they say that they would like to study more interesting, exotic religions. When pressed to explain what he means by this remark, one boy suggests 'cannibalism', to which another responds 'cannibalism isn't a religion, it's a type of cuisine'. (Matilda's High School)

Of course in the everyday transactions between student and teacher there will be humour and misunderstanding, poor practice and good practice but this recognition does not give licence to occlude the very significant and widespread issues of poor translation, engagement and conceptual confusion. Such instances of the treatment of world religions may be notable as examples of poor practices, leading to inadequate understanding and engagement, but they also point to a recurring theme of this volume: often in classrooms across quite different schools, serving quite distinctive community ecologies, students are introduced to concepts and ideas, practices and claims, that are superficially descriptive and offer no particular insight into the theological, philosophical or ethical claims of particular religious traditions. Rather than enhancing students' understanding of and engagement with the 'otherness' of the other, such approaches undermine the notion of a citizenship for authentic tolerance. This occurs where the other is reduced to another 'me', as is the case in the Catholic school where the wearing of the niqab becomes appropriated as an ethical resource for another tradition, rather than as a particular religio-cultural social practice within its own traditions. It also arises where the beliefs and attachments of the other are reduced to morphologies. This failure to treat religious and religio-cultural practices as ends in themselves not infrequently led to a somewhat bland and disengaged treatment of 'other people's beliefs'. Without a genuine encounter with the otherness of others' beliefs, or indeed highlighting the strangeness of students' own beliefs, students often find that their important questions go unanswered. This points to a genuine problem, which remains present even in many more considered and reflective attempts to broker genuine engagement with religious beliefs in the classroom.

The dominant picture of RE in our study, as well as the reports of the DCSF (Jackson et al. 2010) and Ofsted (2010) suggests that specialist teachers are largely committed and professional in their approaches to RE, and are aware of the obligation to nurture positive engagement with students. However, to acknowledge this is not to ignore those sometimes poorly articulated features of a particular religious education that render even committed teachers powerless. Nor is it to suggest that the struggles teachers have are insubstantial.

The growing pressure of examination entry and success may well contribute, as in the Buddhism example, to the continuing failure of RE to present religious concepts in the depth required for effective engagement. But this alone cannot account for such palpable failures to communicate a resonant, complex and intellectually satisfying account of religious belief and practice or indeed of otherness. As we discuss in the previous chapter, a perception of the inexorable advance of secularization (Bruce 2002) militates against effective religious education because the students have too little acquaintance with religious conceits. However, the kinds of difficulties and challenges we witnessed during our study have echoes in much earlier work (Kerry 1984; Egan 1988) and this particular version of the secularization thesis will only take us so far. In some of the schools in our sample, teachers encountered a struggle in overcoming overt hostility to religion in general, and Christianity in particular – where such hostility existed, a different model of RE could often be observed, which involved treating the study of all religions as a study of the beliefs of others. This could take either a sensitive and thoughtful approach, such as might be seen in one school that introduced Christian theology by focusing on the role of Christianity in the developing world, decentring it from a familiar narrative of local churches. In other cases, this model could remain shallow and condescending; only introducing students to external practices without engaging with the reasons why anyone might view the world from a faith perspective. In the course of our ethnographic work we regularly observed teachers respond to students questions about the verisimilitude of particular religious events such as the parting of the Red Sea by having recourse to naturalistic (often pseudo-scientific) explanations of causality. Of course, it can be argued that any resource can be well or badly used, but – taken in conjunction with conversations and pedagogies that appear to evade theological explanation – we see the emergence of a recurrent trope around the failure to engage with the epistemic challenge of religion.

Different communities: Different approaches

The epistemic and ethical weaknesses illustrated to this point in the study are not the whole story. For some 20 years there has been an increased emphasis on diversity in educational provision across the United Kingdom, although this has taken different forms in the constituent nations, with an emphasis on institutional convergence in Northern Ireland (McAdam 2011), and on diversity of institutions with divergent faith, community and founding ethos in England

(DCSF 2007). Many of the schools in our sample had a unique ethos, responsive to complex demographic challenges in the school's selection criteria, or in the local catchment area. Here and there religious education could be seen to be responsive to such local conditions, where the community is substantially and overtly religious (even where the school is not itself religiously denominated). Moreover a number of school leaders described the subject as a prominent vehicle, in some cases *the* prominent vehicle, for community cohesion, the moral and social development of their students, and a range of other civic entailments. Again, in many cases, learning about the other, whether that other was present in the school or only outside the school gates, was considered to be key to both of these entailments. Two different models of practice were observed. The first was based on engendering a respect for the other, where the other was not present, through study, asking speculative questions, and through field trips or observation. The second was concerned to broker a space of encounter within the classroom, where students could open up about their deeply held concerns, discover commonalities and share differences; where students encountered diversity within the school. Nonetheless, even when schools actively value both religion and diversity, as in the case of one school which enthusiastically sought to promote intercommunity relations and ease tensions as part of the outworking of its Christian ethos, the pressures of examination competitiveness continue to intrude, as a member of the school's leadership team explained:

> It would be lovely to think that many of our parents send their children here because it's an integrated school. I firmly believe that the majority of people would send their children to our school because it's a successful school, it gets good marks. It can keep children . . . and turn them into successful learners, to high achievers . . . that's the law of the jungle, that's why parents would send their children to our school, and then, secondly, yes, it's an integrated school. (Dungally)
>
> [The headteacher of a large London community school recounts] . . . how central RE is to his agenda for the school. He tells me of his own work in combating a rising tide of racism in the local community, at times literally turning back racist elements of the community at the school gates. RE, tolerance, and improved learning environment are firmly interwoven in his account of the school's recent successes, turning the school from the verge of special measures (<15% GCSE pass rates) to one of the most successful in the area. (Brockton Community School)

Juxtaposing this ethos of commitment to community integration as a civic aim with the 'law of the jungle' in this way provides an important perspective on the challenges faced by RE. The reliance on examination-focused learning outcomes, examination-board approved materials and the content and aims of the examined curriculum in setting the agenda for RE, even in schools with committed and engaged teachers and clear leadership, would appear to have a distorting effect on learning. A review of available examination-board approved textbooks revealed that these focused overwhelmingly on either Christianity alone or Christianity and Islam. And, as we discuss in Chapter 6 on texts, this has been both a challenge and an opportunity for classroom teachers.

At one school in East London, which worked to forge explicit links between RE and community cohesion in an area of racial tensions, effective teaching proceeded from a position of committed openness, embracing controversy. The school offered a philosophy and ethics paper and a Christianity paper as part of their GCSE syllabus, and the head of RE, drawing on his own personal identity and disposition, employed a Socratic model of reflective questioning, at times eliciting the complex from the facile. As Mr C, walked down the corridor a student comments 'Mr C is good at confusing us', to which Mr C responds, 'Yes, because life is confusing, there are *never* any easy answers'. This challenge is repeated by Mr C in the everyday transactions of the classroom. Hence:

> With a low ability Year 9 class, Mr C is discussing God's attributes, Chloe says: 'He's got a beard', to which Mr C replies: 'Couple of interesting things . . .' and points out to Chloe her assumptions that God is male and human. (Brockton Community School)

While this approach does not deal explicitly with the theological, it at least can be recognized as an attempt to deepen understanding towards a level of abstraction beyond the literal. Students in Mr C's classroom approach RE from different community perspectives, often their language comes pre-evaluated and loaded with meanings from different religious belief systems, in particular from London's black-majority Pentecostal churches. In employing a more philosophical approach to his questions, Mr C is careful to adopt a pedagogical humility, allowing students to bring the language of their own understandings to the conversation, then challenging them, within that world-view, to move outside the familiar in order to engage with underlying truth claims and to see the contradictions between world-views. This approach brings about confrontation and paradox, but rarely resolution.

One example of the ways in which these philosophical and theological language registers challenge one another, opening up spaces for students' personal and intercommunity exploration, is presented below. The example is taken from a community school in a racially divided area of multiple deprivation in London:

Mr C:	'If God loves me, he wants to stop me dying of cancer, he wants to stop me feeling pain. If God's all powerful, he is capable, he is able to stop me dying from cancer. So what would any logical, reasonable person conclude from the fact that God can stop me but hasn't?'
Teje:	'That that was how you're meant to die.'
Mr C:	'Well, I don't think that's the logical/'
Teje:	'Well, does you believe in death?'
Mr C:	'Believe in death?'
Teje:	'Aye'
Mr C:	'I don't know how you/'
Teje:	'Like you have to die at one point. . .'
Mr C:	'Does everybody have to die?'
Sammy:	'Yes'
Mr C:	'If God is all powerful, could God not have created a world in which nobody dies?'
Teje:	'He never done that though, you have to die!'
	Two girls laugh at the intensity of Teje's statement.
Sammy:	'Yeah but that world before like heaven and hell, so if this world was perfect, what was the purpose of heaven and hell?'
Mr C:	'That's an interesting question we're going to come back to that.'
Jacob:	'Cos God created the world, but Satan/'
Mr C:	'God loves everybody [pause] question mark.'
	Four students say together: 'yes'
Mr C:	'Right, so if God loves everybody, why does he send some people to have sticks poked at them for all eternity, that doesn't sound like/'
Sammy:	'Cos they done bad . . .'
Azim:	'I don't know about the Bible, yeah, but in the Koran it says, it says yeah that through the hard times you have to, you have to stay patient [Sammy: 'Yeah'] an' if people die you're not going to go 'aw I don't believe in God' and all that, cos that's your problem and you're gonna go to hell for that. And it clearly states like bad stuff happens.'
Mr C:	'So essentially what you're saying is that evil is a test of faith?'
Sammy:	'Yes'
Azim:	'Yes'
Sammy	[to Azim]: 'I like that, you know.' (Brockton Community School)

In the classroom conversation, Sammy and Teje's account of faith takes as obvious a Christian anthropology and eschatology, the realities of the soul, its death and judgement. Death, as a natural process, is part of the supernatural, already invested with religious meaning. Mr C's questioning proceeds from a philosophical logic, treating God as an ideal, rather than revealed, being. Without the humility of each to accept and work within the frame of reference of the other, each side's approach is rendered meaningless by the other. In this brief conversation, two world-views meet – the God of Mr C's logic, the God who 'could', and the God of Teje and Sammy's faith, the God who made things as 'meant' to be. This opens up a paradox, in which each side's questions appear strange to the other. Instead of seeking the kinds of oppositional dichotomies which are often rewarded in GCSE examinations, 'some Christians believe x, other Christians do not' – dichotomies that were all too evident in many classroom encounters across schools – here Mr C facilitates an opening up of a space where the different epistemic roots of Sammy and Azim's beliefs can be exposed.

The mutual interruptions in the dialogue illustrate the teacher's preparedness to enter into this space of paradox, deliberately nurturing a discursive equality with his students, while remaining in control of the questions they address, consciously modelling the embracing of the strange: an invitation to which his students respond. It is the students themselves who must make the journey into this space, exposing their own beliefs in dialogue. In this environment, different faith positions find common ground, arguably mutually enhancing one another, as Azim's intervention from within a Muslim frame of reference, suggests but doing so in a way that avoids compromising or reducing one world-view to a cipher for or epiphenomenon of the other. No final resolution is possible, although both sides are allowed to exercise critical reason, nor is any final reduction of faith to the categories (naturalistic or otherwise) of reason attempted. But neither is there any movement towards a resolution of conflicting claims.

It is, however, in the recognition of mutual *strangeness* that transformations can occur. Within this particular school, racial tensions and discipline problems have been resolved in recent years, with the headteacher describing RE as foundational to his approach to these, often apparently intractable, problems. A former humanities teacher in the school, the headteacher had actively nurtured the notion of safe space for discussion within his own department, and sought to make use of RE and the humanities more generally, to encourage open dialogue. Far from turning RE into a form of 'therapeutic education' (Ecclestone & Hayes 2008), however, the school sought an authentic engagement with the complex and deep commitments held by students. While this approach did not focus exclusively on examination performance, it does stress the intellectual rigour of the subject, and RE was one of the highest performing subjects in the school.

What emerges here is a manifest commitment to the not inconsequential responsibility of RE to introduce young people to authentic understandings of religions. Such an approach recognized from the outset that not only is our society diverse and at times disorienting, but also that any social grouping, and the individual member is ever subject to a sense of incompleteness. Complexity and unfamiliarity are an inherent feature of human existence, not as a 'problem' to be solved, either through final synthesis (Conroy 2009) nor by putting aside deeply held values in public spaces (Stern 2007), as a mode of being to be recognized and embraced as an essential feature of living in a pluralistic society. As we discussed earlier and will continue to explore, too often, as a consequence of resource pressures and intellectual impoverishment, classroom RE is an exercise in foreclosure. Standard accounts of multiculturalism have been subject to significant critique in recent years for creating a climate of separation (Guardian 2005; Cameron 2011). Where effective pedagogical engagements emerge they draw upon a committed pluralism, which actively values difference, complexity and change, enabling diverse groups to work together to realize a common good without putting aside their fundamental character (Kassam 2010). Such pedagogies are not only compatible with examination success, as demonstrated by the high rates of success in the schools in which they are observed, but act as midwife to the effective integration of social and civic aims with an openness to personal spiritual and moral development and exploration.

In order to enact the kind of approach illustrated above, a high-trust environment must already exist within the classroom. Those teachers and classrooms that made manifest this kind of 'pedagogy of encounter' did so in ways consistent with the deeply held commitments of their own teachers and students. The influence of local factors makes it difficult to refine this pedagogy into a singular set of rules that might stand as advice for all RE teachers. It conforms in many ways to Conroy's (2004) account of a liminal pedagogy, breaking through at the boundaries of the curriculum. No RE curriculum could be, or ought to be, composed entirely of such encounters, as much substantive grounded knowledge is required before such discussions can take place. But such encounters are necessary, erupting into the mundane, if students are to be challenged to take seriously the beliefs of others, and likewise to recognize the strangeness of their own positions. It is not a pedagogy of grand epiphanies, but rather of quiet confidence, enacted by teachers who are willing to broker a depth and authenticity of encounter in the RE classroom, and to model that depth of enquiry themselves. This can lead to a progressively deepening series of meetings with the socially and spiritually unfamiliar.

A further example, which belies the more prevalent record of field experience alluded to above, was to be found in a trip to a Hindu temple by students from a Muslim-majority school. The head of RE tells the ethnographer that this trip started as a response to a lot of prejudiced attitudes from students, whose only experience of Hinduism came from Bollywood or from rumour within their own community.

> Upon first entering the worship area, the girls are visibly frightened. They cling to one another, whisper to one another, bite nails, fiddle with pens, etc. Two girls look down with disdain at a worshipper sitting cross-legged on the floor. The girls write on each others' backs as they complete the task they have been set . . . There are moments of recognition . . . Two girls look at a display in the temple exhibit which tells a story about loyalty, one says 'that's nice', another immediately responds 'no it isn't!' . . . Some of the girls gather by a mirrored section of the museum, they talk about their experiences . . . On returning to the worship area, the girls appear less apprehensive . . . One girl sits on the floor of the worship space and looks up at the carvings. (Linden Girls)

What was particularly interesting here was that the apprehension and dislocation experienced by the female students found some amelioration in the mirrored space, which appeared to function as surrogate school female-student washroom – that is as a refuge from the intensity of the formal spaces where students had to be on their guard. Here they appeared to become more relaxed at seeing themselves in the mirror with their classmates. It is difficult to measure precisely the effect of this firsthand experience in transforming students' understanding in a largely silent place of worship. Clearly, some girls assumed the role of moral guardians of the group, mocking or rebuking the *other*. This went unchallenged until it began to interfere with the respectful appreciation of others. The shift from disdain to appreciation proceeded not from a phenomenological 'bracketing out' of the self – there is no implication that the girl sitting on the floor is acting as a 'Hindu for the day', she remains entirely within her own identity and position in the world. Rather, in the unfamiliar place of encountering the other, the girls remain entirely themselves, aware of personally held commitments, but, for those who accepted the invitation, came the capacity to enter into a space of more comfortably understanding the other in their otherness. What indisputably underpinned the possibility of encounter was a subtle pedagogical framing of social and liturgical practices, theological insight and behavioural management.

The two, at times contradictory, examples elucidated above – of loud, mutually interrupted conversation, and of largely silent apprehension – illustrate the significance of a space of symbolic exchange in Religious Education. Baudrillard (1993) regards religion as an 'anti-discourse', a silence in which the presence of the Final Reality itself resists any attempt at signification. Baudrillard stresses the power of this extreme end of language as fundamental to the value and meaning of symbolism, resisting simplification and trivialization. The significance of the use of silence, the teacher's comfort with uncomfortable silences, and the appropriate breaking of silence, in meaningful RE, is illustrated in the following encounter in Dungally College:

Mr D shows the class a DVD, *Time for Peace?* produced by the Presbyterian Church in Ireland. It is composed of news clips from the troubles, set to a U2 soundtrack – the students are attentive throughout and at the end there is silence.

Mr D respects the silence, but after a few moments says 'Now, first thoughts?'

'Beatings'

'It all still happens now'

Connor says 'See that name, Michael Mooney [a man killed during the Troubles, his story is featured in the DVD], his son lives on my street.'

Mr D asks 'Does it all feel far away?'

'yeah'

Connor argues:'No, cos there's still dissident Republicans, that's why they're bringing in the Brits again, not to walk the streets again, but MI5 or SAS or that.'

Mr D addresses a quieter girl by name: 'Keosha, I'm really interested to hear what you think when you see that?'

Keosha:'J's [just] upset.'

Connor:'It's not really different . . .' [interrupted]

Iain:'See if you wore a Celtic top round where I live, you'd be shot in a minute . . .' says there are paramilitary 'top men' [senior paramilitary figures] who live in his neighbourhood . . . Mr D asks Iain to explain what 'top men' are to anyone in the class who didn't know . . . (Dungally College)

Students are sharing their own experiences, every one of them has a story to tell about the way sectarianism and *the Troubles* have affected them. At the end of the discussion, Mr D says, 'I wanted to bring what Jesus told into a modern context'. Of course Mr D draws upon the expressly and particularistic Christian impulses that suffuse religious education in Northern Ireland. Here, beginning with the resource itself, media footage is transformed by its context from a transitory carrier of meaning to something of significance in the moral discourse. The use of media footage in classroom discussion appears again and again in RE pedagogies, with mixed degrees of success. As we will see later, on the one hand media portrayals of religion itself, and 'religious issues', can risk trivializing the realm of religious experience, and media portrayals of some issues are so stark as to come pre-evaluated, such as in one instance of the use of highly emotive images and sensationalized reports from the 2008 US presidential election in constructing a classroom wall display on abortion (discussed in Chapter 3). On the other hand, when appropriately situated within the context of a difficult narrative, such as the parable of the Good Samaritan – the topic of the lesson in which the above encounter takes place – such an approach again makes the two familiar narratives (Jesus' parable and the Troubles in Northern Ireland) strange, allowing both to be viewed from a new perspective.

This example illustrates what has long been held to be the civic aim of Religious Instruction/Religious Education – inculcating students with a clear sense of *christian* values and virtues (Copley 2008). Recent years have seen the subject of citizenship appear on curricula across the United Kingdom, in many ways supplanting the claims of RE with regard to civic virtue. In various ways many teachers remarked that in some important respects citizenship had taken over the work that RE used to do on topics such as discrimination and sectarianism. The pedagogic encounter reported above illustrates a form of engagement with religious parables on a level which enlists the deeply held experiences of students, neither a form of 'civic' religion, the preaching of a bland gospel of tolerance, nor a simply political citizenship lesson.

The general message is perhaps best summarized by the first word from a student: 'beatings'; violence is a part of human experience and the experience of these young people. The content has a reality in the lived experience of the students. Unlike some other school contexts, where death and suffering existed only in the mediated experience of the world through news and global communication, and in which a depth to moral discussions did not seem to penetrate, a depth and maturity of understanding surfaces in the careful consideration given to silence between each student's response. The reality with which the media content is imbued in this context is illustrated by Connor's contribution, first of an experienced reality: 'his son lives on my street', then of a reported reality: 'they're bringing in the Brits again', bringing the outside world of students' lives into the religious discourse. In this encounter, the loaded dialect of the students is allowed to pass without judgement, reinforcing both strangeness and familiarity: 'Brits', 'top men'.

Mr D succeeds in mediating a space between silence as an exercise in authority, and the chaos of instantaneous debate – a liminal space for the exploration of personal encounter with the object of study. The brevity with which language begins to impose itself on silence illustrates the importance of this limitation and the difficulty with which students can speak about these difficult and controversial issues. Mr D introduces contradiction, asking, in spite of Connor's comment to the contrary, whether it feels 'far away', demonstrating a respect for contrary positions, even if only represented by the single word that follows. Mr D also restrains the hyperbole of Iain's statement by asking deeper questions, encouraging him to analyse his own view of reality. Mr D's own stated purpose in managing this difficult encounter is itself of significance – to 'bring', as a gift, not to judge or to examine or rationalize, but to 'bring' the stories of his students, and the media stimulus for those stories, into encounter with 'what Jesus told'.

Similar examples of this kind of encounter can be found in schools in very different contexts. In the different context of St. John Fisher students are encouraged to contrast the images and messages about sex and love in popular culture with Catholic teaching on the theological meanings of sexual love. A school in a suburban/rural area in the South of England encouraged students to consider animal welfare issues in the light of passages from Jewish, Christian and Islamic texts. In all of these cases, both students' lived experience and the multiple meanings within religious texts are allowed to speak for themselves in a pedagogically managed encounter, distinct from the predetermined aims of a religious studies reduced to 'respect study'.

Such an approach requires ongoing layers of critique, however, if it is to engender continuing progression and avoid becoming a bland civic virtue education, indistinguishable from citizenship education. Returning to the integrated school above, the parable of the Good Samaritan becomes a foundational parable for this institution, aiming as it does to bring together communities in conflict. In the more senior years, students risk being desensitized to the now familiar discourse of 'The Good Rangers Supporter' (the title of a Year 8 student's illustrated work which the ethnographer found pinned to a classroom wall). Here, effective RE requires a continuing depth of engagement with the multiple layers of meaning within religious texts:

> With a Year 12 class, Mr E reflects on the shallow use of the parable of the Good Samaritan in the lower school, he says the parable 'is the RE teacher's dream . . . you do this in junior school and you get Celtic and Rangers . . . but I kind of think they miss the point of the story . . . "and who is my neighbor" . . . the person who asked the question is a teacher of the law, almost certainly he's a priest [or] a levite . . . Jesus is having a dig at the man that asked him the question' – Mr E goes on to point out that the story is told to a crowd, not on a page, says it is over-used by politicians, most notably by Margaret Thatcher. To this, Shane responds 'I hate Margaret Thatcher', and there follows a brief discussion on Thatcher's legacy in Northern Ireland, interrupted by the end of period bell. (Dungally College)

In drawing attention to the subversive dimension of Jesus' message in its context, Mr E effects a further layer of displacement, removing the parable from the ownership of the now settled patterns of discourse within the integrated school. In taking the story out of the hands of the 'teacher of the law', Mr E executes a re-calibration of his authority; a levelling of his own status as a teacher. His reference to Thatcher's personal and idiosyncratic interpretation of the parable to the Church of Scotland General Assembly opens up the discussion to the appropriate use and misuse of religious texts to serve political ends, precisely the kind of problems which the Delphi participants raised about the instrumental use of RE for civic ends. A familiar discourse, a lynchpin of integrated schooling, is once again enstranged from its familiar context and presented in a dynamic way. In contrast, some scripted tasks, based too heavily on the commonplace understandings, can fail to cohere.

These examples serve as an important lens through which to evaluate some of the broader themes which emerge across the whole sample set. What is harder to identify are examples of effective Religious Education for engagement with values in places where religion no longer functions as a context for mediating the world. In areas of overwhelming secularization, such as the North East of Scotland, teachers often find themselves struggling to present religious perspectives as valid and relevant, brokering an encounter with religion as the beliefs of an absent other. In this situation, content knowledge about religion can serve to encourage sympathetic understanding, or to reinforce the otherness of the believer.

But, even in those classrooms where positive constructions of otherness surfaced, inconsistencies and flaws could also be seen which can render the learning experiences transparent and facile. Should these encounters fail to find traction with the lived experience of students, the potential for genuine engagement with the strangeness and subversiveness of religious concepts, our own and others, risks being turned into a lesson in pretence, an exercise in superficiality. Some barriers to the effective development of such an environment for analytical skills may clearly be seen from the evidence. In particular, some students are reluctant to express themselves or to work in less traditional ways, and class size and general levels of mistrust between teacher and students can preclude some such approaches (Baumfield et al. 2011). Further, in many spaces the *immanentization of the transcendent* makes it difficult to introduce students sympathetically to religious concepts (Lundie 2011), with students finding it easier to settle at the level of content knowledge without seeking a depth of understanding. In many ways, the examination focus, which lies like a shadow over this volume, can exacerbate this risk, by encouraging students to accept facile explanations rather than challenge. Nurturing genuine depth of understanding of diverse religious and philosophical perspectives leads to interest and valuing of RE, and in turn to examination success, while examination success is neither necessary nor sufficient as a predictor of genuine depth of understanding. The risk of students seeing through the facile and reductive conceptions of religion presented in the examination curriculum is illustrated in the following comments from a focus group with Year 10 students in a Muslim-majority school in London:

Student 1: I think with RS, you know like when you look at the Koran and everything . . . you know when we interpret the Koran, it's different in RS than at home because at home we've been taught . . . we've got books that interpret it anyway . . . but in school we take it literally. Whereas you know in the Koran, you shouldn't take everything literally. So, that's something different . . .
I: So, you think it's taken more literally at school that it is at home? Ok, well that's interesting. And would you feel comfortable to say to your teacher, well that's not what I've been taught before?
Student 2: No. We'd get in trouble, probably.
I: Really?
Student 1: No, we wouldn't get in trouble. We might . . . I dunno.
Student 3: I think the stuff the school teaches us . . . I think we have to kind of accept it when we're in school because that's what comes up in exams. (Linden Girls School)

Such comments are particularly poignant given the stated purpose of the RE teachers, interviewed in another focus group:

> Ms A: Yes, we've talked about this at length before, haven't we? . . . I mean I've been here, however many years I've been here . . . and the level of knowledge and understanding of Islam has got less and less and less and less . . . to the point that the number of misconceptions and the amount of misinformation, actually not just misconceptions, misinformation that you have to sort out before you start is . . . I'm quite worried about it actually from the point of the community . . . you mustn't lose the focus on the knowledge and understanding is very important because they've got such a void.
> Ms B: It's also . . . you know when you told them well this is what the Koran says, or this is what this religion says and they'll go, *'really?! Wow!'* That's nice. That feels quite nice. (Linden Girls School)

In contrasting the students' and teachers' accounts of the purpose and practice of RE in this school, a disconnect can be seen between the students' understanding of Islam in its cultural and traditional context, and the teachers' description of this context as cultural 'misinformation', 'misconceptions' distorting Koranic teaching. The teachers' approach, which they describe as challenging these misconceptions, introduces a judgement into the classroom environment, which places this closer to the 'respect study' model of pre-evaluated ends, than to the open-ended pedagogies of encounter described earlier. Unlike Mr C's classroom, these disconnections do not emerge in the classroom, but are instead suppressed by the students' 'acceptance' and the performance demands of examination success. The students' sense of a disconnect between the Islam of the classroom and their deeply held beliefs is not explored openly, as students do not feel they have been invited to challenge the values and constructions presented to them by their teachers:

> Ms B says 'I know all of you are, to some extent practicing [Muslims] . . .'
> While Ms B is out of the room, one girl wearing a hijab turns to her neighbor and asks 'Why does she assume we're all practicing?'

What has been presented so far illustrates the key distinction between a pre-evaluated religious education for civic virtue, whether that is understood as the virtues of a 'good Christian', 'good Muslim', and so on, or an overarching value of tolerance, reinforced through 'respect study', and an active engagement with the deeply held faith values of students. It is necessary for RE teachers to recognize that religious language is no flat assemblage of descriptions (sociological, psychological or culture) but is suffused with spiritual and moral depths for believing students, which runs deeper than examination performance. Subtleties in definition require excavation; controversy and counter-cultural challenge embraced and entered into deeply, not merely 'accepted'. The fine line between success and failure in such pedagogical engagements can be marginal, and a dullness about detail can compromise the most important personal and spiritual aspects of the content. In a Year 9 scheme of work about the attributes of God, taught at a school in East London, one teacher's well-meaning approach to controversy illustrates what is meant by this dullness as to detail:

Ms F: 'You can be as controversial as you like.'
Audrey: 'What does that mean?'
Ms F: 'It means you can say anything you want.'

. . .

Jack: 'What about the father of Jesus?'
Ms F: 'I'm just gonna put "Father" [on the board]'

There are a lot of group discussions arising out of students' ideas, this is generating background noise in what is intended as a whole-class discussion, Ms F sits at the front desk, with her arms folded, she looks fed up. 'Is it possible to have a discussion with you lot?' (Brockton)

While this teacher does well to invite controversy, Ms F's depiction of this as a removing of all barriers, 'saying anything you want' as opposed to the sensitivity to discursive limitation illustrated by Mr D, and in contrast to Mr C's aversion to easy answers, creates a reductive atmosphere. The concerns raised in recent Ofsted reports (2010) and by our Delphi participants about the failure of much RE to engender a sense of progression may often amount to the consequential effects of such an uncommitted pluralism, whereby the acceptance of all views entails the valuing of none. The teacher's description of this enumeration of unevaluated anything-you-wants as 'a discussion', further fails to engender a sense among students that they ought to value their peers' contributions.

Ms F's response to Jack's comment neutralizes the conceptual apparatus which Jack's words potentially carry, reducing them to empty abstractions. A key detail is elided in reducing Jack's conception of God to 'Father' – while a universal fatherhood is of significance to many religions' accounts of God, the particular significance that this carries within Christianity in the unique claim to Sonship of Jesus is foundational to Christian understandings of God as Trinity, as incarnate, as well as of humanity's relationship to God through adoption, sonship, redemption.

Further, the elision in this encounter, not only of the Christian narrative in Jack's comment, but also of the spontaneous discussion which may subsequently arise (where, among other episodes, we find, one girl arguing vocally with her neighbours that God is a murderer, because of the apparent commanding of genocide in parts of the Old Testament), represents an exercise of teacher authority in the service of 'coverage'; the determination to cover the syllabus by the end of the lesson. Feedback from students gathered during the project's launch of findings conference (Conroy et al. 2011) suggests that the pattern observed above, of students having meaningful conversations with one another, while teachers ignore these either out of professional embarrassment to engage with controversy, or based on a determination to achieve predefined outcomes, is not uncommon in many classrooms. Overcoming this temptation is a challenging task for any teacher, particularly when constrained by time and examination requirements.

Moreover, it can be very difficult for some teachers to adopt the kind of epistemic humility required for the effective discussion of controversy and deep commitment in the classroom. A teacher at a controlled secondary school in Northern Ireland, for example, explained to the ethnographer that he did not expect his students to always agree with him, and invited them to question his (evangelical Christian) perspective. While students in focus groups at this school discussed finding faith difficult and uncertainty about their own beliefs, a combination of the teachers' forceful personality and the students' fondness for the teacher meant that these doubts did not emerge in the observed classroom encounters. What is true of teachers in contexts of high levels of religious identification, belief and practice can equally be true of teachers functioning in secular contexts. A teacher in a school in the North East of Scotland, for example, introduced the sociology of religion to students through a study of Celtic and early tribal religions, producing a framework for the study of religion as distant from students' life experience, and associated with pre-modern accounts of the world.

Conclusion

What is presented here may be described as recognition of the possibility of exposing religious concepts and deeply held values to critical analysis while standing within a religious discourse. Rather than trying to reduce these values to reason, as in some philosophy of religion approaches, or trying to 'bracket out' ones personal beliefs, as in phenomenological models, such an approach momentarily exposes everything the rules exclude and conceal, enabling spaces of paradox to open up. Hence the teacher affords students the opportunity to challenge cultural norms and rules from within a recognition of culture, belief and the individual. In this subversive process, the teacher uncovers their own underlying assumptions, exposing both teacher and student to a process of levelling, the subversive elements of religious narratives are foregrounded, and the civic uses of religion exposed to critique. It is this facilitating that simultaneously challenges impoverished versions of civic education and opens up the potential space of encounter with the other.

Just as the possibility of meaning includes the possibility of failures of meaning, the possibility of encounter with transcendent truths and irreducible strangeness clearly entails the possibility of encounter with 'false transcendence' (Girard 2004). So too the encounter with the teacher and examining authority, or injunctions against the intolerant and the controversial, as the final end of RE can present a barrier to authentic encounter. The teacher who operates only within an institutional culture points a student to the *habitus* of that culture with its limitations of imagination (Bourdieu & Passeron 2000), but the teacher who brokers an encounter with a transcendent strangeness can at times point students towards the metaphysical, the limits of hope (Kant 2008).

It is common to criticize RE for attempting to indoctrinate students, either from a particular faith perspective (Narisetti 2009) or with a reductive and relativistic education for 'tolerance' (Felderhof 2007). None of the schools in our study fell into the former category. All were either places of vigorous debate and committed pluralism in the RE classroom, or examples of the kind of bland misrepresentation criticized above. In the latter case, there is little threat to students' deeply held beliefs, as these pedagogies are rarely engaging, and their 'easy grace' rarely convincing. By taking seriously the reality of deeply held individual and cultural beliefs, some schools instantiated a place not only of interpersonal and intercommunity encounter, but a place of encounter with the 'enstranged' self, embracing the strangeness and irreducibility of one's own commitments, including commitment to secular world-views. Teachers in these contexts were willing to enter into discussions of personal value, engage in talk which went beyond abstracted academic content, and recognize and accept the value-laden nature of their own and their students' language.

At its worst, the teaching of 'other people's beliefs' can present an alienated picture of the religious believer as a depersonalized and deracinated caricature, defined solely by his or her religious identity. Equally, in an attempt to predetermine the values and beliefs which students will develop through the study of religions, a diluted and bland picture of religious teachings can be presented, which fails to engage with the genuine otherness of religious value systems and narratives (including the Christian narrative) to the value systems of contemporary British society. Where this happened the pedagogy failed to effect a transformative encounter, falling flat, being dull to detail, seeking to bracket out personal responses to value judgements or to exercise excessive control over the meanings given to religious concepts in the classroom. Given that most of the teachers observed in our study held qualifications in the subject, no clear distinctions could be drawn in these resepcts between specialists and non-specialists. Such a committed pluralism, as opposed to a pretended neutrality, is essential if RE is to broker an effective engagement with 'other people's beliefs' as well as with students own search for meaning, without reducing religion to bland civic entailments, which are all to easily seen through by the students themselves.

6

Religious Education and the Nature of Texts

Introduction

Textbooks hold an ambiguous position across the educational continuum, from the beginnings of formal provision through to higher education. They are simultaneously prominent and ubiquitous, and displaced and derided. In the context of higher education, specific, well-known and well-used textbooks may be influential in the recruitment or retention of student populations, and yet the processes of research assessment in the United Kingdom do not place high value on textbooks in general, instead excluding them from definitions of research itself (Baumfield 2006). John Issitt (2004, 683) notes that this low status results, in part, from 'disciplinary histories that cast discovery and breakthrough as having far more value that careful expository teaching'. Unlike many other subjects in the school curriculum, such as History or Chemistry, there is no clear place within universities where Religious Education as a discipline finds a home. Despite this attitude, scholars from diverse fields, including Theology, Sociology, Religious Studies and others, continue to write textbooks which set out the parameters of particular fields of study and make assertions about the state of *the* discipline. These become part of the fabric that, in turn, defines areas of study. Consequently attention to the processes of production and use of textbooks is clearly important to any understanding of the nature and definition of the discipline(s) that help shape Religious Education as a social practice.

In retrospect, it is unsurprising that we might devote a chapter to the ways in which texts are used in religious education. Initially we harboured something of a passing interest in texts as a resource upon which the teacher could lay their hands, and which would be part of the firmament of teaching and learning. But the imperative to explore the place of the text in its own right emerged only slowly, and as a response to its increasingly evident importance as more than a resource *simpliciter*; a neutral object to be manipulated or a thing upon which certain intellectual and affective activities are inscribed. Instead of being constructed as passive objects, organized and manipulated by the teacher, texts emerged across the varied contexts of our schools as *actors* in their own right. As we have seen elsewhere in this study we did not start with an explanatory theory into which we subsequently attempted to fit the data. Nevertheless, as we proceeded, actor-network theory (Callon & Law 1997; Latour 2005; Fenwick & Edwards 2010) emerged as a helpful explanatory heuristic, which assisted in the recognition and acknowledgement of texts as significant actors in the classroom. Here we attempt to illustrate the ways in which these texts *act* in the classroom as carriers for the impulses and imperatives of other, somewhat vicarious, actors. In this particular regard texts are interesting if complex mediators of the drives and positioning of what have become commercialized examination companies, where even the state-sponsored systems in Scotland and Northern Ireland (Scottish Qualifications Authority [SQA] 2012) find themselves subject to the imperatives of business expansion. As we note in the next chapter the examination system itself, has become an extraordinarily powerful actor in shaping the social practices of religious education, and texts of various kinds have, we suggest, become yet other actors mediating but rarely radically altering the power of the dominant actors that have become the examinations *companies* and their commercial owners.

Religious education is, in some important respects, quite unexceptional and enjoys similarities to other disciplines or fields of enquiry in school in as much as it is shaped and defined by its textual content. By this we do not wish to suggest that it is only shaped by such content or indeed to delimit in a too narrow fashion what it is we mean by textual content (Conroy et al. 2012). There are varied kinds of texts that influence and help shape the spaces of Religious Education. The extent to which, for example, we should consider handouts, PowerPoint presentations, posters and displays, videos as well as artefacts as 'texts' is an important consideration. As might be expected in the contemporary classroom, it was quite rare to see textbooks being used unmediated by other resources and explanatory devices. Whatever the complex range of resources deployed by teachers, the role of textbooks in particular, with their strong links to exams, speak in particular ways to the emergent purposes of Religious Education during its final, compulsory, stages; they represent complex actors in the transactions between classroom actors (teacher, students and school managements) and the increasingly performative character of official expectations with their strong pressures of measurable educational outcomes.

The relationship between teacher and text is complex and, in the course of our work, we witnessed many examples where teachers' relationship with textbooks was one of avoidance and amelioration as well as utilization and adaptation. In one school, the Head of Department 'explains that the department doesn't work much from textbooks, this [he suggests] is his influence and his choice. The only textbook they do occasionally use is: Joe Jenkins' 1992 text, *Examining Religions: Contemporary Moral Issues*' (Jenkins 1992) (Dundoon). Such decisions about textbooks in particular reflect a somewhat more dynamic relationship between the teacher, student, text, examination and policy than might often be supposed. Teachers' choices about texts, and their decision to exclude and occlude – as well as their indebtedness to the text – points to a kind of dance between the actors. In probing the project's ethnographic data we find that it reveals some of the ways that teachers implicitly or explicitly *exclude* textbooks from the classroom experience, with justifications ranging from economic limitations to personal intention and suspicion about both the quality and the *intention* of the text. Hence, a somewhat paradoxical picture emerges whereby textbooks, with their necessary link to examinations, continue to play a defining role, yet their actual presence in day-to-day teaching in classrooms is by no means given. The sometimes engaged, sometimes ignored text reflects a 'dialectic of presence and absence' (Battaglia 1997) in which the displacement of the text as an object has significant effects on the power relations and culture of the RE classroom and of the relationship between teacher, school, politics and examinations.

What textbooks 'do'

As we have suggested texts as non-human participants in the activity of learning within a classroom can be understood, according to Latour, as *mediators*; that is,

> [They] cannot be counted as just one; they might count for one, for nothing, for several, or for infinity. Their input is never a good predictor of their output; their specificity has to be taken into account every time. Mediators transform, translate, distort, and modify the meaning or the elements they are supposed to carry. (Latour 2005, 39)

So it is that textbooks as mediators are more than the passive carriers of inert ideas in the daily enactments of the curriculum. Rather than merely 'determining' and serving as a 'backdrop for human action', [textbooks as] things might 'authorize, allow, afford, encourage, permit, suggest, influence, block, render possible, forbid, and so on' (Latour 2005, 72). Textbooks are not merely a vehicle for 'the curriculum' to be achieved in mechanical fashion. As Richard Edwards rightly points out, in education 'the curriculum' is often discussed as a macrostructure which might somehow produce similar results if greater standardization were to be achieved (Edwards 2011). If we want to be more specific in our investigation and ask questions such as: 'Which curriculum? Enacted where? In which classroom? To what audience? By which teacher? With which resources?' then we need to consider the active (or otherwise) difference that textbooks make. In this way, it may become possible to view textbooks as part of curriculum-making which is:

> multiply ordered, assembled, distributed and enacted through a range of material semiotic networks within which any object is interconnected, linked to institutional structures, everyday practices, and policies in different domains. (Edwards 2011, 43)

Even where teachers exercise agency in the construction and exclusion of textbooks from the curriculum, texts can still be understood as an 'absent presence', an actor within the construction of the pedagogical site, notable by its absence (Lefstein & Snell 2009). What then, can we say about textbooks as part of this interconnected texture of the classrooms forming the basis of the ethnographic study in the *Does Religious Education Work?* project? What is it that we find textbooks 'doing'?

As we turn our gaze more myopically to the connections and encounters that may be observed, the data is varied. At times, textbooks are prominent; at times they do not appear at all; or they may sit passively on shelves or in pupil rucksacks. For instance, the image here (Figure 6.1) shows a set of textbooks laid out for an open evening, and yet the ethnographic record would suggest that fieldworkers had never seen most of them used in the classroom. Such an image suggests the department markets itself to parents based on these texts – they represent a level of financial resourcing of the subject, in turn reflecting the status bestowed on RE by management. Clearly textbooks are used within RE classrooms, though questions may be raised as to whether in particular instances they are supporting learning aims or encouraging a form of passive exercise on the subject matter. We also need to ask, what factors might prevent the use of textbooks in the classroom, and under what circumstances are they specifically excluded from the learning environment by teachers? With regard to the first issue, there is the very practical problem of resources, and how these are or are

Figure 6.1 Departmental display – parent evening

not allocated for Religious Education. In one of our project schools, a Head of RE recounted a telling tale about how they were attempting to work with a mere £2 per head for resources (though this was not the smallest per capita allowance seen in the schools in our study with some operating with budgets under £1):

> They [pupils] trash resources when they're coming through because it's only RE and you get stuff written on, scribbled on, and because you're doing the same thing with like four classes in a week, you can't give them that resource . . . They are only seeing you once a week, so you're not an important bit on their timetable. If their bag is heavy, they're not going to bring the book. You just need to bite the bullet and keep paying for it. (Northwest)

Doubtless, resources are an issue across subject areas, but this particular Head of Department's view indicates a strong feeling that RE is marginalized: 'it's only RE'. While not universal (and certainly church schools in the study tended to spend rather more on resources than their common school counterparts), this sense of the impoverished resource base in the subject was certainly commonplace. As another Head of RE (Longwood) commented in relation to resources and their replacement of textbooks with their own materials:

> It's all done from my own stuff, all mine . . . I use quite a lot of powerpoint with question sheets, but we don't really have a set textbook. There is a set textbook,

> but can't really afford to buy it because if we bought it we wouldn't be able to buy
> the Key Stage 4 books which we needed and the syllabus changed . . .

Here, we find other types of resources emphasized above texts, alongside the issue of funding. If teachers produce all of their own materials, this will ultimately be more beneficial to school (and RE) budgets. But concerns about textbooks are not merely a matter of economics. A number of teachers in our study expressed their own disquiet at the quality of text provided, most especially with regard to those created to serve the examinations system (see also Jackson et al. 2010).

At the other end of the spectrum, the ethnographic data provides examples of pupils being asked to read and work directly from textbooks, with little or no input from teachers, as if the textbook were a substitute for the human teacher; a situation at times accentuated by the presence of supply teachers – as this extract from our fieldnotes highlights:

> Texts related to the examination board are used and, while these can allow scope
> for variation in how the material is explored, there is also evidence that where
> less experienced teachers or cover teachers are involved in delivering RE, these
> texts in themselves do not always provide guidance on how expanded activities
> can be developed to enrich learning.

One Head of Department indicated that workbooks published by the exam board are so detailed that the more able top band students can do them on their own – *so that lesson time can be used for more worthwhile, educational RE* (Matilda's High). We will return to the issues of 'worthwhile, educational RE' in distinction from content revised for exams, but for now let us note that textbooks appear to afford a kind of self-contained sufficiency, though often exemplifying potential weakness in the areas of expansion and depth. Yet, even with such examples of textbooks coming close to serving as teacher in themselves, and in so doing permitting and enabling certain activities in the classroom to take place, the textbook did not have it all its own way. As much as the text was an attempt to shape the teacher's practice so too, on occasion, the teacher would be seen to resist using the strategies of supplementation and adaptation. Hence, the threat to return to the textbook, to individual, silent, work, was used as a vehicle to sustain good behaviour in group work on more than one occasion. While this approach was, and is, by no means exclusive to Religious Education, given the aims which many RE teachers claim to foster, of 'personal search', debate and imaginative engagement, successful engagement through the use of this threat may be a pyrrhic victory for the RE teacher. One head of RE reflects on their early career and the move that they made away from reliance on textbooks to building up their own lessons:

> I [am] reluctant to teach like I would teach when I first started at this school. It's almost like you walk around and everyone is sat inside and they've all got a textbook out and they're all writing and I almost felt that I should be like that, but then I suppose . . . it took me a few months to actually realise that didn't work and I was just really uncomfortable with it and . . . I think it [working without relying on textbooks] works because the results are paying off. (St. Athanasius)

Teachers in our study harboured deeply conflicted relationships with texts, most especially examination texts. On occasion the text could be a productive agent in the classroom but equally, many felt a sense of discomfort with the role of the text as performative agent. Within the interconnected mix of texts, texbooks, handouts and so forth a textbook may be considered a tool for adaptation, most especially where teachers have been 'trained' to work in this way (Rymarz & Engbretson 2005). Such practices might allow 'resources to support and facilitate teaching rather than dominate it' (Richards 1993, 13). Indeed, one teacher, described a kind of liberation in moving away from following textbooks closely in teaching:

> I think it affords a kind of freedom not to be tied to a textbook. It also pushes you to a kind of challenge in each lesson, to draw from different resources. So I think it makes for a more interesting and varied lesson and learning experience for the pupils. I wouldn't like to think we would have a situation of saying 'here's a textbook; that's to last till Christmas'. I think it's quite mundane and I think it doesn't allow for the creativity in the classroom which we enjoy at the moment in bring in, mixing different resources. I think that's important: keep the mix, keep them fully engaged. (St. Bede's High)

The freedom that this teacher felt afforded in moving away from the text was in constant tension with the sense of needing to compete on the exam stage, and it is to this we now turn.

Textbooks and examinations in Religious Education

As we have already intimated for secondary education in Britain, there are particular connections between textbooks and exams. Often the authors of textbooks are teachers whose strong links to the examinations process are paraded as part of their credentials as author, as in the case of a popular set of textbooks used by regional schools participating in the project research. These were written by a teacher of Religious Studies who had worked for the *Qualifications and Curriculum Authority*, providing substantial consultation in the processes of setting, vetting, moderating and marking exams. In many cases, these connections are regarded as a promotional resource for publishers marketing new textbooks. The close and complex relationship between commercial interests, examination boards, textbook and authors (as classroom teachers) cultivates a circular system whereby the core content of textbooks becomes closely aligned to the imperatives and structure of examinations, each informing the other and producing a situation in which it may not be necessary for those involved in particular subjects such as RE to reach very far 'outside' the boundaries of what is, provided in textbooks and written material produced for exam preparation and revision. In this context, the content of textbooks is more likely to reflect that of similar textbooks on the market than matters of developing concern in research disciplines (Engebretson 2002).[1]

On more than one occasion, however, this nexus of competitive examination providers and approved commercially available textbooks was not only subverted but directly influenced by teacher practice. This appears to be most clearly the case where market forces alone failed to dictate a competent effort in exam formation – such as in the case of a Muslim majority school teaching a new syllabus on Islam which had yet to be finalized by December of its first year of operation. The same Examination Board had made available exemplar materials and textbooks for its more popular courses (Christianity, Philosophy and Ethics) much earlier, but had yet to address the Islam course. Taking the initiative, teachers at Linden Girls' School had organized a conference for all local schools teaching the Islam option, at which they presented their own teaching materials, and to which the chief examiner would be invited. Teachers at this school represented this as an opportunity not only to gain guidance from the examiner, but to influence directly the writing of the examination syllabus and subsequent textbooks. While such practices were rare, evidently they do demonstrate the collaborative and indeterminate nature of these seemingly fixed external factors, albeit an indeterminacy which reduces the closer schools travel towards the market-determined centre of gravity of RE curriculum options.

The growth of the examination-tailored text is hardly the exclusive domain of religious education, but the explicitly performative character of the contemporary text aimed at 16-year-olds has marked a decisive break with historic texts in religious education, where the text previously acted as a gateway into questions of meaning and metaphysics as well as opening up the claims of transcendence and theology. When we compare the claims made by texts published in the 1980s to those used more recently there is a marked change in not only the structure of the text but also in the primacy of the visual over the written. Moreover, if we compare three texts from the early 1980s, the early 1990s and the 2000s a noticeable shift of emphasis emerges as regards to purpose.

Geddes' and Griffiths' (2003) *Revise for Religious Studies GCSE* informs the student that, 'This book tells you exactly what you need to know and learn for your exam because it is written specifically for your course' (cover). Harrison and Kippax's (1996) *Thinking about God*, penned in 1996, 'provides you with a complete RE GCSE short course. Focusing on questions and issues faced by everyone, it is interesting and stimulating for all students' (cover). More than ten years earlier, Collinson and Miller's (1981) *Believers* suggests that their book 'aims to give pupils a stimulating and sympathetic insight into the variety of ways in which ordinary people approach their God' (cover). Of course it would be methodologically naïve to suggest that each book set out with the same purpose in mind, but that is precisely the issue – the displacement of texts concerned to attend to the thing in itself with those designed for an altogether more proximate and performative purpose highlights a marked shift in the normative and pedagogic character of the text. And, lest it be thought that the exercise was overly selective, the schools in the study had large numbers of texts expressly badged as exam texts, such as Watton's (2005) *Religion and Life* 'endorsed' by Edexcel, which had been 'extensively updated to match more exactly the most current version of Unit A' (cover). Moreover, nowhere on the flyleaf description do we move out of the realm of the performative but are to be re-assured that the author is 'an experienced Senior Examiner'. Mayled and Ahluwalia's (2002) Discovery is also written by 'experienced examiners to meet the requirements of revised OCR GCSE Religious Studies specification B' (cover). What is of interest here, as we discuss later in Chapter 7, is the way in which the text itself is both changed by, and in turn changes, the nature of the activities of teaching and learning. In its foregrounding of the visual, its elevation of the pericope, the priority afforded the visual coupled with data recall as well as the occlusion of argument, the changing nature of the text represents an attempt to structure the engagements in the classroom in quite specific ways.

There is an almost ineluctable logic to having those involved in the examination process writing textbooks. If pupils and their teachers are impelled to work towards the ultimate goal of passing exams, then authors who are involved and familiar with the exams process may be best placed to guide them towards the fulfilment of that goal. As Issitt points out, textbooks must sell to be viable, and observes that we should not be surprised to,

> find that some modern textbook authors are senior examiners on exam boards – what more convincing a sales pitch could there be in our target-driven management-accounted educational world than a textbook written by the chief examiner of a board?

A recognition of the pragmatic connections between exams and texts, should not lead to understating the import of the issues which this symbiosis throws up. That is, if 'the textbook . . . establishes so much of the material conditions for teaching and learning in the classrooms', often defining 'what is elite and legitimate culture to pass on', then the scrutiny of textbooks and their role within learning environments is part of a discussion of the very nature of texts and their role in setting out the shape of disciplines and practices therein. The subjection of religious aims to those of the examination can be seen in activities such as a powerpoint presentation used at Dungally College – a memory test for the GCSE paper on St Mark's Gospel, the task is presented as 'Who Wants to Pass GCSE RE?' – in the style and register of high-stakes TV gameshow, 'Who Wants to Be a Millionaire?' Here the text mediates and reinforces quite subtle if important connections between popular culture and the examination process itself.

What textbooks aren't able to 'do'

In the course of our investigations, it became noticeable that there was a tendency of the text (as resource) to gravitate towards generalization. If we can speak about textbooks as mediators, we can also understand them as *panoramas* in the sense in which Latour uses the term when he observes that they allow spectators, listeners and readers to be equipped with a desire for wholeness and centrality. It is from those powerful stories that we get our metaphors for 'what binds us together', the passions we are supposed to share, the general outline of society's architecture, the master narratives with which we are disciplined (Latour 2005, 189). In the case of the text in the classroom, these are actually *intended* to provide us with a view of the whole, an impulse that may be found behind the production of various other resources in a classroom.

Textbooks highlight the 'gap of execution' between the 'generic you' they are meant to speak to, and the actual interactions between – both human and non-human – participants in a course of action: the mediators active in a lived classroom (Latour 2005). In actual experience, resources may mislead and misinform as much as they aid and educate. The 'generic you', able to pass an exam, may not actually meet the intended aims and outcomes of Religious Education as a subject, in particular the more pluralist aims associated with personal search for meaning and embracing diversity, which emerged in Chapter 5 as heavily foregrounded in teachers' and policy makers' discourse.

Understanding textbooks as panoramas highlights some of their limitations; the difficulty they have as a genre in accounting for locality and specificity. Even when they do attempt to do so, our recurring questions again become relevant: Whose locality are they attempting to reflect and engage? 'Whose curriculum? And, whose real world?' (Macintyre & Hamilton 2010).[2] Put another way, 'Whose confession? Which tradition?' (Thompson 2004) does the textbook attempt to represent in a faith-based or independent school setting?

The disconnect between words and world is notable in certain key examples – the Head of RE at Dundon Grammar pointed to materials designed for an English GCSE course, as an illustration of his reasons for avoiding textbooks wherever possible:

> Different religious views, Hindu, Christian, Jewish etc. mingle[d] with quotes from popular songs and movies as part of an approach to 'inspire' around moral issues . . . One activity suggests 'using some of the words and phrases below . . . make up a text message about love'.

Such attempts to mix contemporary culture with religious world-views are rarely successful. At worst, they can lead to Religious Education being freighted with a host of other aims, including citizenship and sex education, leading to a failure to either accurately represent the perspective of religious faith or the world-view of the students.

The disconnect often encountered between the personal, the world of lived experience and the activities and depictions in textbooks is illustrated by a scripted task undertaken at Dungally College in Northern Ireland on the topic of sectarianism:

> There is a visible lack of purpose while students are rehearsing the dialogue they have been given . . . One boy gasps in mock horror as a girl reads the word 'fenian' in her script. The dialogue seems clunky and there is a lot of repetition . . . At the end of one play, George says, quite accurately 'that's the same as the last one'. It takes about 12 minutes to complete the task, the teacher, recognising

that this missed the mark, moves straight on to the next activity without pausing for discussion.

Unlike other discussions and activities on the same topic, which were designed by the teachers in this school, this failure to connect with the student experience in a way that brokers encounter with lived reality leads to a discursive closure (Conroy 2004). In these kinds of closed activities, students encounter religious and social themes as banal and reductive. In this case, the activity fails to live up to the reality of a pluralistic encounter which happens every day in an integrated school context. In other cases, such as in the GCSE Religious Studies classes observed at one Muslim-majority school in London, the reductive ability of the textbook leads to students learning examination content which, interview transcripts reveal, they viewed as not only simplified but incorrect.

Pupils may have a desire to see 'themselves and their aspirations represented' (Macintyre & Hamilton 2010), but can a textbook ever do this well? On occasion, as in the instance below, we can see that some teachers share the antipathy of students to the emergence of faux (vernacular) relevance in many textbooks:

> Ms Harper at Kinraddie Academy drew my attention to the dialogues which she cringed at, as did her classes. The lowland Scots speech in the dialogues was both cheesy and not idiomatic in the North. There was a perceived Central Belt bias in the exam syllabus and in the textbook materials written for it. (From ethnographer fieldnotes)

If we begin to see challenges to ideas about 'nationhood', and that of a national curriculum, where '"England", "Wales", "Scotland" and "Northern Ireland" may yet, for their populations, remain powerful defining principles of identity, [however] they will not remain the only ones???' (Newby 2005, 297), how can textbooks 'keep up' with such changing and diversifying notions of identity? In such a situation, where textbooks are extremely limited as a genre, the responsibility lies with the teacher to 'fill in the gaps' of what the text is not able to provide; to make learning 'local' and 'relevant'.

The delicate balance of interconnectedness in a classroom can be heavily reliant on teachers, perhaps especially in the areas where textbooks are inadequate. One teacher describes attempts at teaching 'personal search' and making material 'relevant' to pupils.

> When a non-specialist teaches, eh, that element of personal search is sometimes missing. Now I can remember having a discussion about a member of staff in the

Humanities department who was, not this year but the year before, helping us out with the 2nd year class, and he was teaching Islam as if, em, it was Arabs and camels, right, not something that touches the humanities curriculum at all. Now, em, and he said he enjoyed it, and the kids enjoyed it, yes, but it's just information-topping-up, it's not trying to relate that to what it is like to be a Muslim in 21st century, what it is like, why there is conflict in the world between, eh, Islam and Christianity. How much conflict there really is and how much it is exaggerated by the media, d'you understand, I mean teaching Islam as if it's something that happens in a foreign country to foreigners strikes me as a bit like. We have, you know, they've got some out-of-date textbooks in Modern Studies where, um, Russia is still referred to as a Communist country, now, it's as bad as doing that, it's as bad as teaching the kids out-of-date Modern Studies, if you don't make some attempt to make it relevant today. (Teacher, Kinraddie Academy)

This example touches on another issue: aspects of Religious Education which textbooks don't actually cover – those relating more closely to the *meaning quest* and personal search in RE; the goals of personal ethical development. In the 2010 DCSF sponsored study of resources used in RE provision Jackson and colleagues observe that:

> At KS4 the books' contribution in these areas [five named areas: personal and moral development; social and cultural understanding; community cohesion; global understanding; spiritual development] was found to be implicit and their potential subject to teachers' drawing out of relevant material and offering students opportunities to engage with the content provided. Personal and moral development, spiritual development and community cohesion emerged as areas attended to by fewer than half of the books reviewed for KS4 and post 16. (Jackson et al. 2010, 69)

If texts do not cover these areas, and many don't, they become totally reliant on teachers and their classroom practices. Returning to the idea mentioned earlier that textbooks achieve a certain purpose in relation to exams, but do not represent 'worthwhile, educational RE', we can see that attempts at 'information-topping-up', and instilling in pupils the ability to make generalized statements on exams, can be distinguished from the loftier aims or RE, from what 'should be' happening within the subject area. Hence,

> [Mr Jenkins] does not think they [textbooks and workbooks] represent good RE but he knows that if the pupils do exactly as the books instruct them to do then they will pass/get a goods grade. (Matilda's High School)

Clearly, if textbooks are 'telling' us something about the shape of the discipline, this uncomfortable dichotomy between what textbooks and exams 'do' and what 'good RE' *should* 'do', is part of the troubled landscape that comes into view. Perhaps this also leads to a danger identified by Mary Hayward in relation to the representation of religion within syllabuses for Religious Education: that there is a danger that religious education implicitly assumes an apologetic role for religions. Divorced from the contexts which shaped and shape them, from a world in which they are inevitably enmeshed and act, both for good and for ill, religions are rendered simply 'safe', a 'good thing' (Hayward 2006).

If textbooks, as good panorama, but poor communicators of specificity and locality, tend towards generalizations and views of the whole, there is the danger of missing the complexities of religion. Opportunities to enquire more deeply may be missed, and examples which are problematic or difficult, or that don't fit naturally into 'the curriculum', may be avoided and excluded from the subject matter.

The history of the text is, in important respects, a microcosm of the history of Religious Education in its progression from authoritative, biblically grounded non-denominational Christian religious instruction, through a more exegetically shaped engagement with the Bible as text, to a multi-faith approach to religious belief and practice where the religious text is more frequently than not lodged inside a pedagogical text. These shifts in the role played by religious texts have been precipitated, and simultaneously marked, by changes in pedagogic and developmental psychological attitudes, perhaps most significantly articulated by Goldman (1968). But such changes have not been uniform or consistent; the older forms of engagement with text emerge spasmodically. Bible, Qur'an, the Tripitaka and other texts appear in varied ways playing disparate and complex roles. Moreover when we expand the definition of 'text' beyond the literary, students also engaged in complicated ways with objects associated with sacredness in various religious traditions, including Puja sets and Murthis, Seder plates, Icons, prayer mats and prayer beads (see Figure 6.2, a teacher's desk at Brockton School).

Some displacement occurs in Religious Education in the separation of the object from the conditions in which its sacredness is constructed in the life of the believer (Banks & Morphy 1997). This transformation occurs when the sacred text, as teaching aid, acquires a different status in the classroom and demands a different kind of attention. We witnessed this in the concerns which students voiced at one Muslim-majority school (Linden School) about handling the Qur'an without first washing, and the various approaches teachers took to reassure them

Figure 6.2 Staff base display

about the legitimacy of this practice when engaging with the text in the classroom. By not engaging in ritual washing, the uses of the Qur'an in school were explicitly removed from their sacred use. In another school, in Scotland (Burns Academy), a teacher was reluctant to have students use the New Testament they were given by the Gideon's Society in the classroom, while acknowledging the centrality of biblical passages to a range of work in the curriculum, again suggesting a separation between the devotional and academic use of the text.

We observed practices which engaged with the 'givenness' (Milbank 1993) of religious texts that were, ironically, often prompted by examination requirements. Sometimes, this looked nothing so much as a form of 'proof-texting' or providing isolated quotations in support of a particular position. This could be seen in the following samples:

1. [During a scheme of work on euthanasia, the teacher] directed students to move onto [1] Corinthians 6:19. [The teacher] read the text and then suggested that the essential piece of information that students could draw out of this was that the 'Body is a Temple'. (from ethnographer field notes, Castle Grammar)

Mr Cantle asks his class what they need to write in answering a question on animal rights . . . John responds 'quoting Genesis 1:26'. (Brockton)

2. Interviewer: What is it that you need to learn?

Male 1:   Stories

[unclear]

From the Bible . . . Some of them are a page long and they're like size 12 [font].

Interviewer: And you need to know it all?

All: yeah

Male 2:   More or less word for word.

Female: We have to summarise it and . . . (from GCSE student focus
               group, St. Athanasius)

3. Female student: here is a focus on Christianity in RE mainly because of the examination syllabus. There is coverage of other world faiths for the lower school at A level pupils learn about Buddhism. There is also a reluctance to alter the syllabus because it is what has been done and appears to work well in terms of RE GCSE performance. As the HoD states 'I think we would almost be stabbing ourselves in the foot to change it. . . .'

Year 7 and 8 what we have been doing there's a syllabus RE1 and RE2 which is just basically taking issues and looking at them from different religious points of view, so it's very broad. Then in Year 9 we do a focus on Islam and Judaism and then after Christmas we start them on their GCSE, that's purely because in my opinion we don't get enough contact time with the students to give them good grades, so if we start earlier and now its up to 12 modules in their GCSE, it's gone from 10 to 12 and we're losing something like, over the two weeks, we're losing 20 minutes. (Longwood)

4. Mrs Hove plays a game called 'stand up, sit down' with her GCSE class: if students get a question right, they can sit down. The questions are mostly factual recall [about the Gospel passage and its context, e.g:] . . .

'Who was Jairus?'

'Why did the Jewish officials have a problem with Jesus?'

'What was wrong with the woman?'

'What was wrong with that in Jewish society?' (St. Athanasius)

Not infrequently teachers expressed frustration at examination curricula which required these attenuated approaches to sacred texts. Among the examples here, only the first, drawn from a Northern Ireland Grammar school where the teacher is an Evangelical Christian, reflects the teacher's substantive preference. The fourth case is of interest in suggesting that school leaders and class teachers alike feel heavily constrained by the requirements of the examinations and where 20 minutes appears to be critical to success.

The predilection for the literal was subverted by a number of teachers; one in a Catholic school, taught a scheme of work which engaged historico-critical method in an investigation of the historicity of the Judas narrative which required student to operate at a level significantly beyond that required by the examination syllabus; that is, beyond the skills of summarizing and contextualizing. Such examples not withstanding, we did find that a lack of teacher confidence could stifle these kinds of complex engagements with text:

> Because you could just read [the Bible] and interpret it fairly superficially. You could be a little more historically critical about it and with the older kids I do try and be, so I will sort of bring in some information about, you know, what was going on at the time when it was written, why it was written . . . And that's quite an advanced thing to do, I think, and actually I don't really do that until year 11 really . . . But when I'm looking at the Qur'an I don't do any of that because I just don't have the confidence and literally we [*unclear*] to give it some context which is useful. (Linden)

This lack of confidence in the handling of texts refers back to the problem of the breadth of academic expertise discussed earlier. Few teachers have academic expertise in all of those religious traditions they may be called upon to teach, but many have sufficient awareness that this expertise is not easily transferable. At other times, students subverted the presumed authority of texts, for example by defacing them, or by a complicit silence. The gap between the notional authority of a sacred text for the purpose of 'exam RE' and the 'real world' of lived experience of students, was prevalent in a number of schools. It was explicitly addressed (in a variety of contexts) by recourse to personal reflection and exposition. Such approaches can be separated into those which use an inclusive language, which presumes consent – 'what can we learn from this text?' – and those which presume a more phenomenological detachment – 'what might a Muslim learn from this text?' Examples of the former type can be seen in these varied scenarios:

> 1. Pupils are looking at passages from the Qur'an, in pairs. There is silence. The teacher says [about the text] 'What is God saying?' (Linden)
>
> 2. [A teacher in a Catholic comprehensive school] tells me if her pupils tell her they don't believe in God, she tells them to treat Mark's Gospel as an academic text, but tries to resist this approach. Many of the questions in the scheme of work presume consent, e.g.
>
>> 1) Explain how Jesus' suffering shows that God loves us . . .
>> 4) How did Jesus' death achieve atonement?
>> 5) Why can Jesus empathise when we suffer?   (St. John Fisher)

3. The third slide contains a starter activity, a quote from the Qur'an:

Serve Allah as if He were before your eyes. For if you see him not, He sees you.

Describe what the above quotation means for you. Think about what it is saying about the implications for a Muslim? (Linden)

A worksheet on Hinduism shows an illustration of a Murthi and asks students to focus on one of the objects associated with the god Ganesh, and give an example of a situation where a Hindu could draw comfort from it. (Armourer's Guild)

Expanding the text as actor

Given the common practice of teachers constructing and scavenging materials out of the fragments of everyday life, it is important to continually remake the notion of the text and what its introduction into the space of the classroom might portend. When textual materials that would not normally be defined as 'academic' but perhaps, as in the case below, are more properly described as popular, their role as actor becomes yet more complicated. As popular cultural texts, such as celebrity gossip magazines, are introduced into the classroom they press themselves into the identity of the subject, remaking its shape and purpose. Let us explore for a moment the following episode;

[The teacher] has to carry a box of resources to this class from her registration class in her own room. There are some behaviour difficulties. At 9.10am Mrs Dixon gives one pupil a 'first warning' for disruption. The pupil talks back angrily, says 'Jesus Christ', he is given a second warning for his behaviour, though the blasphemy is not explicitly addressed by the teacher. Later in the lesson, [she] does give a pupil a warning for using the F word in class.

[The teacher] talks over low-level chatter to review the previous lesson and introduce the next task. The teacher has brought a pile of magazines (Heat-type gossip magazines mostly) for pupils to use. The task is to look at examples of good and bad female role models, following on from a previous lesson on gender stereotypes. Mrs Dixon models a good example of a previous class's work. The pupils are to work in groups, and they choose their own groups to work in, pupils take some time to move around the classroom into groups. The teacher gives pupils creative freedom, but tells them they can ask if they don't know what to do and would like more structure. The task, which is mostly about cutting out and sticking, lasts from 9.10–9.40. The entire lesson is a preparation for next week. (Dundon)

As with any record of the transactions of a classroom, much is going on; equally much is going on that we fail to capture in the written record. Moreover, there is an ever-present danger of generating overdetermined readings of social practices and actor engagements. Being aware of this, we nevertheless consider the introduction of the resource box of magazines and materials into a pre-existing world as shaped, however obliquely, by some students' belligerence and the teacher's engagement with that belligerence. The relationship between a number of the actors is pre-existing and the materials enter into this existing (in this case, authority) relationship. The challenging, if not particularly unusual, behavioural relations between student and teacher arguably provide not just a backdrop against which these texts are introduced but actually shape the kinds of texts being introduced. For example, in a broad spectrum of the schools in our study there was a tendency among some of the teachers to introduce popular videos that exemplified a particular ethical theme (e.g. a scheme of work at Brockton which used *The Boy in the Striped Pyjamas*; a scheme of work on euthanasia at Kinraddie which began with the film *Million Dollar Baby*). The video would then be shown in its entirety over a couple of periods and there might be a Q and A session at the end of the showing. On numerous occasions, videos were deployed as a displacement strategy to secure certain behavioural compromises. But it would be wrong to assume that every deployment represented a defensive strategy – on other occasions teachers introduced accompanying worksheets with the video showing but, curiously for students nurtured in the complex web of multi-media multitasking, many complained that they couldn't simultaneously address the questions and watch the video. Here again the dynamic relationship between text and subject is evident. In all of this, questions as to purpose, efficacy and intellectual challenge surface, and indeed the relationship between the disciplinary challenges faced by the teacher and the kinds of intellectual, affective and other entailments posed by the materials becomes obvious. Hence, we might ask, 'does the issue of gender in popular culture become a religious educational issue?' No doubt there are possible and reasonable answers to such a question. We might, for example, explore the gendered nature of religious institutions and the relationship between such gendered identity and popular culture. The text would then offer an interesting counterpoint to traditional ascriptions of gender identity. But the arresting feature of this episode is the way in which those opportunities are ignored in favour of the re-inscription of popular text as a reflection of the students' interests.

Textbooks, authorship and authority

While questions of authority echo below the surface throughout this discussion and elsewhere, we have discussed the gap between the discursive practice in schools regarding belief and doctrine, and that of the home; a gap identified by the students themselves (Conroy et al. 2012). Once again, the role played by the text and the relationship between text and reader differs significantly as between classroom and home. Here students give voice to the limitations of textbooks in terms of religious perspective:

> the people that write the textbook, they're not generally from that religion, I think whatever religion it is, for example Sikh, I think a Sikh person should write that textbook. (Linden Girls School)

Such a student concern with the effectiveness of the text as a vehicle for understanding religion in its particularity points to the broader concern about ways of thinking about religion taken up by another student who, with regard to teaching Islam, observes that, '. . . whoever's teaching would have to be able to fully appreciate the, not the idea, but the style of thinking and such' (Pupil interview, Gorston).

While expectations for both textbook and teacher are high in the two instances here, it may be that on many occasions neither is well-equipped to address the complex issues of perspective and experience. Questions of authorship and authority which surround textbooks are resolved in a range of ways, which in turn surface the structure and purpose of the subject in a range of school contexts. In Catholic schools, materials approved by the Bishops' Conference or Diocesan guidelines often manifest a particular aspect of the Church's authority structure. In one case, students in a Catholic school in Northern Ireland have a lesson on Islam from a book written for the Catholic sector, illustrated by a picture of a Muslim woman wearing a Niqab (face veil) and abaya (body covering). In another case, a Catholic school in inner London had purchased a full class set of the *Icons 1–3* textbooks so as to satisfy the diocesan inspectors, but these were rarely used, as the teaching team considered them too basic. In the case of the London Catholic school, teachers made an explicit attempt to move through the Diocesan approved course with some alacrity, allowing more time for alternative activities, focused on an alternative examination syllabus, and its board-approved textbook, which students viewed as more relevant and engaging.

As we have already noted, decisions about curriculum were often informed by the commercial availability of board-approved textbooks, but beyond their performative character such texts often raise challenging questions about the nature of the authoritative (authorial) voice. In *GCSE Religious Studies B: Philosophy and Applied Ethics for OCR B Revision Guide*, written by an experienced examiner in order to help students achieve examination success, the author goes beyond the structuring of the text into 'bite-size chunks'. It 'gives students confidence in knowing what the examiner is looking for through providing examination guidance' (Mayled & Anderson 2010, cover). Even as we acknowledge that this is a revision text, we must also be aware that its form and discourse points to an important transfer of authority from the text itself to another actor. Here the text acts, not as an embodiment of knowledge of religion – nor indeed the capacity to evaluate its claims – but as a vehicle for the authoritative hold of the examiner over the students. None of this is to suggest that assessment is an inappropriate entailment in a classroom, it is rather to observe that here the text acts in the service of the 'system' rather than either the student or the religions(s) being studied.

Alternative approaches, however, also exist, and at least two teachers in our sample had contributed to published textbook series which promoted such alternatives, with one school (Dungally) launching its own certificate programme accredited by the Open College Network, complete with companion course materials. These alternative approaches often stressed the same kinds of sympathetic approaches to the lived experience of religion which students told us they would have appreciated. The difficulties in enacting such approaches in the face of a textbook market driven by examination pressures has, however, tended to result in marginalization.

Ironically the dominance of the *official* authorial voice is subject to some scepticism from other parts of the official community. In their 2010 report, Ofsted noted that very often 'teachers lacked confidence and were reluctant to risk new approaches . . . teachers relied too heavily on published schemes of work or poor quality worksheets' (Ofsted 2010, 19), and despite the 'vast number of resources . . . pedagogical skills are needed to turn web resources into useful and productive teaching' (Jackson et al. 2010, 204). While the inspectors might recognize the shortcomings of many texts, and indeed teachers' engagements with those texts as they often appear in the lived experience of the classroom, they are powerless to offer much support in the resistance to poor texts. And the reasons for this can be found, as we point out in Chapter 2, in the complex and conflicted policy space inhabited by religious education. In this, inspectors play a complex role, simultaneously, if inadvertently, upholding the dominance of the examination regime and chastising teachers and schools for their perceived inability to respond adequately

Figure 6.3 Newspaper wall display

to its imperatives. Recognizing that shared understanding emerges through the interaction of resource, teacher and student in the cultural domain of the school, it is necessary to pay attention to context. In what contexts are the texts intended to be read? In what contexts do they appear in the curriculum? How does this differ depending on the discursive structures which constitute the intended context (such as browsing YouTube), the normal school classroom and the RE classroom? The 'different' status enjoyed by RE pedagogy compared to the rest of the curriculum is addressed in Chapter 7, and the displacement of sacred texts from their sacred context has already been considered above. Figure 6.3 offers a further illustration of the displacement of media texts in the RE classroom. Frequently, journalistic sources are employed in this or similar ways, transplanted from the impermanence of being tomorrow's chip wrapper to the permanence of the classroom wall, the scheme of work. The act of bringing these texts into conversation with the permanence of students' transcendent value frameworks effects a profound change in the nature of the texts themselves. During a GCSE class on euthanasia as a moral issue, for example, after introducing several passages from the Bible one teacher,

> briefly mentioned that this type of topic was in the media at the minute, and
> indicated that there were two topical issues, one involving a rugby player, and

the [other a] woman who wanted to argue that her husband should not be held criminally responsible if he assisted her to commit suicide. [The teacher] did not dwell on these themes, nor use them as a means of debate. (Castle Grammar)

The dynamic relationship between these media texts, the teacher as mediator, the Bible as sacred text, and the GCSE syllabus, demonstrates the complexity of intertextuality in the construction of the RE curriculum.

While resource constraints, discussed elsewhere, have a limiting effect in certain contexts, in others a plethora of resources may give some teachers an illusion of control, while in fact not departing from rigidly defined pedagogical norms:

1. While pupils are working on their assessments, the teacher updates a PowerPoint presentation of fasting, he has a copy of Lynch et al [Lynch, Orchard, Weston & Wright *Religion in focus: Islam in today's world* (1999), John Murray: London] in his hand, peruses Mrs T's bookshelf (in whose classroom he is working), flicks through *Lynch*, puts it back on the shelf and picks up Green [*Islam (GCSE Religious Studies for OCR)* (2001), London: Hodder & Stoughton]. (Linden)

2. Mr D explains to me that the department doesn't work much from textbooks. This is his influence and his decision . . . much of the material on sex and relationships in the scheme of work seems to have come word-for-word from Walker, J (2001). (Dundon)

3. [The school] produces its own scheme of work from scratch, drawing from a range of resources. Pupils are given 2 workbooks for each unit, one for classwork and one for homework. Extensive use is also make of the VLE. (Dungally)

In the first two cases, teacher control only serves to disguise the pervasive role played by textbooks as source material. In the last case, as an example worksheet (Figure 6.4) illustrates, the format and pedagogical structures of the textbook are perpetuated by the framing effects of resource design. Although Virtual Learning Environments and interactive tasks provide opportunities to subvert such approaches, the limits of teacher confidence and student expectation make this very difficult in practice. The lack of a singular, clear and coherent shape to the learning aims of RE, beyond the satisfaction of examination board requirements, further compounds the problem of devising and delivering creative and innovative curricula that stretch students' knowledge and understanding.

The possibility of such approaches having meaning, connecting with the 'real world' of student experience, is not guaranteed by the use of materials from media

Crime and Punishment

Everybody has a slightly different opinion about what is right and wrong

Everybody in the country makes is part of society. Society decides on what should be the law. Some laws have been laws for years and years. Some are quite new.

If you break the law you are doing something society thinks is wrong.

If you break the law you are committing a crime.

Here are some different reasons why people commit crimes.

greed   revenge

boredom   influence of TV

sense of injustice(it's not fair)   poverty

drug addiction

Breaking the law can range from parking where it says "no parking" to murdering someone.

Here are some different crimes. For each one say why you think the criminal committed the crime.

1. A woman finds out that her husband is seeing another woman in secret. She puts poison in his tea.

....

....

2. A truck full of live cows is trying to get on a boat. A young woman stands in front of it to stop it getting on. She is arrested.

....

....

Figure 6.4 Worksheet

with which students are familiar. Contested meanings, and the RE classroom as a space in which texts of various kinds (including multimedia sources of various kinds) interrelate, require high levels of teacher confidence. The influence of a range of resources in the classroom, whose provenance is either unclear or linked entirely to the examination syllabus, while not constraining pedagogy in itself, has the potential to disempower all but the most confident of teachers in practice, with the cultural domain of RE defined rigidly by what supports, or does not support those examined ends.

Conclusion: The textual shape of Religious Education as a discipline

We can think of textbooks – or more widely the textual content of RE – as an interconnected part of the way that the curriculum is enacted. Investigation of textbooks brings to the fore important questions which are related to the very shaping of disciplines, questions about the view of 'reality' presented, as well as orientation, philosophical underpinning and role in constituting knowledge of a 'subject' (Nicholls 2005). Textbooks clearly 'do' something as mediators within many learning experiences, as our observations indicate. However, this does not mean that their presence should be assumed, or that the interactions between text and teacher, pupil and resources, are in any way simple or straightforward or could produce the same results in different settings. Textbooks as a genre, and as panoramas, do not account easily for particular localities. Nor do they often reach further afield than their ties to exams, beyond 'covering' the material required for repetition. And in this way, many of the aims and ambitions of RE provision can be left to the inclinations (or otherwise) of teachers.

A range of practices of engagement with religious texts were observed, which include the use of quotations from texts embedded within textbooks, slides or handouts, or the use of copies of the Bible or other religious books, and which include critical and interpretive considerations, as well as approaches to text in terms of its givenness. The way such appropriquination to text operates when textbooks are involved, in particular when the textbook has its own kind of authoritative 'givenness' as the official approved text of the examination board, lends itself to a different kind of analysis to that of engagement with religious texts.

'Interest', 'variety' as well as 'creativity' in approach appear to characterize both teacher and pupil opinions of how RE operates, or, at least, how it should operate, in relation to the deployment of different forms of textual resource across a range of contexts. One pupil speaks from their perspective on the kind of approach adopted by some teachers:

> In RE you watch videos and stuff just to help you understand more. If you're just reading you can't see a picture in your head, but if you watch a video of how they celebrate certain religions and stuff like that it's more clear to you, so it's a better way of learning. (Burns)

Another pupil stated that:

> There's a teacher [RE] who makes us do projects and like videos and stuff like that which helped us learn as well as have fun at the same time, and stuff which made us learn and made us interact, so it was easier to learn that way. (Burns)

In 'having fun', and through encouraging interaction, teachers are seen to be utilizing and creating materials which are relevant and conducive to learning in their particular settings.

And yet, however stimulating an environment this may create, questions could be asked about how well teachers are trained and equipped to work in this way; perhaps more tellingly, we should not imagine that departing from the use of textbooks and bringing in other resources always improves the learning experience. In the following example, PowerPoint slides are equally capable of presenting confusing issues and providing misinformation to pupils.

> Many Christians hold fundamentalist views about one part of the Bible but not about another. E.g. Catholics tend to hold fundamentalist views about the Last Supper and many Protestants hold fundamentalist views about the Creation Story.
>
> (From standard PowerPoint resource for teaching Christianity and Scripture)
> (Dungally)

A set of questions can be put to this: Which Catholics? Which Protestants? Where? Which 'part of the Bible' did they read? How did their reading of one 'part' compare to another? What statements did they make? What did they say their views were? How can any particular view be identified as 'fundamentalist'?[3] Textbooks can also contain such sweeping statements, and often include images depicting festivals or practices of named religions with no specificity or identification of context (Figure 1.2). Who is being photographed? Where?[4] Misrepresentations, imprecision and inaccuracy can be found in many of the resources used in classrooms, whether published textbooks or other materials.

However, by considering the role of not just human, but material actors like textbooks, we are positioned to realize the potential of life that 'occurs *before* and *alongside* the formation of subjectivity, across human and non-human materialities and *in-between* distinctions between body and soul, materiality and incorporeality' (Anderson & Harrison 2010 , 13). Perhaps, on a more hopeful note, textbooks may provide opportunities for Religious Education yet.

Notes

1 We should certainly ask whether this is a worrying trend. Should there be more collaboration between teachers who write textbooks and reflect pedagogically, and researchers who move the subject matter into new areas in developing work?

2 See also David's discussion of how generic images of the 'normal case Other' such as we find in textbooks have the 'power to both create and confirm stereotypes'. If images appear in a contextless manner with no indication of their origin or value as sources, they can be misleading and meaningless (David 2000).

3 Would it not be a more profitable approach with regard to (in this case) Christian material, to look much more closely to specifics, and to take the view that "'Christianity" is not "bigger" than a local interpretation of Christianity, a local reading of a biblical text, but there will be particular connections that allow us to suggest that the local interaction is in identifiable ways "Christian."' K. Wenell, 'Ears to Hear': The Bible.

4 See in particular Robert David's study of 'contextless' archive images used in secondary textbooks (David 2000).

7

Stories We Tell Ourselves:
Making Sense of Religious Education
in Communities of Practice[1]

From its inception, this project was designed to garner a nuanced understanding of the lived experiences of the participants. As we moved forward, it became increasingly apparent that the nested identity of Religious Education as a social practice reflected its *sui generis* status within British Religious Education. The recognition that this very particular nested identity involved practices within practices led us to wish to drill down, exposing, as we went, the sedimented layers of social practice. The layers include those stories that we tell ourselves about our identity and moral purpose and the concomitant organizing and pedagogic decisions we make on a daily basis as a result of those narratives. The layers also include the effects of legislative and political imperatives, which we, in our turn, internalize in our communal discourse.

While we did not spend 3 years working with any individual school, we were fortunate in being able to work for three years with teachers, advisors and teacher educators, and gain insight into the relationship between the intentions, enactment and outcomes of the provision for Religious Education in secondary schools in the United Kingdom. The professional Religious Education community is small, with members belonging to intersecting networks with connections that are strengthened by a sense of the subject as occupying a precarious position in the curriculum of mainstream schools. The sense of a closely configured community was manifest in our Delphi seminar (Baumfield et al. 2012), where those who are influential in the mediation of the subject are able to move seamlessly into and through the world of providers and teacher educators, local authority and church advisers. The sense of the fragility of Religious Education, which appears repeatedly in this study, is echoed in other recent work, such as the National Association of Teachers of Religious Education (NATRE) report, on the impact of the introduction of an English Baccalaureate on Religious Education. The NATRE reports (2011, 2012) illustrate among other things the sharp decline in compliance with the legal requirements for Religious Education. In the 2012 report, one teacher's comments echoed those of many in saying, 'I feel that RE is being marginalised in schools, with less teaching time for this crucial subject. It makes me so angry that the EBAC is pushing RE out. I know of schools where there will be no RE.' The size of the community allied to a kind of heightened sense of moral purpose, and sense of being somewhat under siege, has tended to create something of a 'guild mentality' among many professionals working in the area.

This chapter draws upon three sources of data from the project to access the processes by which the participants make sense of RE in their professional practice. First, we looked to the Delphi seminar; secondly, we explore teachers' perspectives on the efficacy of their practice; and, finally we explored the impact of examinations on both the aims and the practices of Religious Education. While we have variously touched on each of these sources in the course of this volume, here we attempt to bring them together in order to shape a narrative that reveals not only the sedimentary layers but also the striations that fissure the layers.

The Delphi process and the 'broken middle': Tensions within professional narratives on Religious Education

Although somewhat dispersed and isolated within their schools, RE practitioners generally enjoy productive relationships with faith community organizations, university centres for the academic study of religion, philosophy and theology, and faculties responsible for teacher education across the United Kingdom. It is the integration into these external networks that facilitates the exchange of ideas and perspectives on the implementation of policy, and this plays an important role in the forging of professional identity. While, as we have seen earlier, sharply contrasting views of the nature and purpose of the subject exist, this well-established 'guild expertise' of professional collaboration and networking supports members of the Religious Education professional community in their response to change. The Delphi seminar, with which we opened our fieldwork, had, as a central motif, the concern to surface and elucidate the opinions and claims surrounding the aims of Religious Education, as articulated by those involved in the mediation between policy and practice. To re-iterate, the seminar lasted two days and involved 13 participants, 11 of whom had been Religious Education teachers in schools earlier in their career. Eight were involved in initial teacher education, five held policy development roles and five had held positions of responsibility in professional associations for RE. A number of the participants had dual roles with at least three teaching theology in University departments of Theology and/or Religious Studies, including one who taught Islamic theology.

Designed to engage expert opinion on controversial issues, the Delphi method helps us recognize that a constitutive feature of expertise can be its heterogeneity. We were particularly interested in how an expert panel – drawn from both secular and faith school education sectors from the three different legislative contexts of Scotland, Northern Ireland and England – would distil occasions for consensus and dissent that would arise through the iterative rounds of questioning and reflection.

The initial stimulus for the discussions was a series of questions reflecting issues identified from our review of current research in RE.[2] The resultant questions were distributed to the participants prior to the first seminar, and their initial responses formed the agenda for the opening session. Analysis of the discourse of our seminar reveals a tendency to refer to prior, shared experiences and the use of anecdotal descriptions drawn from practice as a vehicle for the advancement of a particular viewpoint. Anecdotes tended to focus on examples of pedagogical or policy intentions of which participants disapproved, rather than on examples of good practice. Indeed, one colleague gives quite precise voice to what was a general mood among participants when observing that, 'the anecdotal stuff for me is much more powerful.' Furthermore, during the discussion of the attributes of a teacher of Religious Education, stories about how *not* to teach Religious Education were recited and discussed frequently, with only fleeting and infrequent references to instances illustrative of *good* practice. It was as if participants sensed greater opportunities for unity in their collective creation of, and opposition to, negatively imagined classroom scenarios, than in establishing conceptually and pedagogically common ground. Recourse to anecdotal discursive patterns precluded criticizing or calling into question individual accounts and was reminiscent of the pedagogy we observed in the Religious Education classroom, where generating multiple perspectives through questioning and the valuing of personal opinion frequently took precedence over any engagement in robust argument or the formulation of criteria by which to judge religious concepts and practices. Two overarching tropes were present in the discourse over the two days of the seminar. One conveys the idea of the pedagogy of RE as a subversive activity consciously directed towards 'messing with their heads' by challenging preconceptions and subjecting social structures to radical critique. The other is that of inclusion, in which all perspectives can be accommodated within the Religious Education classroom.

The pattern of interaction during the seminar tended to conform to what Scheele (1975) defines as an episodic Delphi encounter. According to this profile, participants continue a discussion in which they have had prior involvement, either with the other participants or with similar groups of professional colleagues and so resist redefinitions. Finding this pattern of discourse is not surprising, given that participants were familiar with one another; a familiarity that has been at least in part shaped by the overlapping nature of responsibilities and attachments in a small professional field. However, contrary to Scheele's characterization of such encounters, the group did not resist redefinitions but positively embraced shifting definitions and the flux of opinions within Religious Education. Ambiguity seemed preferable to seeking clarification and a certain professional courtesy was evident. Nevertheless, on closer examination, the apparent coalescence of opinion breaks down when the proximate purpose of Religious Education is considered in terms of the relationship between education and personal belief, and the scope for religious nurture in the classroom. In the discussion of actual examples of practice, what was particularly interesting was the way in which putative agreement as to the broad aims of the subject and conversational patterns that resiled to anecdote and the *via negativa*, masked disagreement. Moreover, as we noted earlier, many in the group were wary of any attempt to investigate the efficacy of Religious Education. Members were fearful that empirical investigation in classrooms guided by the question 'what works?' risked becoming reductive and would fail to capture what is important about the subject. This tendency may account for the Religious Education community's sense of its own and the subject's fragility, and the solution could lie in being prepared to grapple with how to establish a basis for action and reflection in what philosophers term the 'broken middle' (Rose 1992). Functioning in the broken middle requires negotiation of the territory that lies *between* the opposition of overarching beliefs and fragmented, individual contingencies. It is a process of constructive doubting rather than superficial agreement. The aim of dialogue is to enable things to be taken apart, unravelled, in order to diagnose what may be wrong; to form judgements between competing ideas and to act. Negotiating between statements of abstracted, absolute positions and relativist contingency, in order to find a basis for moving forwards together, is demanding and requires the capacity to challenge and be open to challenge. Religious Education, as is so often the case, highlights the tensions of working in the midst of oppositions and pluralities, but the confidence to recognize that there is a broken middle could become the common ground for practitioners trying to make sense of Religious Education. Certainly, the group identified a broken middle with regard to the chasm existing between the claims of Religious Education and the practices in the classroom. Yet for all the identification of inadequacy and incoherence, there was little sense that members of the group were, in any meaningful way, a part of what they themselves considered to be a failed dynamic. Indeed, fault was clearly attributed to two sites: the failure of policy makers to keep abreast of the shifting social fabric – which, in turn, gave rise to significant shifts of focus in the subject – and the poverty of knowledge about both religion and human (ethical) development and engagement.

Is RE working? Teacher perspectives on classroom practice

It was important in the research fieldwork phase to capture the teachers' perspectives on the question of the efficacy of RE and their views on the trajectories from intentions, to the enactment and the evaluation of impact at the micro level of daily practice in the classroom. The practitioner inquiry strand was developed alongside the teacher questionnaires and interviews because we wanted to know about teachers' interests and the accompanying issues in learning and teaching in Religious Education that they considered to be a priority. We also hoped the inquiries would provide case studies that could be used by other teachers, and that the experience of conducting an inquiry would itself build capacity for evidence-informed practice within the professional Religious Education community. Teachers whose classrooms featured in the ethnographic study of students' experiences of Religious Education were invited to a workshop in each region to explain what would be involved in undertaking an inquiry, and it was stressed from the outset that participation was optional. Members of the project team facilitated the planning, but the teachers individually and personally determined the focus, scope and duration of the inquiry. The emphasis was on the particular issues they were facing in their schools and we stressed that, above all, whatever they did should be manageable. In total, 16 teachers decided to carry out an inquiry, and the questions they decided to explore are listed in Table 7.1.

Table 7.1 Practitioner inquiry questions

Focus	Report
Why are high attaining Y10 pupils disaffected with RE?	Yes
Has the introduction of philosophy for children led to more quieter/ more reserved pupils making contributions to lessons?	No
What is the impact of lessons based on multiple intelligences (in the context of a whole school approach) on the engagement of students in RE?	No
What is the impact of active learning in religious, moral, and philosophical studies lessons?	Yes
Can S1–S3 students' analysis and evaluation skills be improved?	No
What is the impact of ICT in RE on attainment, attitude, and engagement?	No
Will S3 pupils be more engaged during the visit to the oratory if the planning and delivery is completed by their peers?	No
Which cross-curricular areas in curriculum for excellence relating to citizenship can be developed through core RE in S4?	No
What is the impact of the use of Quizdan software on pupil engagement in RE lessons?	No
Does the use of ICT improve the engagement of pupils in RE lessons?	No
Does RE contribute to making you a responsible citizen?	Yes
How can the experience and participation of pupils in prayer within the classroom be enhanced?	No
What is the best way of developing critical skills with higher pupils following an examination syllabus?	No
How effective is note-taking as measured by pupil performance in Y11 GCSE assessment questions?	No
What do staff feel to be the impact of roll out of the revised curriculum on planning/teaching in Y8 and Y9?	No
Does the development of 'connected learning' with Y10 students empower them to take ownership of their learning?	Yes

Given that the schools involved were sufficiently confident about Religious Education to agree to be research sites for the extensive classroom ethnography that formed the core of the project, the response to the inquiry strand was disappointing. Over the last 30 years, there has been a growth of interest in developing evidence-informed practice in education, and the benefits for teachers' professional development of taking an 'inquiry stance' (Cochran-Smith and Lytle 2009) has been widely discussed. Reference to the importance of engaging in and with research can be found in the standards for Initial Teacher Education in each of the jurisdictions of the United Kingdom, and feature in policy guidelines for developing the teaching profession for the twenty-first century:

> Exploration of theory through practice should be central
>
> . . . emphasising effective professional practice, reflection, critical analysis and evidence-based decision making
>
> (Donaldson 2011, 42)

Within Religious Education, there are some notable examples of teacher inquiry having an impact on practice. For example, teachers in the North East of England developed the case studies for the book *Thinking through RE* (Baumfield 2002); the Westhill Seminar Series has supported teacher research for a number of years (Stern 2006, 2010) and the Warwick Religions and Education Research Unit incorporated a European action research community of practice as part of the project titled 'Religion in Education: a Contributor to Dialogue or a factor of Conflict in transforming Societies of European Countries' (REDCo) (O'Grady 2010). The National Association of Teachers of Religious Education also administers an annual bursary scheme to fund teachers undertaking curriculum development in their schools. Such provision has had some success in enabling teachers to contribute to our understanding of Religious Education in practice and in addressing the need for independent research to test the claims made for particular approaches – as highlighted, for example, by Michael Grimmitt in his review of pedagogy:

> . . . There is no empirical evidence of the reasonableness or otherwise of the claims that each project both implicitly and explicitly makes about the viability of the pedagogical procedures or strategies that it adopts in accordance with its central pedagogical principles in order to meet its aims. (Grimmitt 2000, 22)

We also thought that more teachers would want to take an active part in shaping the research into the controversial question of the efficacy of Religious Education, rather than being merely our 'subjects'.

The inquiries can be grouped into five areas:

improving the engagement and motivation of students;
incorporating whole school initiatives into the teaching of RE;
responding to the reform of the secondary school curriculum;
raising attainment in public RE examinations;
enhancing student experience of religious nurture in faith schools.

We need to exercise caution in drawing any definitive conclusions from this list of questions, but it is worthy of note that the concerns for the most part lie outside anything substantive regarding the content or approaches to teaching Religious Education as a subject in its own right. It is hard to escape a sense of the teachers reacting to external demands and grasping at anything that might improve the attitudes of students and secure their engagement in lessons. Notable by its absence is any reference to pedagogies based on particular approaches to Religious Education, such as the interpretive approach developed by Warwick Religious Education Project (Jackson 1997), theological approaches such as the Stapleford Project's 'concept cracking' (Cooling 1994) or critical realist approaches as developed by the Spiritual Education Project (Wright 1993). This observation on the focus of the teacher inquiries resonates with the findings from the classroom ethnography and analysis of textbooks, where little evidence could be found of any specifically grounded theoretical basis for teaching Religious Education and where no reference was made to expert opinion. It would appear that the robust debate which is so much part of the fabric of the research and teacher education community, regarding approaches to Religious Education, has little enough purchase in the daily lives of teachers in secondary school classrooms. In mitigation, it should be acknowledged that the tendency for practitioner inquiry to be conducted without being contextualized in existing research is not unique to Religious Education, but the lack of any reference to debate about pedagogical approaches, distinct to the subject content, is a concern. In making these observations, we are not suggesting that the teachers' practice is devoid of a general theory of the purposes of Religious Education. Rather, in these instances, there appeared to be no connection between the general purposes of RE (e.g. that children take religion seriously or that they understand others' faiths and so forth) and more specific theories about the nature of religion, religious attachment and belief, and concomitant epistemologically coherent pedagogic responses. Consequently, the focus tended towards the management of Religious Education, framed by the material conditions of schooling. These findings echo I'Anson's (2004) small-scale study of Religious Education students who, from the outset, are caught between the 'modernist' account of purpose in Religious Education, designed to 'shore up' the institutions of civic liberal society, and the 'postmodern' analysis of the fragility of those institutions and our analyses of them. In the context of teacher education, where they inhabited the worlds of both university and school students, the students attempted to negotiate between such competing imperatives. Full-time professionals located in school tended to drop the pedagogically and epistemologically more troubling framings in favour of the more prosaic and 'manageable' perspectives, given the external pressures. It is not difficult to suggest possible, and very practical reasons for the focus on issues extrinsic to Religious Education, not least of which may be the reduction in the number of specialist advisers[3] and the de-skilling of the teaching profession as a whole in the area of curriculum development.

Perhaps the most powerful influence on the teachers in our study was the increasing demand on Religious Education to act as the 'catch all' for interventions, ranging from community cohesion to healthy eating. We saw staff struggling to manage the multiple entailments placed on the subject while managing heavy teaching loads, often in small, under-resourced departments. Competing pressures on time was the main reason proffered by the teachers involved for the poor completion rate of the inquiry projects; of the 16 who began an inquiry, only four were able to complete the cycle and submit a report. However, active engagement with the process was not limited to those who managed to complete the 'full cycle'. Follow-up interviews with all of the teachers involved in the inquiry strand indicated that even those who did not write up the report gained from the process and the benefits confirmed what we know from reviews of research on the role of inquiry in professional development. The reward mentioned most frequently by teachers conducting inquiries was the insight they gained into the thinking of their students through the opening up of the processes of teaching and learning:

> This experience allowed me to appreciate, more fully, the pupil's experience. . . .

They enjoyed working with their students, who were more engaged in the lessons and also revised their estimations of the students' capabilities:

> What was interesting about this experiment was that the pupils were very engaged and, listening to their discussions, were actually thinking through the topics very sensibly. It was particularly noteworthy that the group who had previously been much disenfranchised was as involved as any other.

The teachers also saw that the students were themselves aware of the benefits of their voices being included in the evaluation of the impact of an inquiry:

> They became more aware of their own potential for learning.

> The pupils involved in collating the activity realized the time and preparation needed to complete the task.

Even when the insights into the depth of the disaffection of students might be painful, the process revealed some empathy – as this quote from a student in a focus group that was part of a teacher inquiry suggests:

> The teacher gets angry with us because of our lack of respect for the subject.

Taking a structured approach to the evaluation of an initiative through the inquiry process was also beneficial to colleagues:

> It has been a good opportunity to help the Department monitor and evaluate our effectiveness and contribution to the life of the school and the formation of students.

Evidence from the inquiries was used by teachers to evaluate factors such as the impact of class size on the feasibility of externally imposed initiatives, such as active learning or multiple intelligences, and to modify them so that they matched the needs of their students.[4]

Moreover, we were interested to understand more about how teachers themselves thought about the question, 'Does RE work?' What did they consider to be the weight of evidence needed to make a judgement? The reports and interviews about the inquiries support conclusions, drawn from other studies, that the insights into student learning achieved through improved feedback loops constitute a key factor (Baumfield et al. 2009). In addition, in keeping with other examples of practitioner inquiry, we see very little incidence of the use of existing research or sources of knowledge beyond the immediate context. Tangible impact on the quality of interactions in the classroom remains the most convincing source of evidence for teachers. There are, however, indications that enquiry can enable teachers to be more proactive in the face of externally imposed initiatives. Taking an enquiry stance and testing their efficacy in their own particular context can only be beneficial to a subject such as Religious Education that is too often (as explored in the Forum Theatre) construed as a passive recipient of whatever will not fit elsewhere in the curriculum.

For some commentators, the future of Religious Education as a subject and the future of research in Religious Education are interlinked, and the association offers the best way of resolving the tension between different approaches to teaching the subject (Grimmitt 2000; Stern 2006). They follow Stenhouse (1975) in promoting systematic practitioner research as the most appropriate strategy and the best way to meet the challenges of justifying the role of Religious Education in the contested social circumstances of community schooling. However, while some projects have been successful in motivating teachers to engage in research, others have foundered on the perception that it is unrealistic to expect teachers – already facing the pressures of working with limited resources – to engage in research. It has been argued that too forceful a push for practitioner research in Religious Education could have the unintended consequence of distracting from teaching and learning, and exclude critique by becoming normative (O'Grady 2010). The teachers in the *Does RE Work?* project investigated questions that had a direct bearing on their practice in the classroom, but the majority did not, or felt that they could not, effectively engage with the inquiry strand – in contradistinction to the strong claims of Stern that a life in teaching without research should be deemed unjustifiable (Stern 2010). In most of the schools in our study, the daily practices of the teacher are shaped by a range of prosaic considerations, including (in many instances) meagre resources, squeezed time, some isolation and excessive expectations. These are conditions that are unlikely to conduce to paying close attention to theorists in and of Religious Education.

Managing the impact of examination pressures on pedagogy: A tale of three schools

Central to the purposes of the ethnographic study of the enactment of Religious Education in classrooms was the identification of the characteristics of learning and teaching that marked the culmination of Religious Education in mainstream, compulsory schooling. Before we even began the fieldwork, we were warned (in an interview with professional leaders) that the decision to focus on the experience of students nearing the end of their 'career' in Religious Education would result in a distorted picture owing to the domination of public examinations in this phase of education. Teachers and students alike felt this pressure acutely and commented on the disjunction with how the subject is taught in the years before starting to study for a public examination. Despite this, we considered the selected stage to be a critical time for students' engagement with the subject. Moreover, we also looked at Religious Education across the school and, while the conditions of examination certainly had a significant effect on the practices in the subject, these conditions were not limited to Key Stage 4/S4. Religious Education across the years was impacted to a greater or lesser extent by the same factors. Students who asked questions that were 'off piste' often had them deferred until they returned to pursue Higher, AS or A Level; a practice rather unhelpful to those not opting for the senior examination cycle. Indeed, we might argue that the suggestion, to students, that they would get the opportunity to engage with more intellectually and personally demanding questions only if they came back to pursue study for a further exam, rather undermined the claim that the examination years were unrepresentative! The relationship between statutory and examination Religious Education has shifted over the years as it has become less feasible for schools to offer parallel courses. Meeting the requirements to provide statutory Religious Education, by entering all registered students for a public examination, has had advantages and disadvantages for the status of the subject in schools. Offering an examination pathway for all students in Religious Education means that it has a degree of parity with other subjects in the same phase of education, while meeting the legal requirements. Schools were supportive of Religious Education when examination results could boost the number of students achieving grades A–C, and so improve the place of the school in the league tables. In the early days of mass entry of students for the examination, there was also some evidence of a pull-through to further study at advanced level. However, early gains were undermined by the tendency to expect Religious Education departments to prepare students for examinations without any additional resources and, frequently, with less time in the curriculum compared to other subjects. In one notable example, (Brockton) the head of department (HOD) observed:

> When I first came here I taught the A Level, not me but my predecessor and I taught the A Level after school. So it wasn't even [unclear] . . . So it wasn't timetabled, it was an after school thing. And then eventually I stamped my feet and got it on the timetable and the numbers picked up.

In one regard, we see the extraordinary commitment of teachers in the most unpropitious of circumstances, but we also see the fragility of the subject where the same teacher goes on to suggest that should he or she leave, then the subject would be left with an unbridgeable knowledge gap, likely to precipitate the disintegration of the subject at advanced level. For many of those students who were sitting post 16 examinations, it was not clear that they appreciated being entered for an additional examination and they often lacked motivation. Teachers were frequently faced with a situation in the classroom marked by a wide disparity between those who wanted to do well and those who had no interest in the subject. The situation was complicated further by the competitive relationship between different examination boards, resulting in a trend to trim the subject to match the constraints imposed by large, mixed-ability cohorts of students and a shortage of time to teach the syllabus. Within this overarching narrative of distortion, however, there was evidence of individual teachers making decisions that indicated that there *was* scope at departmental level within schools for a different construal of Religious Education to develop. The following vignettes, drawn from our fieldwork, illustrate how teachers working in three schools in one region of England negotiated the teaching of RE.

Breaking down the subject

What's that subject called that's like RE but in proper depth?

In this school, the Religious Education Department sought to justify the value of the subject in the eyes of senior management by achieving the maximum number of grades A–C for students. Staff managed a sophisticated virtual learning environment (VLE) on which example questions, model answers and tips on achieving maximum marks were posted regularly. Full advantage was taken of the modular structure of the examination to break the subject down into units and subunits, and time was devoted in lessons to analysing performance against marking criteria provided by the examination board. The staff prepared detailed revision booklets that students could buy for each unit. The Department relied on the extrinsic motivation of achieving a good grade in the examination as the main means of motivating students, and also tried to tap into their competitiveness through ranking students and comparing their performance against predicted grades. To some extent, the strategy reflected a wider concern within the school to demonstrate good performance in examinations, because OfSTED inspections had indicated that it might be a 'coasting' school that could be at risk. However, the Religious Education Department appeared to have taken up what could be dubbed a competitive 'league table' approach with some voracity and relied heavily on performance data, not only when engaging with the school management but also as a socio-pedagogical strategy in the conduct of lessons. Interestingly, during the development of the Forum Theatre presentations for the launch of the findings conference, drama students fixed on the way in which exploration and robust or deep discussion – in short, the life of the mind – has been subjugated in Religious Education to the obsession with examinations. As we have seen earlier, the potentially deleterious impact of the examination culture has been particularly strong in Religious Education.

The students interviewed in this school could see the value of studying Religious Education because it encouraged a wider perspective on moral issues and increased awareness of other cultures, but they simultaneously admitted that they found the lessons uninteresting. The main reason given for the tedious nature of Religious Education was that the emphasis was mainly on learning facts and '. . . reading stuff out of books which we have already done.' Subjects were critical of the way in which the particular textbooks used a double page per lesson for each issue to be covered in the exam syllabus. They thought that this format was repetitive and reduced everything to the memorization of facts. The linking of the content of the lessons so closely to the examination syllabus through the textbooks frustrated the students who felt that the questions they were expected to answer on each topic were exactly the same, '. . . once you answered one question it was like the answer to everything else.' They considered that there was little sense of discrimination between religious traditions, '. . . it's the same in every religion.' Students were left feeling that they lacked a frame of reference, a disciplinary structure, within which to think about issues. They described Religious Education as a set of disjointed, repetitive topics that did not make any connection with actual, authentic religious practices or with other curriculum subjects. On the whole, the students were more positive about their experiences of studying Religious Education prior to the preparation for the examination. One student spoke of Religious Education being 'OK' in Key Stage 3, as they were learning new things and had more contact with people who practiced a religion through the programme of visits and visitors. She thought that Religious Education had actually become less challenging now and it was when asked how it could be improved that she asked the question that appears at the beginning of this vignette:

> Student A: What's the subject called that's like RE but in proper depth?
> Student B: Ethics?
> Student A: No
> Student C: Theology?
> Student A: Yes! But I could never do that.

The giveness of Religious Education as an examination subject did not motivate the students. In fact, as we have seen, the converse tended to be true, and the requirement to complete course work and to revise was an unwelcome imposition that used up valuable time that they would prefer to spend on more 'important' subjects. The attempts to make the exam manageable in the constrained time available appear only to have reduced the status of Religious Education. The class was divided on its views as to whether the study of religion should continue as a non-examination subject until the end of compulsory schooling at 16, but, on the whole, it was felt that this may be necessary given the need for all students to be aware of other cultures. Indeed, this particular feature of Religious Education is echoed in the statistical data, where students considered the subject important in nurturing and understanding the need for respect for other cultures. They also enjoyed having the opportunity to discuss controversial issues and thought it was '. . . interesting to think about these things but it's not right to be tested about it.' Not only was examination in Religious Education lacking in structure and boring, it was inappropriate as student opinions and attachments could not be assessed, '. . . there could be no right or wrong answers.' Once again, these features of student responses and engagement echo more general findings from other schools and raise, yet again, the complicating matter of the meaning and purpose of Religious Education.

A space apart

> The GCSE course textbook is written by the Chief Examiner and has everything the students need to know, so we use that for homework and do proper Religious Education in the lessons.

The HOD in this school had recently revised his strategy concerning the examination of Religious Education. He had originally entered all of the students for the examination and this had been effective in raising the status of the subject in the eyes of the senior management in the school. The head teacher welcomed the *fact* that the students were achieving good grades, hence boosting the overall performance of the school in the league tables. However, this strategy, conducing to significant levels of student disaffection, as it did, was beginning to have a detrimental effect on the subject. The HOD was himself unhappy with the constraining influence of the examination syllabus, which he considered to be reductive and instrumental. He faced the dilemma of knowing that if the students followed the textbooks and workbooks written by the chief examiner, then they would be able to achieve good grades in the examination, but that such achievement was to be purchased at the expense of what he considered to be 'good' Religious Education. The Department also had to contend with problems arising from the timing of the module examinations, which disturbed the integrity of the lessons and interrupted the flow of teaching for the year. The compromise reached by the Department was to enter only those students who were in the top two ability bands for the examination and to organize the work schedule so that they could complete the tasks in the detailed workbooks as homework. The lessons then provided a focus for those issues and themes that the staff considered to be more worthwhile as 'educational' Religious Education. On occasion, these were linked to some of the themes covered in the examination syllabus. This approach enabled the emergent ideas to be explored in more depth, and with more subtlety.

The characteristics of the 'more worthwhile' Religious Education, featured in the lessons, included an emphasis on a holistic approach involving 'head-heart-hands' and a pedagogy based on creating a community of inquiry. All of the students were given a laminated yellow card with the Religious Education Department motto, which states that to develop as a whole person you should:

Use your HEAD – think for yourself and think wisely

Engage your HEART – appreciate what it is like to be someone else

Get HANDS on – learn by doing and act on your beliefs.

The other side of the card reminds them of the procedure to be followed when in a community of inquiry. The Department was involved in a number of national initiatives for Religious Education, including the Blair Faith Foundation 'Face to Faith' project and a video link with a school in Trinidad, where a 'virtual' community of inquiry was being developed. The HOD had a definite and overt philosophical approach to Religious Education, in which the priority was to raise awareness of different cultures and promote community cohesion. He also promoted links across the curriculum and tried to involve the local community in the lessons as much as possible through visits and visitors to the school. More than this, the 'invitation' to 'engage one's heart' and 'act on one's beliefs' evokes once more the character of general discussion in the Delphi seminar regarding the importance of seeing Religious Education as 'character forming' and as a site that offers an opportunity for students to engage in moral learning 'from' their educational engagements. The focus group interview with students, however, indicated that they did not understand the intentions of the teachers and would, in fact, have welcomed more structure. Students felt that the aim of Religious Education was not very clear; one student described the lessons as, '. . . random work on people's feelings.' While they enjoyed the opportunity to discuss ideas and liked the 'clashes' and arguments that ensued, they wanted an overview of the subject and closer links between the examination topics and the lessons. The latitude of approach to Religious Education that the school permitted was thought to be double-edged given that, on the one hand, it made it easier to participate and feel relaxed, but, on the other hand, this often meant that there was no sense that there was actually anything to 'learn' in the subject since everyone was entitled to their own opinion. Of all the tropes that emerged across our study, this is perhaps the most substantial, significant and, from a professional educational perspective, the most disconcerting. The Forum

Theatre presentations and consequent high-school student responses strongly echoed the same sense of student dissatisfaction with the practice of eliciting opinion as a pedagogical and substantive entailment, especially when it tended to displace/replace a more content-rich approach. The lack of any sense of criteria to be applied in the evaluation of ideas meant that discussions could not progress and students felt annoyed with their more truculent, opinionated peers who dominated lessons and 'took advantage' of the fact that the teacher was not dealing with 'sure answers.' Again, this sense of stagnation was certainly not unique to this particular school, although its refraction here is complicated by the very self-conscious intention of the teachers to do something different. Creating a separation between the requirements of the examination and classroom RE does not appear to have been very successful as far as these students were concerned. Echoing the statistical findings in the next chapter, neither the 'real RE' lessons nor the examination was taken very seriously and the students reported that, in the recent mock examination, they had been running a bet on who could introduce the phrase 'Gordon Brown's tie' into an answer to a question.

Taking part is the important thing

Teachers in other subjects can't get these students to even turn up for the exam.

The third vignette illustrates the approach to Religious Education in a Church of England Voluntary Aided School that has been formed through a series of mergers of failing secondary schools serving a challenging catchment area. The HOD described the aim of Religious Education in the school as raising the self-esteem of the students and developing the personal qualities encompassed by 'learning from religion'. The priority was to create in the classroom a space in which the bigger social and political issues affecting young people in their daily lives could be grappled with and where everyone had a voice. In this particular school, Religious Education was merged with Personal, Social and Health Education (PSHE) and Citizenship, and was the *only* Humanities subject studied after the age of 14. Students in the focus group were very positive about Religious Education and emphasized the fact that everyone was included and entitled to express their views. The deputy head teacher also praised the inclusive policy adopted in Religious Education and the success of the Department in engaging and motivating even the most challenging students. In a recent module examination for RE, 100 per cent attendance had been achieved, which was outstanding in a school with severe problems with truancy and unmatched by subjects that might be considered more 'high status', such as Maths and English. The difference was, according to the deputy head teacher, that in the school there was no hierarchy of subjects and the students simply responded to the teachers who they felt valued them as individuals. It was not just that the students turned up for the examination, they also tended to do better in Religious Education than in other subjects with a 60% pass rate in the previous year. As he concluded, 'The kids drive the lesson in Religious Education.' Despite such 'official' valedictions, the two staff who comprised the Religious Education Department felt marginalized and undervalued in the school. During the fieldwork, the HOD was in dispute with the senior management team about the policy of entering everyone for the examination regardless of his or her performance and predicted grades. For the head of Religious Education, inclusion should be paramount, especially in a Faith School, while the school management wanted to restrict entry to those likely to achieve grades A–C. The HOD also felt that Religious Education was being judged more harshly than subjects such as Maths and English, which were better resourced, and for which contextual information was included when assessing performance. The second member of the RE staff, a newly qualified teacher, was anxious to find a new post as she felt that the identity of the subject was lost in the merger with PSHE and Citizenship, and she was worried that if she stayed, she would become 'de-skilled'.

Conclusion: Communities of practice

Participation in the practices of social communities shapes not only what we do but also who we are and how we interpret what we do (Wenger 1998). Exploration of the perspectives of policy makers, teacher educators and teachers, as revealed through the data from the *Does RE Work?* project, provides insight into practice as 'the experience of meaning'. We have been able to trace some of the interacting factors that have contributed to the construction of the identities of the participants in the Religious Education professional community. What has been noticeable throughout the accounts in this chapter has been the level of shared commitment at the higher level of aspirations and aims for Religious Education, and an equally intense commitment to the adroit handling of challenging individual situations. However, it is also hard to avoid a pervasive sense of a community of practice unable to arrive at a rationale by which this general agreement at a 'global' level and understanding of particular local circumstances can be drawn together to constitute genuine shared meaning. Consequently, we find a common vocabulary and discursive pattern used to throw a blanket of apparent agreement over deep teleological and ontological fissures in practice. The complexity of the task facing over-stretched, under-rated and frequently marginalized participants in the professional Religious Education community is daunting, as members try to juggle the competing demands made on a contested and controversial curriculum subject. Notwithstanding the existence of a number of professional bodies, the absence of viable structures to facilitate negotiation from the global to the particular creates a sense of a vacuum. This absence can be disguised by a justification based on the grounds that dogmatic certainty is anathema to modern Religious Education, but the eschewing of certainty cannot be at the expense of a willingness to seek definition. It is this vacuum that is sensed by students, seeking structure, on the one hand, and embracing a superficial relativism, on the other, which then undermines Religious Education.

Notes

1   Here too, as a consequence of the detailed descriptions and analysis of particular schools, we have chosen not to identify them, even pseudonymously.

2   What was interesting about this survey of recent and current research was the paucity of substantial anthropological and ethnographical work, or indeed, substantial empirical work. By way of contrast, there is a great deal of normative scholarship promoting particular pedagogic approaches.

3   In the early 1990s, Scotland alone had an Association of Religious Education Inspectors and Advisers numbering upwards of 20. Today it boasts not a single expert adviser. They have been replaced with Quality Improvement Officers (QIOs) with generic portfolios none of whom have a specialist qualification in the field. Yet even as this service diminishes in Scotland (down from 354.6 to 265.9 between 2009 and 2011), there are many who argue that schools can provide all of this themselves. Of course, the diminution of a specialist support service has been yet more dramatic in England, which has witnessed a progressive shift from local government control and support to individual schools. For further discussion of the decline in QIOs, see Buie (2012).

4   These were whole school or local authority initiatives instigated by external advisers or consultants to which all subjects were expected to respond. So, for example, in Scotland there was at the time an emphasis on promoting active learning. See www.educationscotland.gov.uk/learningteachingandassessment/approaches/activelearning/index.asp

8

Religious Education and Student Perspectives

Introduction

In previous chapters we have attempted to understand something of the complexity of religious education in the United Kingdom and explored the way in which the fieldwork was concerned to expose the *inscape* of the classroom and the school with respect to RE. While much of our work was ethnographic in character, we wished to triangulate our observations and analyses so as to enhance our grasp of the complexity of the domain. This impulse led to the development of a survey, shaped by the qualitative evidence from classroom observation. Importantly, we consider that any data arising from the questionnaire needs to be read in conjunction with the other material we have attempted to surface in this study. In understanding more about how the students collectively considered or reacted to some of the themes that emerged in the course of our work, we wanted to include data that would enable us to examine the views of a wider set of students' dispositions and attitudes across the project schools.

Following a consideration of the sample obtained for the survey, this chapter examines some of the findings to emerge from the analysis. We begin by looking at the levels of religious participation among the students and their families, including the extent to which they participate in religious services inside and outside school. Moving on from this, we examine the extent to which schools promote academic improvement and a sense of ambition among the students. One major part of the survey focused on various aspects of school ethos – and the role, if any, played by Religious Education in the development of this ethos. Our initial consideration of school ethos examined the extent to which students feel they have opportunities for engaging in leadership roles within their schools, and a range of extracurricular activities focused on volunteering, charitable work and promoting the environment. We also examined the students' views on whether their schools challenged racism and provided support, of various kinds, for religious groups within the school community.

Another significant part of the questionnaire focused on the role of Religious Education as a curriculum subject. In particular, we wanted to ascertain the extent to which students are provided with opportunities to engage with difference, and how this compares to other curriculum areas. A more general aim of this section of the questionnaire was to explore students' feelings regarding how well their school prepared them to live and work in a diverse society, and what role is played in this task by Religious Education. We also examined the status of Religious Education vis-a-vis other curriculum subjects, and explored the extent to which students considered the practice of Religious Education classes to be distinctive. Given that, in some schools the resourcing of Religious Education appeared to be modest, this question of distinctiveness is of some significance. We were interested in whether, for example, Religious Education classrooms were characterized by a greater or lesser engagement with discussion and active learning. Of course, that they might be so characterized does not, in itself, conduce to effective Religious Education. Indeed, as we saw from a number of focus groups and the Forum Theatre (Lundie and Conroy, 2012) intervention, students do not automatically consider more discussion to equate to 'better' education. In many of the project schools we observed substantial evidence that discussion was a significant feature of pedagogic engagement, but its existence alone could not be regarded as a validation of quality.

Nested identity

The data available from the survey provides extensive opportunities for analysis. However, our primary interest in this chapter lay in the comparative experiences of students from different faith backgrounds. As we have observed in our chapter on policy, the history of the role of the churches differs markedly across the varied constituencies of the United Kingdom. In England, over an extended period, there was a conscious attempt to displace the role of the Churches in favour of local authorities (Gardner et al. 2005). In Scotland, the same reliance on local authority control was mitigated by an arrangement in the early twentieth century with the Catholic Church which allowed for a distinctive category of denominational local authority schools (Cormack et al. 1991; Davis & O'Hagan

2007) – while in Northern Ireland, the Churches, Protestant and Catholic, have always played a much more significant role in school ownership and governance (Gallagher 2004, 2005). When we add to this the post-war growth of religious diversity in Britain, as a consequence of inward migration, then we have seen some evidence of the de facto, and sometimes de jure, emergence of separate minority faith schools (Ritchie 2001; Gardner et al. 2005). One important consequence of the evolution that is visible in our survey sample is that some students have experience of schools with a rich diversity of religions but in which many do not claim any religious affiliation at all, while others experience schools where most students claim adherence to a faith community, even though that is not always mirrored by direct denominational control of their school. This pattern links to ongoing debates on the role of denominationalism in education and the question as to the relative value of separate schools as sites for the promotion of a particular identity as against the common schools imperative to promote cohesion (Lijphart 1975; Berube 1994; Sturm et al. 1999; Wells 2009). While we are not in a position to engage with such big structural debates here, our data do provide an opportunity to cautiously explore some of the impact of these different experiences.

The data in the survey are categorical, thus chi-squared tests were carried out to test for statistical significance. In cases where there was statistical significance for a table, the individual cells contributing to this were identified by examining the adjusted standardized residual value of each cell. This ensured that the cells with adjusted standardized residual values of more than 2 or less than 2 were identified as statistically significant. All attributions of statistically significant differences below relate to cells that satisfied the above conditions.

Sample

All of the project schools were invited to participate in the survey, which was made available online. The achieved sample comprised a total of 535 students, of whom 56 per cent were girls and 44 per cent were boys. Of the total sample, 312 students (58%) attended schools in England, 130 (24%) attended schools in Scotland and 93 (17%) attended schools in Northern Ireland. In England we had respondents from seven schools; in Scotland we had respondents from five schools; and, in Northern Ireland we had respondents from two schools. Three students indicated they were from England, but did not indicate which school they were attending. Although we had targeted class groups across the schools, the number of respondents from each school varied: thus, five of the schools had 13 or fewer respondents, while one school had over 130 respondents; the remainder of the schools had between 30 and 60 respondents.

The students came from a variety of religious backgrounds, as evidenced in Table 8.1. Given the large number of extant faith communities, labelling is always a potential problem. However, acknowledging that many Christians would participate in the survey, we decided to adopt the following approach: students who said that they belonged to a Christian tradition other than Roman Catholicism were labelled as 'Other Christians'; students who said that they belonged to one of a number of non-Christian world faith communities were labelled as 'Other Faiths'; and, students who said that they had no religion were labelled as 'No Religion'.

As Table 8.1 shows, there were broadly equal percentages of 'Catholics', 'Other Faiths' and 'No Religion' students within our sample, and a smaller proportion of 'Other Christians'. Within these categories the 'Other Faiths' group included Muslims (11%), Sikhs (7%), Hindus (4%) and Jews (2%), while the 'Other Christians' group included Presbyterians (4%) and Anglicans (3%).

Table 8.2 shows the denominational profile of each of the schools with 30 or more respondents (the number of respondents for each school is indicated in the first column). These profiles allow us to make another distinction, that is, between the schools which have a high proportion of students who describe themselves in denominational terms and those which reflect greater diversity, and include large numbers of students with no religious affiliation. On the basis of the profiles of our respondents, we identified the following schools as denominationally homogeneous: England 2, Scotland 2, Scotland 3, Northern Ireland 1 and Northern Ireland 2. In addition, we included the students in the school with 13 respondents in this categorization and labelled this school as diverse. This meant that of the total sample, 318 (59%) pupils were determined as attending denominationally homogeneous schools and 199 (37%) pupils were identified as attending schools with diverse communities. However, given that

Table 8.1 The religious background of the students

Religious Background	Number	Percentage (%)
Catholic	162	30
Other Christians	101	19
Other Faiths	134	25
No Religion	138	26

Table 8.2 Denominational profiles of students by school and area

School	Catholic (%)	Other Christians (%)	Other Faiths (%)	No Religion (%)
England 1 (*n* = 43)	5	42	7	47
England 2 (*n* = 133)	4	11	69	16
England 3 (*n* = 48)	6	19	17	58
England 4 (*n* = 59)	12	29	12	47
Other England (*n* = 26)	19	15	50	15
Scotland 1 (*n* = 36)	6	19	6	69
Scotland 2 (*n* = 49)	86	0	4	10
Scotland 3 (*n* = 43)	88	0	9	2
Northern Ireland 1 (*n* = 35)	0	86	0	14
Northern Ireland 2 (*n* = 58)	98	0	0	2

Note: 'Other England' refers to students in schools where the response rate was below 13 students; two students from Scotland were the only respondents from their school and are not included in the data above

the denominationally homogeneous schools represent a smaller proportion of the 24 schools in the study as a whole, the numbers disguise the inability of a much larger proportion of the common schools to support their students in completing the online questionnaire. It is difficult to know why this was the case, and we can only speculate about the relative commitments to the objects of the study. However, what is clear is that the head teachers of some of the schools intervened to suggest that we had conducted enough research. Again, it is partly for this reason that we are using the results for further exploration of the themes that emerged from our overall study, rather than as free-standing entities.

Levels of religious participation

The next area of interest lies in the level of religious practice of the students, both within and outside school. We asked two sets of questions on this issue: the first was concerned with whether our respondents and their families would view themselves as religious, and the second set asked about participation in religious activities outside school. The overall responses to the first set of items can be seen in Table 8.3, which shows that a little over two-thirds described themselves as religious and three-quarters described their families as religious. Perhaps unsurprisingly, the respondents who said they had no religion were significantly

Table 8.3 Reported levels of religious participation

Question	Not at all (%)	A little (%)	A lot (%)
Would you describe yourself as religious?	31	52	16
Would you describe your family as religious?	25	48	27

more likely to describe themselves as 'not at all' religious (75%), when compared with Catholics (18%), Other Christians (19%) and Other Faith students (9%). Perhaps the more interesting pattern emerged among those who took on a religious identity: Catholics were more likely to describe themselves as 'a little' religious (69%), compared with those with no religion (23%); while those with an Other Faith religious identity (33%) were more likely to consider themselves as 'a lot' religious when compared with those with no religion (1%). In those schools serving religious communities, teachers tended to state that they had an important task in nurturing students in the life of their own communities, even where the students themselves saw something of a disjunction. As we have noted elsewhere, however, most teachers working in schools in communities with a more diffuse, if any, religious identity, considered the religious lives of students outside school to be of little import as a professional or personal obligation.

Similar patterns emerged when we asked our respondents to describe the religiosity of their families, although this was nuanced. For this item, those with no religion (66%) were significantly more inclined to state that they were 'not at all' religious, in comparison with Catholics (7%) and Other Faith students (5%). As before, Catholics (62%) were more inclined to describe their families as 'a little' religious when compared with those with no religion (5%); while Other Faith students (49%) were more likely to describe their families as 'a lot' religious when compared with those with no religion (2%). This echoes quite a strong theme in the ethnography, where students in schools serving religious communities had perceptibly stronger religious attachments than students in schools serving broader communities. However, according to the teachers in such schools, religious attachment or feeling does not translate into the students having knowledge about their own tradition. Hence, one teacher observes (Linden):

> . . . you ended up with a community who put religion right at the very top of the ladder, but actually if you ask them to rate on a scale of 1–10 how confident they are about what they know about their religion, they put it down in the bottom three. So, don't know much about it but it's the most important thing in my life.

Table 8.4 Participation in Religious Services outside school

Question	Not at all (%)	Less than once a week (%)	Once a week (%)	More than once a week (%)
Do you attend religious classes outside school (e.g. Sunday school or Madrassa, etc.)?	79	8	9	5
Do you attend religious services outside school (e.g. going to Church or Temple or Mosque)?	47	23	23	7

Table 8.4 presents the responses to the next set of items on religious practice, with an overall picture which reveals that while only a minority of our respondents attend religious classes outside school, the sample is split fairly evenly between those who do not attend religious services and those who do, however infrequently. The deeper patterns in these responses are perhaps not as might be immediately expected: Catholics (89%) and those with no religion (98%) are more likely to say that they do not attend religious classes outside school, when compared with Other Christians (53%) and Other Faith students (66%). These last two groups are significantly more likely to attend religious classes outside school once a week (20% and 13% respectively), while the Other Faith students (12%) are more likely to attend religious classes outside school more than once a week. Of course, in each category, the absolute proportions attending classes outside school were relatively small, a finding that resonates with the more focused study on mixed-faith families by Arweck and Nesbitt (2011). Furthermore, with the exception of some children from minority religious communities (Christian or Islamic), the classroom was the only site for Religious Education. With particular regard to Catholics being less likely to engage in any Religious Education outside school, this is perhaps unsurprising given the perception among Catholic parents that they have 'their' schools to provide for their Religious Education.

For the item relating to participation in religious services, the pattern is somewhat more predictable: those with no religion (92%) are significantly more likely than not to attend religious services at all, in comparison with all the others; Catholics (44%) are more likely to attend services once a week; while Other Faith students (17%) are more prone to attend services more than once a week. Even on the basis of these data, it is possible to identify an important contextual feature: our Catholic and Other Faith respondents are more likely to be in denominational schools, but in the case of Catholics, these are in schools governed by their Church. Thus, while these two groups describe themselves and their families as more religious than the rest, their religious identity and practice is given explicit institutional form in school, for Catholics, but outside school, for adherents of Other Faith traditions.

Ambitions

While the picture of provision across the United Kingdom was indeed variegated, some themes emerged as incontrovertibly key to Religious Education as a social practice, notably the emphasis on examinations, not only as a source of external validation for the subject but also as a motive force for students. The role played by the examination system in shaping the life of Religious Education should not be underestimated and is typified by wallcharts evincing strategies for securing an 'A' (St Athanasius); by games mimicking the television game show, 'Who wants to be a millionaire?'; by teachers concluding feedback sessions with advice on how to secure an A* (Castle); by shaping the pedagogy around what students are 'going to need for [their exam]' (Seggett); by offering multiple opportunities to take examination (Bp Fulton Sheen); and, by Ofsted inspections that align being an effective school with high examination performance (Brockton). This list is indicative and by no means exhaustive. While there were one or two voices of demurral (from church schools) that considered examination offerings as a distraction from what they considered to be the 'core' purposes of Religious Education as religious nurture, most considered them as central.

While ambition per se was not an overwhelming concern for teachers and students in our sample schools, it did feature regularly in both iconography and discussions. With regard to iconography it was not unusual to see schools 'flag' this as central to their values, with one school sporting 'in the main hall 8 flags proudly display[ed] the school values "Pride, Ambition, Respect" . . .' (Ethnographer's notes, Dundon Grammar). Discussions on ambition were common in a variety of classrooms, though on occasion, and somewhat paradoxically, they were cut short by a need to get on with examination preparation. It is certainly the case that the explicit consideration of ambition has become something of a commonplace in our schools; indeed in Scotland a number of the schools in our study had partaken in the government sponsored *Schools of Ambition* programme (Hulme et al. 2009). Moreover, given the vaunted place of Religious Education as a site of challenge, both in the internal discourse of the texts and resources, and in the conversations of students, we were interested in the level of ambition evident among our respondents and their perceptions of whether Religious Education made any contribution to the achievement of these ambitions. This was particularly important given that, in the focus groups, the question of the contribution of Religious Education to the academic ambitions of the students surfaced frequently. So it was that we came to consider further the relationship between RE and ambition. Hence we asked the students if they intended going to university when they finished school, whether their teachers encouraged them in aspiring to do so and whether they intended to leave school and get a job as soon as they could. Of course, it is important not to consider a desire to go straight into the workplace as an indication of diminished ambition. Nonetheless, much of the emphasis in conversations across schools was on the contribution of RE to academic achievement and concomitant ambitions. On all counts, a clear sense of ambition was evident in the responses: 79 per cent responded that they planned to go to university, while 67 per cent said that their teachers encouraged them to go to university and 20 per cent expressed a preference to leave school to get a job as soon as possible.

There were, however, some statistically significant differences among the groups. For example, while overall 58 per cent of students *strongly* agreed that they planned to go to university, the proportion saying this among Other Faith students was significantly higher (69%), while by contrast, it was significantly lower among those with no religion (50%). Among the Other Faith group there was also about half as many students who intimated that they were unsure whether or not they were planning to go to university as compared with the students as a whole (7% versus 14%).

Perhaps unsurprisingly, schools serving strongly middle-class communities saw the conversations about the purpose of RE reflect the broader ambitions of the school and the parents. In such schools there was a complex interplay between RE as a resource and the capacity of students to engage more confidently in critiques of religion. In one such school, where 'many girls have very high ambitions', a sixth former tells [the ethnographer] that she has applied to 'Oxford, Durham, York and LSE and . . . there is a definite middle class confidence about the girls in A level, particularly in Mrs Hallam's A-level philosophy and ethics class' (Ethnographic notes). As they discuss the success imperative, students are also interested and not uncritical of the way in which the examinations themselves shape their intellectual life; a theme that also emerged in the course of the Forum Theatre seminars. As one of the students observed, 'it's not fair, rewarding them for thinking in a particular way that the "institution" (does air quotes) wants, that philosophy is thinking outside the box' (Ethnographic notes: Linden). In these circumstances, RE is no more or less than a chess piece on the board of professional aspiration. As one teacher, Mrs Hallam (Linden), observes, 6 out of 10 'A' level girls are applying to Oxford but as a consequence of 'pushy parents'. We know that she has a deeply ambivalent relationship to the ambitious impulse because she shrugs and wrinkles her nose in a disapproving way when she observes that the students are applying because of parental drive.

When we considered the extent to which teachers encouraged their students to go to university, we detected a difference between those who said that they had a religion and those who reported that they had no religion. The latter were statistically less likely to strongly agree that their teachers encouraged them, in comparison to respondents as a whole (22% vs 29%). Similarly, they were statistically prone to disagree that their teachers encouraged them, again in comparison to the respondents as a whole (16% vs 10%). In this regard, the teacher from Holy Cross School observes that in the attempt to interlink RE, PSHE and citizenship 'the main aim is to raise the students' self-esteem and encourage higher aspirations.' While the relationship between religion, education and ambition is complicated, these findings echo a number of studies (e.g. Green & Cooling 2009) which suggest that religious schools conduce to better performance. Perhaps for our purposes, it is more instructive to turn to Schagen and Schagen's (2002) work, which suggests that while 'on the whole faith schools seem to make very little impact . . . there are exceptions to this general rule whereby students in faith schools of all types *were encouraged* to take an additional GCSE.' This was confirmed in the recent research, which showed that faith schools are ahead of ordinary comprehensives in terms of total point score (but not average point score) and number of GCSE entries. There were no statistical differences among the groups with regard to the proportion who said they wanted to leave school and find a job as soon as possible.

When one poses the question, 'does x work?' there may be, as we have already noted, a considerable set of subordinate questions as to what kind of 'work' is entailed here. The growth of the importance of performance in the Programme for International Student Assessment (PISA) in educational planning and development (OECD 2010) coupled with more local concerns about the social and economic consequences of educational failure (Burns 2012), suggests that discussion about efficacy in the curriculum cannot avoid some consideration of the relationship between particular educational activities and the 'adult' world of employment. Given the foregrounding of examination success in many of the schools we explored, it might have been thought that this would portend

Table 8.5 Participants' responses to statement: 'Religious Education will be useful when I am applying for jobs or university'

Response	Percentage agreed (%)
Strongly agree or agree	27
Don't know	36
Strongly disagree or disagree	38

a significant interest in RE as a site which could contribute to their future employability. However, in only a couple of cases did teachers or students explicitly consider the 'relevance' of RE to employability. In one focus group (Wallace), there was some discussion of its usefulness in equipping students for the world of work. Here RE was considered to be complementary to the study of psychology given that they both deal in the engagement with, and analysis of, complex human problems. There was a tendency for older students (16 years of age and upwards) to entertain a more positive view of the contribution of RE to their becoming adult. Despite these occasional forays into the 'world of work', there appeared to be little connection between the strong focus on examination success and future employability. This might lead us to consider that the robust emphasis on the examinations across many of the schools was motivated by teachers' desire to see these as a resource to be deployed in securing the position of the subject in the very competitive environment of school resource allocation.

The relationship between ambition, examination and employability can be considered to be complex. Given this complexity, we were particularly interested in discovering whether or not students considered RE to be useful when applying for jobs or for university (see Table 8.5). There was an interesting degree of spread in the responses, with over a third stating that it was not important or that they were unsure, while over a quarter thought it would help. Interestingly, there was little difference in this pattern across the religious groups. The Catholic respondents were somewhat less likely to disagree with this contention, in comparison with respondents as a whole (13% versus 19%), but there was no overall statistical significance in the pattern.

School ethos

As we intimated in the opening chapter, the *habitus* of the school (its social practices, its organizational entailments and so forth) are enormously important in shaping attitudes to, and engagement with, RE. This habitus, this 'affinity of style', as Bourdieu (2005, 45) describes it, has become a defining conceit in a school's representation to itself, as well as to the world beyond. A school's self-definition, its self-representation, is to be captured in its ethos. Discussion of ethos was substantial across the schools in our study, and for many of the teachers and students the relationship between RE and general school ethos was considered to be of some import. While the issue tended to be raised in various ways by teachers, some students also offered comments on the ethos of their school and its relationship with RE. Sometimes, ethos was used to describe, explain or articulate attitudes to examination success, while on other occasions it was associated with the perceived contribution of RE to a particular religious culture. Yet, in further instances, it was related to the cultivation of an open or pluralist culture. Hence in Gorston, one teacher observes that,

> a lot of our students, their home life is very much based around religion and also it's really good because lots of parents will say 'well we understand the importance of my son or daughter's learning of other religions, so that they will respect them'. We did a big thing in Year 7, it used to be RE and you should respect everyone and now it's RS respect study and respect is the core. Again it's the ethos in the school, so it ties in really well.

Of course, the switch here from RE to RS also portends shifts in ethos and can be considered as part of a much wider change in the practice of RE and its relationship to the imperatives of the school as a whole. Perhaps unsurprisingly, church schools would appear to have offered a more extensive account of the relationship between RE and school ethos than their non-denominational counterparts. Given that most of the discourse around ethos appeared to be substantial and significant, and officially generated, we were interested in the extent to which this flowed into student attitudes. Hence we generated a series of items concerned with gaining a fuller understanding of students' views on the ethos of their school. The first set of items related to the role accorded to students in the school and proactive measures promoted by the school, while the second set of items was more specifically related to religious aspects of school life. This first set was quite important given that most students see their schools as reasonably progressive places – where collecting for charity is fostered; students are supported in on leadership roles; racist attitudes are challenged; and environmental awareness is encouraged. That said, it is noteworthy that the items which received the lowest levels of endorsement both relate to students, with just over half of the students saying that their school takes their views seriously and

Table 8.6 Percentage of students who 'Agree' or 'Strongly Agree' with each item

Item	Percentage of students (%)
My school organizes collections for charities	82
My school encourages students to take on leadership roles	70
My school challenges racist attitudes	69
My school encourages caring for the environment	67
In my school students' views are taken seriously	56
My school encourages students to carry out volunteer work in the community	40

fewer than half stating that their school encourages them to carry out volunteer work in the community. This last observation is quite significant, given that in the interviews with teachers the role of RE as a resource for developing human community and relations was often foregrounded.

There were some differences in perceptions among the students on some of these items (Table 8.6). For example, Catholic students were significantly more likely to say that their school organized collections for charities (95%) than students with no religion (73%). This echoes other findings that suggest that Catholic schools reinforce a range of positive attitudes to religious and moral values (Francis 2002). Interestingly, while only 3 per cent of students strongly disagreed that their school organized collections for charity (and no Catholic students said this), 9 per cent of students from Other Faiths strongly disagreed that this happened.

Following this, there were some statistically significant differences among the groups on the following three items: dealing with leadership roles, racist attitudes and caring for the environment. However, this often seemed to reflect differences in the strength of feeling among some of the groups of students, rather than fundamental disagreement between them. Students from Other Faiths were more likely to say that their schools encouraged them to take on leadership roles: where 14 per cent of the students overall strongly agreed that their school did encourage them to take on leadership roles, this was true for 22 per cent of those from Other Faiths, but only 7 per cent of those who had no religion. Similarly, these same students were more likely to say that their school challenged racist attitudes: among Other Faith students, 37 per cent strongly agreed that their school challenged racist attitudes, compared with 28 per cent of the sample population as a whole.

From Bath to Bradford, Agreed syllabuses in England and Wales strongly and explicitly promote RE as a vehicle for anti-racist attitudes. Hence the Bradford Agreed Syllabus proclaims that, 'promoting social and ethnic harmony is a moral imperative for Bradford schools and RE has a significant contribution to make to this' (Bradford Standing Advisory Council for Religious Education 2011, intro). In the daily experience of the schools in our study, efforts to instantiate this general claim were part of the fabric of conversation captured in the statement articulated by teachers (in this instance in Longwood School), that an aim is to promote pupils' skills and ability to play a role in their community and wider society.

The importance of RE in addressing multiculturalism and tolerance was highlighted in myriad ways and various places in Longwood. Indeed, this rationale was said to be a key factor in the re-emergence of RE in the school's curriculum. Some seven years previously the then Head of Department of RE encouraged the SMT to see that the subject could be one of the strategies to address the issue of multicultural tensions in the community. In the majority of the schools in our study, the purpose of RE as a vehicle to tackle multicultural and anti-racist attitudes was foregrounded. However, there were sites of resistance, with individuals and groups of students suggesting that it hadn't changed their attitudes. Indeed, in many instances, students from religious minorities suggested that teachers simply didn't understand their communities' religious beliefs (Conroy et al., 2012). Given the importance afforded to Religious Education as a means for tackling racism and nurturing positive attitudes to other cultures, it is perhaps somewhat surprising that almost a third of students in the survey across schools were not persuaded that their schools did this.

In relation to their school caring for the environment, students with no religion were significantly less likely to strongly agree with this claim (14%), when compared with students as a whole (20%). They were also more likely to disagree with this claim (17%), in comparison with students as a whole (11%). As with the previous item, a small minority (9%) of the students from Other Faiths strongly disagreed that their school encouraged caring for the environment, but this was statistically higher than for students as a whole (4%) or for Catholic students (1%).

Schools of very different kinds considered that they had an obligation to serve their community. Indeed, many considered RE to pre-eminently focus on obligations to the community. Examples of the outreach imperative typically saw teachers shape the curriculum around the religious beliefs and attachments of the local community. This of course evinces the belief enshrined in the principle

Table 8.7 Response to the statement: 'My school encourages students to carry out volunteer work in the community'

Response	Catholic (%)	Other Faiths (%)	No Religion (%)	All students (%)
Agree or strongly agree	48	40	28	40
Disagree or strongly disagree	19	31	37	28

Note: The patterns of responses for the Other Christian students were similar to that for all students

of the Agreed Syllabus that RE reflects the preoccupations and patterns of the local. But were students actively encouraged to engage with the community? We asked students whether or not their school encouraged them to carry out volunteer work in the community. There were differences overall among the groups of students and we have tried to capture the nuances of these in Table 8.7. It should be noted that we have excluded the Other Christian students from this table, as they showed no significant differences with others, and we have also excluded the proportion of students in each group saying that they did not know if their school encouraged volunteer work in the community (in each case it was approximately equal to about a third of the group).

There are three distinctive patterns of response illustrated in Table 8.7. First, a distinctive pattern emerges for Catholic students who are statistically more likely to agree or strongly agree with this claim, and also are less likely to disagree or strongly disagree, in comparison with all the other groups of students. Second, and by contrast, students with no religion go in the other direction, with a significantly larger percentage disagreeing or strongly disagreeing that their school encourages volunteer work in the community, and significantly less agreeing with this claim. Third, the students from Other Faiths groups contain respondents of both kinds: that is, like the Catholics they are significantly more likely to agree that their school encourages volunteer work in the community, while at the same time significantly more of them disagree with this claim. The most likely explanation for these patterns is that while the responses of Catholics and those with no religion reflect a broadly consistent pattern of experience across schools (and one hinted at in work by Francis and Robbins (2005)), it seems likely that for those from Other Faiths, their experience varies across schools.

The broad patterns outlined above were reinforced in the comparison of students in diverse or denominational schools, in which the more engaged experience appeared to be recounted by students in denominational schools. Thus, whereas 47 per cent of students in denominational schools strongly agreed that their school organized collections for charities, this was so for only 23 per cent of students in diverse schools; 24 per cent of students in denominational schools strongly agreed that their school encouraged caring for the environment, in comparison with 12 per cent of students in diverse schools; and, while 31 per cent of students in diverse schools disagreed that their school encouraged students to carry out volunteer work in the community, this was so for only 16 per cent of students in denominational schools. Despite teachers in many schools feeling and expressing the imperative to support the cultivation of particular ethical values in students, there did appear to be a more consistent approach to this in religiously denominated schools, and those serving strongly religious communities such as St Bede's.

The final set of questionnaire items in this section relate to a variety of ways in which religious values might form part of the ethos of the schools. This was a matter of interest given the claims by many teachers and professionals, alluded to in the opening chapter, that RE was more than an opportunity to impart some facts about, or understanding of, religion. However, in quite a number of schools, such an impulse was in competition with the desire to secure good examination passes. Moreover, in a number of instances, RE was seen to overlap with a desire, more or less specific, to secure the spiritual growth of pupils. Consequently, we wished to understand more fully the extent to which students actually considered their school as a site for expanding the opportunities to learn *from* religion. Table 8.8 illustrates the proportions of students who agreed or strongly agreed with a series of propositions that emerged from these considerations. While most students reported that there was someone in their school to whom they can talk about religious or moral questions, and just about one half of students stated that there was somewhere in their school where they could go for quiet reflection or prayer, only a minority

Table 8.8 Percentage of Students 'Agreeing' or 'Strongly Agreeing' with the each item

Item	Percentage students (%)
There is someone in my school I could talk to about religious and moral questions	63
My school has somewhere I could go for prayer or reflection	46
The RE teachers normally take Assemblies in my school	27
Religious charities work with students in my school	27

said that RE teachers normally take Assemblies in their school, or that religious charities work with students in their school. Certainly this echoes the desire of many teachers to see assemblies as acts of collective worship which are at some remove from the RE class, despite the sense that RE is expressly intended to contribute to the overall personal and spiritual development of students. But, in many of the schools, assemblies still functioned, at least from a producer perspective, as sites for ethical and religious reinforcement, with the latter foregrounded in church schools. And indeed teachers, across a wide range of our schools, directly and indirectly considered charity to be a substantial activity and responsibility, with teachers repeatedly positioning their school as an ethically determined space. As one teacher opined, it is about the school's senior managers:

> They have to support a subject like RS to be in the place that we're currently at and I do go to schools where they've got one man and a dog department and a very low esteem and I think the other thing I would say and it's not just the teaching, it's everything else you build around it and there's a huge focus on charity. (Gorston)

Responses to the item on whether students have someone they can go to talk to about religious and moral questions appear to illustrate some of the key differences in the circumstances of minority students. For example, while 63 per cent of students overall agreed that there was someone they could talk to on these matters, among Catholics the figure was higher at 78 per cent, but among students from Other Faiths it was lower, at 51 per cent. In other words, a denominational school serving its own community is more likely to provide ethical and religious support for its students. That is not to say that schools do not provide some level of support, even in circumstances in which the school is not run by a denominational authority. We can see this in Table 8.9, which demonstrates the pattern of agreement and disagreement with the second item

Table 8.9 Responses to the item: 'My school has somewhere I could go for prayer or reflection'

Response	Catholic	Other Christian	Other Faith	No Religion	All students
Agree/strongly agree	85*	17*	52	16*	46
Disagree/strongly disagree	9*	67*	30	54*	37

Note: *statistically significant

above, that is, whether schools have somewhere for students to go for prayer or reflection. As we can see from Table 8.9, the proportion of Catholic students who agree that this facility exists is significantly higher than other students, while the responses for Other Christian students and those with no religion are significantly lower.

A small, but statistically higher, proportion of students from Other Faiths said that RE teachers are more likely to take Assembly in their schools, in comparison to all other students. Perhaps, not surprisingly, a much higher proportion of Catholic students (51%) say that religious charities work with students in their school, in comparison with all other students.

Curriculum areas

As we have seen in the opening chapters of this work, a key theme emerging from conversations with staff and students is the relative position of RE. In most of our schools, including church schools, many teachers complained that the subject was not considered to be as important as many others. Such sentiment has a considerable history with Greer (1972) observing that, even in Northern Ireland, RE was generally considered to be a 'cinderella' subject, at least in 'controlled' schools. Consequently, we were interested in the role of the curriculum in schools and the comparative impact of RE as a curriculum subject. Participants in the Delphi seminar foregrounded the function of RE as a vehicle for educating about multiculturalism and pluralism (Baumfield et al. 2012), hardly a contentious claim given the plethora of papers on the topic. This ubiquitous concern with multiculturalism, which we have discussed elsewhere in this volume, was also evident in the discussions and focus groups with students. We were therefore concerned with understanding how widespread was their sense of RE providing a preparation to live and work in a diverse society. We began by asking students how often they read about the experiences of different cultural or religious groups in a range of curriculum areas. Table 8.10 indicates the proportion who said that they read a lot about other groups. Two features of this table are immediately striking: the first is that so many reported that they have read about different cultural or religious groups in RE classes; the second is that so few say this about all the other listed areas of the curriculum. There is little variation across the denominational groups on these responses, except that Catholics were more likely to say they dealt with diversity a lot in History (23%), while those from Other Faiths were significantly less likely to say this

Table 8.10 Percentage of students who agreed that they read 'a lot' about experiences of different cultural or religious groups in different subject areas

Subject	Students (%)
Religious Education	44
History	17
Personal and Social Health Education	9
English	8
Modern Languages	7

(8%); and, those with no religion were significantly more likely to say they dealt with diversity in English (12%).

Given that it would be well nigh impossible to pick up any introductory text on education that failed to offer a significant discussion of the topic, its perceived near absence from the curriculum experience of the students is indeed remarkable. Table 8.11 further focuses on this issue by displaying students' views on how effectively they have been prepared to live and work in diverse societies, partly through being provided with opportunities to engage with diversity in their classrooms. The contrast with the findings of the earlier questions (as seen in Table 8.11) is that a little under two-thirds of students reported that they are comfortable working with students from different backgrounds in their classrooms, but only about a third say that school has helped them get along with members of different religious groups or prepared them to understand or work with people from different religious backgrounds.

On the one hand, Other Faiths students were more likely than students as a whole to say that school has helped them 'a lot' to prepare for working with people who are different from them (46%), while those with no religion were significantly less likely to say this (26%). On the other hand, while they said that they feel prepared to work in diverse contexts, the results also suggest that they were not taught to understand diverse perspectives. When asked whether lessons at school had helped them better understand points of view different from their own, Catholics were more likely to say that the lessons did help them a lot (43%), while those from Other Faiths were significantly less likely to say this (23%). While we do not wish to overdetermine these results, we do know from other studies that good education can significantly contribute to positive attitudes towards the other (Hornberger 1982). Moreover, Contact Theory (Allport 1954; Pettigrew & Tropp 2006) would suggest that mixing with the other is likely to conduce to having more positive attitudes towards them. Indeed, Breen (2009) argues from a localized ethnographic study that cultivating a respect for, and a need to live with,

Table 8.11 Percentage of students who answered 'a lot' to the following items

Item	Students (%)
In your classroom, how comfortable are you working with students from different cultural or religious backgrounds?	62
When you get a job, has your school prepared you to work with people who are of a different religious background?	34
Do you think lessons at school have helped you to better understand points of view different from your own?	33
Do you believe your school has helped you get along better with members of other religious groups?	30

Table 8.12 Responses to the question: 'Do you believe your school has helped you get along better with members of other religious groups?'

Response|	Students in diverse schools (%)	Students in denominational schools (%)	Significance
Not at all	27	16	*
A little	48	50	Ns
A lot	25	34	*

the other is a motive force in Catholic schools, but we believe that such an impulse is far from universally evident in Catholic schools (McGovern 2010). Ironically, we are faced with some fairly uncomfortable possibilities about the efficacy of our endeavours to educate for engagement with the other in common schools!

When we examine some of the responses to the third question above, we find another interesting, if perhaps counterintuitive, answer. As we can see in Table 8.12, when asked whether school helped them get along better with members of other religious groups, students in denominational schools were significantly more likely to affirm this experience, in comparison with students in diverse schools. Of course it is possible that students in denominational schools have imbibed the discursive practices better than other cohorts, and there is some evidence to suggest this as a possibility (Conroy et al. 1998). Certainly the classroom engagements and teacher discourse in such schools were no less occupied with considerations of multiculturalism than was the case for schools in general.

Religious Education as a curriculum subject

Perhaps the dominant consideration for professionals, teachers and students across the three years of the study is the place of RE in the firmament of education as a whole. In one sense, this entire study is a reflection of concerns about status. In the Delphi seminar, our participants considered the status of the subject at some length. While the picture was nuanced, certain themes emerged that re-surfaced in the ethnography, with respondents deliberating on the absence of religious literacy as a proximate cause and consequence of any putative failure of Religious Education. However, any such epistemic failures had to be juxtaposed with what one participant vocalized as the main culprit in such perceived inadequacy of status, when she observed that 'non specialism is one of the major barriers to the subject, and that school leaders don't rate the significance of Religious Education and . . . treat it in a way that they wouldn't dream of treating another subject' (university lecturer and senior figure in professional development). On this theme, another senior figure (former Chair of a national organization) opined that head teachers do not register shortages of RE teachers because RE is 'used as a timetable filler'. It would be absurd to think that such senior figures in the field were not more absorbed with what constituted good Religious Education and, as we have discussed earlier, this was an area of substantial contestation. These status anxieties resurfaced in myriad ways in the schools – from the dependence on non-specialists, considered to be largely inappropriate, through impoverished resources, on to student indifference. Against such a background, it was important to further explore questions about the status of Religious Education as a curriculum subject. Table 8.13 shows that a little over one-half of the students responded that Religious Education was 'interesting', a little under a half said it was an 'important subject in their school', and somewhat fewer considered it to be 'one of the easiest subjects to pass'. There was a difference among the students in their judgement of the importance of Religious Education, with a significantly higher proportion of Catholics agreeing or strongly agreeing that it is important in their school (68%), compared with students with no religion (32%). Of course, given that church schools' very being is rooted in religion, it is remarkable that almost a third did not agree that it was important in their school. Once again, this echoes the ambivalent attitudes in some church schools and, in the iterative process of dissemination, the comments

Table 8.13 Students who 'Agreed' or 'Strongly Agreed' with the following items

Item	Students (%)
Religious Education classes are interesting	55
Religious Education is an important subject in my school	48
Religious Education is one of the easiest subjects to pass	44

from a senior church official who observed that a number of Catholic schools, with which he dealt, did not hold Religious Education in high esteem.

These two groups (Catholic and No Religion) also differed in their judgement on whether Religious Education classes were interesting, with more Catholics than those with no religion agreeing that they were. However, the overall pattern fell just short of statistical significance.

It might be suggested that many of the issues raised in this volume, with respect to Religious Education, feature as issues, challenges or concerns across the curriculum. As we have suggested already and illustrated elsewhere (Conroy et al., 2012; Lundie and Conroy, 2012), the comparison fails to hold good on a number of counts. Despite the complex strategies adopted by many professionals to 'normalize' it, Religious Education is seen to be different. It was this enduring sense of difference that motivated us to explore a little further students' judgements on RE's relative standing in relation to other subjects. For what may be considered as mainstream subjects, the pattern was clear and differed little across the groups. For example, 68 per cent of students said that Religious Education was 'less important' or 'much less important' than Maths or Science, while only 8 per cent said the reverse. Similarly, 69 per cent of students said that Religious Education was 'less important' or much 'less important' than English or History, with 7 per cent saying the reverse. The pattern of judgement between Religious Education and Citizenship/PSHE was, however, more varied and interesting. Hence, as we can see in Table 8.14, while the modal response was to say that they did not know whether Religious Education or Citizenship/PSHE were equally as important or not, Catholics were more likely to rate Religious Education as important, in comparison with students from Other Faiths and those with no religion.

Table 8.14 Students responses: 'Importance of Religious Education compared to citizenship/PSHE'

Response	Catholic (%)	Other Christian (%)	Other Faiths (%)	No Religion (%)	All (%)
Much more important	20*	20	9*	9*	14
More important	28*	19	22	17	22
Do not know	40	46	47	52	46
Less important	4	9	10	10	8
Much less important	7	7	13	12	10

Note: * indicates statistical significance

These broad patterns were largely confirmed by a further set of questions where we asked the students which subject Religious Education was most and least like. There was a clear consensus that Religious Education was least like Maths, with almost three quarters of the students mentioning this subject. A further 12 per cent said Religious Education was least like Science. By contrast 3 per cent said that Religious Education was least like Modern Languages and only 2 per cent said it was least like Citizenship/PSHE. The pattern was confirmed when the reverse question was asked, with 54 per cent saying Religious Education was most like Citizenship/PSHE as a subject, 15 per cent saying it was most like Modern Languages and 14 per cent saying it was most like History. Overall, the pattern of responses just reached statistical significance: the modal category for all students as the 'most like' subject for Religious Education was still Citizenship/PSHE, but Catholics were significantly less likely to say this (41%) when compared with Non-Christians (66%).

Pedagogy of RE classes

What emerged from the varied strands of our investigation was the diversity in pedagogic practice. However, it was found that teachers, often in quite challenging circumstances, were committed to the social and pedagogic purposes of Religious Education. As one head teacher (St Bede's) stated, 'staff and students see the role of RE as going beyond the classroom and permeating the school community.' Or again, as the deputy head teacher of another school (Wallace) observed, the purpose of RE was 'to raise awareness, give a background to many cultures that do exist in our country but maybe as minority cultures, minority religions in this country, but I also see the gaining of skills, based on computer skills in researching skills, evaluating skills. I see that side of RE as well.' However, such apparently laudable attachments had to sit alongside the students' observations that the purpose was often simply to pass the examination or indeed, on many occasions, that it was pointless. Because of these conflicting impulses and descriptions, we wished to explore further students' views on the nature of classroom practice in Religious Education and the perceived impact of such classes in preparing them to live and work in a diverse society. The first of a series of questions asked students for their views on the wider social impact of Religious Education. Table 8.15 reveals that over three-quarters of our students agreed that their teachers promoted better understanding of difference and that Religious Education as a subject contributed to this process. Furthermore, only

Table 8.15 Students who 'agree or strongly agree' with the following statements

Statements	Students (%)
My teachers encourage me to understand people who are different from me	78
Religious Education helps people understand others who are different from them	77
Religious Education encourages people to stay with their own kind	25

a quarter of our students agreed with the suggestion that Religious Education promoted an exclusive, inward orientation. For all the limits of situation and place, of personal disposition and resource, of epistemic and cultural confusion, respondents generally saw their teachers' efforts as positive with respect to education for otherness. This is an important finding, given the very complex, contradictory and conflicted nature of much that we observed.

It was only with respect to the last of these statements that any statistically significant differences emerged. In the overall sample, 8 per cent strongly agreed that religion encouraged people to stay with their own kind. This view was held by significantly more of those from Other Faiths (14%) and by significantly fewer of those with no religion (2%). Of course, it is not possible to establish causal relationships here. However, given that the state schools we looked at included some serving communities whose population largely comprised of Other Faiths, it may be that the force and shape of the community at large, and concomitant attachments of students, determined the sense of 'staying together'. This pattern was even clearer when we compared the views of students in diverse classes with those in more religiously homogeneous spaces. Among those in diverse classes, 15 per cent agreed or strongly agreed that Religious Education encouraged people to stay with their own kind, in comparison with 32 per cent of those in denominational contexts. Similarly, while 25 per cent of those in diverse classes strongly disagreed with this statement, only 16 per cent of those in denominational classes strongly disagreed with it. In other words, students in denominational contexts were somewhat more likely to say that Religious Education encourages people to stay with their own kind. Perhaps this is not surprising since it was clear throughout the study that whatever concessions have been made over time to the evolution of Religious Education as an educational rather than catechetical or evangelical engagement, church (especially Catholic) schools, foregrounded the cohesion of their credal attachments. St Bede's was

Table 8.16 Occurrence of exploration of controversial issues

Type of class	Students (%) who stated that this occurred 'a lot'
Religious Education	40
Citizenship	27
History	16

fairly typical in this regard, where the aims of RE were to impart knowledge and develop skills to primarily understand their own faith, the perspectives of some other Christian and world faiths and to develop as an active member of society, living according to Catholic values, or their own positive values if not a Catholic. As the Head of Department observed, 'our format in the RE classroom is where they get to learn the vocabulary and the terminology and maybe to identify certain aspects and then they go out the classroom better able to engage in a religious aspect, they're given that knowledge in the classroom.'

RE was often considered by teachers and our Delphi professionals to be a site, possibly *the* pre-eminent site, for raising difficult and controversial ethical and social issues. Indeed, one teacher (Brockton) claimed that her university tutors explicitly told their students 'to be controversial in the classroom'. Hence, it was important to get some broader sense of the students' perceptions on the extent to which controversial issues were addressed in various curriculum areas, including Religious Education. From Table 8.16 we can see that students were more likely to say controversial issues were discussed in Religious Education classes, when compared with classes in Citizenship or History. This view of Religious Education classes was expressed by significantly more Catholics (52%) and significantly fewer students from Other Faiths (26%) in the sample.

Following on from this, we posed a series of questions about the nature of the Religious Education classroom, as we were interested in the extent to which students perceived their class to encourage discussion and debate. Before doing this, we wanted to check if the students felt that the language of Religious Education classrooms was in any way confusing. However, fewer than one-in-five students agreed that this was so. In Table 8.17, we see the responses to a series of items on the type of teaching styles that students experience in Religious Education classrooms. The most striking feature of these responses is that students describe Religious Education classes as places where there appears to be a lot more discussion and engagement with teachers, in comparison with other classes. By contrast, less than a third of students report that they write a lot more in Religious Education classrooms. We also deliberately asked two questions which contained

Table 8.17 Content of religious education classes: Responses to statements

Statements	Students (%) who 'agree' or 'strongly agree'
In RE we discuss issues a lot more than in other classes	69
In RE we listen to the teacher talking a lot more than in other classes	53
In RE we just talk about issues all the time	37
In RE we write a lot more than in other classes	30
In RE we watch videos all the time	20

a negative connotation. However, fewer than two-in-four students agreed that in Religious Education classrooms they 'just talk about issues all the time', while only one-in-five said they watched videos all the time. Hence, it would appear that, not only do the students say that Religious Education classes are more interactive than other classes, but they also suggest that the nature of the activity undertaken is not simply for its own sake, or to use up the time. While the relative consideration afforded to the role and function of discussion in Religious Education is echoed in provision in other parts of Europe, this should not be seen as a validation of its pedagogic or developmental efficacy. As we have discussed elsewhere, it is too often that teachers struggle to effectively use the open-ended question to good pedagogic effect. However, it is clear that discussion is much more commonplace in Religious Education in UK schools than in many other polities, where students sometimes appeared a little nonplussed by the invitation to express their opinion. In her recent ethnographic study of dialogue in Estonian schools, Schihalejev (2009) points to the difficulties in a culture unused to the open-ended invitation, 'Whenever the teacher asked an open question about students' opinions or preferences, they seemed puzzled and switched off' (282). This insecurity in an adequate knowledge base rarely appeared to trouble students in UK schools. Moreover, looked at less benignly, the one-in-five students who report that they spend a lot of their time 'watching videos' certainly echoes our findings that even in these 'committed' schools, where most students were studying for public examinations, time-filling activities were certainly not unknown.

Catholics students were significantly more likely to agree that in Religious Education classes they discuss issues a lot more than in other classes (56% of Catholics versus 44% overall). Similarly, while 53 per cent of all the students agreed or strongly agreed that they listen to the teacher talking a lot more in Religious

Education classes, this was so for 70 per cent of Catholics. Catholics were also significantly more likely to strongly disagree that they write a lot more in RE class (17%), in comparison with the sample as a whole (11%), although more of them also agreed that they 'just talk about issues all the time' (48% of Catholics versus 37% overall). However, while 30 per cent of the students overall strongly disagreed that they watch videos all the time, this was so for 41 per cent of Catholics. It would appear that in the Catholic schools, teacher–student discussion was the dominant mode of pedagogical engagement. Again, reports of the precedence afforded discussion cannot and should not be taken as an indicator of the quality or efficacy of such discussions and, as we have discussed earlier and elsewhere (Conroy et al. 2012), discussion can mask substantive and pedagogic weaknesses.

Two interesting patterns emerged when we compared the responses for students in diverse schools with students in denominational classes. In diverse schools, 14 per cent agreed that they spent a lot of time writing in RE classes, but this was the case for 26 per cent of those in denominational classes. Also, in diverse schools, 28 per cent of students agreed or strongly agreed that they spent all of their time watching videos, compared with 15 per cent of those in denominational schools. The corollary of this was that 21 per cent of those in diverse schools strongly disagreed that they watched videos all the time, and in comparison, 36 per cent of students in denominational schools strongly disagreed that they watched videos all the time.

Overall, the data suggest that students see Religious Education classes as distinctive, interactive and perhaps, in a number of instances, as more engaging than many other classes. When we consider this in the light of other data, it may be that the freer pedagogy of Religious Education classes reflects the lower significance and standing of the subject. However, if the class were simply seen as a waste of time, then more of the students would have been likely to say that their class time was spent in dull and uninteresting activities, such as simply watching videos, and this is clearly not the case. Furthermore, there is some evidence that Religious Education is taken a little less seriously in schools with diverse students populations, and that Catholic students experience the most positive and active pedagogy in RE classes.

Conclusion

As we have suggested throughout, this chapter cannot be read as a free-standing analysis of student attitudes, but must be understood as a refraction, albeit important, of the overall investigation. What it does do is provide an analysis of survey data from a sample of 535 students drawn from 14 schools in England, Scotland and Northern Ireland. A little over two-thirds of our sample described themselves as religious and a somewhat larger proportion of our sample described their families as religious. Most of our students hoped to go to university and felt encouraged to do so by their teachers. Most students described their schools as reasonably progressive places, where racism is challenged and support for the environment is encouraged. However, only a minority of students said that their schools encouraged them to carry out voluntary work in the community, and this was most often described by students from Catholic or Other Faith backgrounds. In fact, the various extracurricular areas appeared more likely to be encouraged in schools with a denominational enrolment. Where the experience of Catholic students differed from that of students from Other Faiths was that the former were more often in schools which the Catholic Church owned, or had a formal role in the management of, and consequently was able to provide stronger direct institutional support, and indeed a more highly specified direction to the practices of Religious Education.

Religious Education is a subject which is not rated as highly as most other curriculum subjects, although there is some evidence that it is linked, by many students, to Citizenship/PSHE. These potential links reflect the emergent struggle between traditional (Religious Education) and 'modern' (Citizenship) subjects (Watson 2004; Freathy 2008), both of which seek to address values and principles, but are set in different contexts and draw on different concepts, claims and literature. Religious Education does emerge, in comparison with other curriculum subjects, as an area where students say they have an opportunity to learn about the experience of different cultural and religious groups. Ironically, this may be linked to the lower status of the subject as a whole, but contrary to this, we see that the subject is rated as both more important in denominational contexts and as contributing more to preparing for diversity. Such intimations are linked to a further interesting finding which emerged from the data: contrary to those who criticize denominational schools, students in denominational contexts are generally more likely to say that their school helped to prepare them to live and work in a diverse society. That said, this last finding may be tempered a little by another that students in these contexts were also more likely to say that Religious Education encouraged people to stay with their own kind.

Overall, the survey data suggests that Religious Education maintains an interesting position in the school curriculum: it is considered by many students to be distinctive, with a more active pedagogy and a more engaged approach to wider societal issues. While students generally rate it as less important than most other curriculum areas, they do not describe it in terms to suggest that it is viewed as a 'time-filler' in the curriculum. Rather, there is a sense that it plays a more significant role than most other subjects in preparing young people to live and work in a diverse society. Given that Citizenship education has emerged as a new topic across the United Kingdom, it is also interesting to note the linkage made by students between these two areas and to wonder whether or not these two subjects may yet compete for the same educational terrain.

Conclusions: Imagining and Re-imagining Religious Education

A few years ago, over lunch, a very senior social scientist expressed some frustration at the inability of educationalists to tell politicians what worked. 'They just want to know', he observed, 'which approach to literacy is best.' While the frustration may be understandable, the belief that politicians want a straightforward answer to a straightforward question is rather less so. It is less so because the conditions within which the question might be asked are not abstractions, detached from politicians' own normative predilections and attachments, but concrete consequences of choices that they, together with others in a polity, take. How else are we to explain the emergence of a major research programme devoted to the advanced study of religion after many years of benign neglect, except by recourse to the coalescing of personal, professional and political interests (Ball 1997). Of course, it might be suggested that the politicians recognized the political importance of enhancing our understanding of religion in an era of substantial international instability, a proximate cause of which, it is often suggested, is religious conflict (Huntington 1996). While this explanation enjoys some plausibility, it can hardly be the whole explanation, given that international and local conflicts suffused with religious claims have hardly become less substantial or significant in terms of world order. Rather, the rapid downgrading of religious education (a cipher for the earlier political belief in the importance of the religious) in England marks a shift in politico-ethical attachment that is personal yet indicative of systemic weakness.

These observations are a prelude to recognizing that the question, 'Does RE Work?' is not amenable to a straightforward yes or no; however much politicians and policymakers might like it to be otherwise – not, as we have attempted to illustrate, because it is impossible to answer the question, but because the terms of reference within which Religious Education operates and its consequent objectives are so multiple, diffuse and fluid as to make it well nigh impossible to offer anything like a comprehensive answer. Does this then mean that the title of this volume is no more than a rhetorical device that is not susceptible to a reasonable answer? We would suggest not. While acknowledging that there is no simple answer, asking the question in this way helps to clarify what would constitute *working*. After all, in our Delphi seminar, as well as in a wide variety of transactions in the classroom and observations of both students and teachers, there was no shortage of claims as to what kind of understanding, attitudes and dispositions Religious Education was supposed to realize. Having looked carefully at the question and the kinds of observations and reflections offered in this study, it would be easy to claim that perhaps Religious Education *does not* work and that threats to the subject lie in its being reduced to the communication of the kind of vague, facile and anodyne stereotypes intimated above, and let matters rest there. Attractive though such an acknowledgement might be, it is insufficient to the task. Rather, what we witnessed suggested that in trying to cover too many bases Religious Education, as practised, often failed to adequately cover very many, if any, of these. Religious Education teachers often felt under exceptional pressure, significant numbers of them appeared to be insufficiently sophisticated in their understanding of religion, resources varied enormously but were, most especially in the common school, often inadequate and the examination system *acted* in ways that were unlikely to conduce to effective learning.

In the course of this volume, we have attempted to lay before the reader an account of Religious Education that documents the modes and manner of its daily transactions in a diverse range of school contexts. We do not suggest that these are *universal* but would claim that they are *indicative*. Their indicative status is authenticated by the depth and triangulations afforded by the linguistic ethnography, alongside the quantitative and hermeneutical methods at the heart of the enquiry. Of course, not *all* Religious Education is dysfunctional, but here we have tried to illustrate the very real and substantive challenges that arise out of its specific forms of cultural and pedagogical engagement. The data provide abundant examples of teachers rising successfully to these challenges with genuine ambition, while frequently having their efforts frustrated by systemic shortcomings and structural obstacles. Some of this ambition is certainly frustrated by the performative imperatives of an examination-driven curriculum, and the cultural anxieties about the role and position of Religious Education as a subject. None of this should be considered, however, as a counsel of despair but, rather an invitation to re-imagine the rationale, objects and pedagogies of and in Religious Education, present and future.

In much of what we unearthed, there was minimal evidence of the use of primary religious texts as a resource for understanding the claims and experiences of religious communities, their histories and theologies. Here text is taken to include not only scriptures but theological, religiously philosophical and other primary texts. Where such textual engagement was in evidence, it tended to be perfunctory and tokenistic with an emphasis on literalist proof texting and sampling. It is not difficult to trace the origins of this eschewal of the text, which in contemporary Religious Education has its roots in the developmental psychology of Goldman (1968), the rise of child centredness (Hull 1984) and the egalitarian re-shaping impulses of phenomenology (Smart & Horder 1978). Here the fear of literalism, coupled with an anxiety that attention to the Christian scriptures and attendant theological texts would be considered inappropriately partisan, drove teacher education to devalue the text as a prized source and resource for religious understanding in the classroom. Chater and Erricker (2012), in common with some of the teachers in our study, conclude on the basis of developments of this kind, that the epistemic conditions of late modernity are such that the text is irreversibly evacuated of its traditional prestige and indeed should be replaced by an entirely personalized form of experiential RE. From our observations, such pessimism is both unfounded and likely to exacerbate the conditions it seeks to remediate. For one thing, it is clear that for a cross-section of students in our study, who were located in schools with quite divergent characteristics, the text retained its religiously inflected status. To marginalize the significance of texts in this fashion therefore, makes Religious Education vulnerable to a disarticulation with the lives of students and the communities they inhabit, imperiling the requirement for education to connect with, and explore meaningfully, the lived experience of learners. Even for those pupils without express religious attachment, this narrowed attitude to texts ignores a key responsibility of Religious Education – to introduce the originary sources of religious meanings as understood in the life-world of the believer.

While this trend can be firmly located within the specific pedigrees of Religious Education, it has an undeniably wider genealogy in the recent histories of modern education. Modern Religious Education, in common with many of the established critical-interpretive disciplines of the 'forms of knowledge' curriculum that emerged from the democratic educational reforms of the post-war period, is subject to two powerful and, we propose, overlapping impulses. In the first place, the inexorable rise of the culture of performativity, characterized by regimes of inspection, regulation, examination and related instruments of late modern societies of control, impinges directly and damagingly on Religious Education. This is pervasively visible in the reductive treatment of religious text, practice and reflection throughout classroom learning and the implicit subordination of these to the examination requirements and outcomes by which subject recognition is now routinely conferred and maintained across the contemporary curriculum.

The second driver has emerged from a superficially quite contrasting set of educational values, commonly associated with progressivism and now evident as the prevailing methodological orthodoxy across the social sciences. This is the practice of 'social constructivism', which since the 1970s has assumed a constitutive role in the understanding of pedagogy, classroom learning and disciplinary knowledge production at almost every level of education. The signature features of constructivism – with their antifoundationalist emphasis on the joint construction of meaning, the fluid dynamics of classroom rationality, and the interactive relations of teacher and pupils in the shared pursuit of meaning – combine to reinforce a conception of Religious Education that is insensitive to foundationally distinct religious and metaphysical worldviews and which frequently deprives the subject of key elements such as authority and propositional content.

These seemingly opposed ideological influences, bearing down upon the curriculum, in fact collude in destabilizing the teaching of Religious Education. Performativity attenuates meaning through the artificial imposition of measures of effectiveness at variance with depth and complexity of the subject, while the uncritical embrace of social constructivism gives permission to a reductive depletion of the *value* invested in meaning. While these pressures are common to the humanities and social science curriculum in the contemporary school, in the case of many curriculum areas, justifications amenable to the expression of core aims and consonant with such reductive pressures regularly emerge. Although detrimental to meaning and propositional content across a range of subjects, these influences need not fatally undermine the fundamental purposes of, for example, literary or historical studies, which can retrieve a viable rationale from their second-order contributions to functional outcomes such as literacy skills, interpretative evaluation and even employability. Whenever Religious Education has recourse to similar remedies, however, these second-order justifications are secured at the cost of a fundamental redefinition of the meaning and purpose of the study of religions. Rather than abandon the text in the name of second-order goals, we would propose a refurbished approach to the text as one of the planks in a re-imagined Religious Education whereby, as they move through the high school, students are invited into a critical engagement with primary texts.

Such primary texts will, of course, include sacred texts but should not be limited to these. They should include first hand encounters with theological, liturgical and ethical texts from varied traditions. This goes far beyond the, nevertheless important, injunction of the Religious Education Council that teachers should 'check whether resources draw on primary sources, which contribute to accurate representation of religious traditions and may foster pupils' interpretive skills'. (REC n.d.). As students move through school, the nature and range of texts should include theological, sociological and psychological resources, incentivizing a better engagement with a small number of high-quality texts.

Our focus on the final phase of compulsory Religious Education was, some might suggest, bound to have a distorting effect on perceptions of the subject and the nature of the learning and teaching. After all, the argument goes (and indeed was often articulated by teachers and students in our study), much more interesting work is carried out in other years when students and teachers are under less pressure. While, in a fairly obvious sense, the first part of this claim may well be true (that exams distort) and Religious Education is clearly not immune from the generalized pressures on both curriculum and pedagogy, the second part does not axiomatically follow. If RE teachers and leading professionals consider the examination system, the kinds of questions proffered to students and the kinds of responses expected, to be so profoundly flawed, who is to blame? Have not examinations and syllabuses been written by professionals? Are there not better ways to think about assessing students? Indeed, we might ask, are there not better ways of asking particular kinds of questions than would appear to be in the often desiccated and dislocated questions that skate along the morphological surface of religion? Might we not consider locating religious and theological claims within an evolutionary or genealogical paradigm? By this we mean that locating the evolution of ideas in their historical context and tracing their connections as responses to historically prior ideas may offer the students a more robust notion of how religious ideas are formed. It would also facilitate the development of their sense of the ways in which religious beliefs confirm and compete within and across traditions as well as how they impact on, and are impacted by, a range of social and cultural forces. With few exceptions, the teachers in our study considered the short courses, which have of late expanded exponentially, to be too compressed, too superficial and somewhat ineffective in cultivating anything like religious understanding or literacy. Despite their very serious reservations, teachers continued to submit their students in large numbers. They did so on the (understandable) grounds that examination success was critical to the position of the subject in *their* schools and with students where the subject was often not highly regarded. 'Submission' here covers some interesting territory – in 'submitting' their students teachers were themselves routinely 'submitting' to a system in which they had little faith as either a social or an intellectual exercise.

This is hardly the first study to suggest that there might be some problems with high stakes testing (Clarke & Gregory 2003; Nichols & Berliner 2007), but here it becomes ever more apparent that many public tests fail to either nurture students' abilities or assess their capabilities. Moreover, it is clear that the relationship between commercial examination companies, authors and the classroom is not self-evidently conducive to effective education or to the cultivation of religious literacy. By the same token, we find teachers who compromise themselves in the hope of retaining the position of their subject in what can be a somewhat inhospitable environment. In making these observations, we are again not offering a counsel of despair. Rather we believe, from our engagement with pupils, teachers and schools, that it is possible to assess RE in a manner that has intellectual and ethical integrity. This would entail a concern to be true to the subject under scrutiny and would require assessment instruments that invited students to attend to primary sources as well as to the nature of religious and theological language, and the genealogy of religious conceits. With regard to the last of these, it was evident that much Religious Education failed to locate religious ideas in their historical and discursive contexts, and that such a positioning could offer an enhanced understanding of how religious ideas and their accompanying expressions emerged. This would stand in stark contrast to the kinds of litanies of beliefs, practices and vocabulary that too often stood in for religious literacy. In those classrooms that bore witness to the possibilities of RE, teachers were unafraid to engage in complexity, to extend students' vocabulary and widen their conceptual horizons. Such practices included challenging many of the ethico-emotional attachments which students (and teachers) substituted for *knowledge* and *understanding*. Some of the most interesting practices were seen in schools where teachers worked with the students on understanding the functions and functionality of analogy and religious symbolism as core skills very early in the curriculum.

One of the most significant claims for Religious Education was that it should be an educational resource in challenging racism and promoting multiculturalism. At the level of an ethical entailment in a complex plural society, this can hardly be unreasonable. The charge to take seriously racial, sexual and religious subordination is as necessary as it is complex, given the ways across the generations in which white male sexual power had been transposed into white racial power (Pinar 2006). The complicity of religions in systems of sexual and racial abuse is a legitimate site for interrogation in the classroom. However, to treat such matters with the cultivated attention they deserve requires an altogether more robust account of how religious claims intersect with social practices. It is certainly the case that some schools (those serving communities with religious identities – not at all the same thing as religiously denominated schools) considered education in religion as one of the foundations of multicultural education. But, as we have tried to illustrate, this frequently found little enough resonance in the daily lives of the students; something that was also picked up in the Forum Theatre reflections. The failures to distinguish properly between civics, ethics, religion and education are both a methodological problem and a philosophical conundrum around what might constitute viable 'religious literacy'. The question then remains, whether or not the best way of approaching multiculturalism through the RE lens is the descriptive or even the ethical. In the senior school, might it not be better to develop courses that pay attention to the complex intertwining of doctrine, power, race and culture? In this way, we might be able to combat the sense that emerges throughout this study of a flattened religious landscape.

Perhaps the most salient feature of our excavations, and one that underpins much of our deliberation here, is the question of language. This is hardly surprising if we treat Pinker's claim that we are verbivores with any seriousness. At one level, what we witnessed repeatedly were teachers' conflicted efforts to bring a religious language to bear in a radically desacralized space. Exacerbated by resource and time constraints, this proved extraordinarily challenging. Being unsure how to approach traditional religious (theological) language, teachers tended to concentrate on a descriptive language, *a naming of parts*, so to speak. A richer use of language was apparent here and there, often reflecting a more philosophically sophisticated account of religious beliefs and attachments. It is ironic that much of the language that was made available in the classroom was descriptive and centred on data transmission and recall. But, for as long as this stage of education is dominated by flawed and etiolated examinations that obsess over the parts while ignoring the whole, it is difficult to escape from the facile and the superficial. There are epistemologically, discursively and culturally more interesting ways of configuring the curriculum around what it is to think and speak about religion that are more faithful to the landscape of the thing itself. These would include acquainting students with the genealogy of religious concepts and their linguistic forms, and exploring the relationships between linguistic and semiotic representations of religion. The very best teachers are already engaged in opening up new linguistic and conceptual horizons to students. Too often however, real opportunities are glaringly missed as in this instance, where the teacher (Castle) casually observes that he was unsure as to why lots of things happened up a mountain. One of the students suggested that maybe they wanted to get closer to God. The teacher then asks 'is that what you think? I thought God was everywhere so why go up a mountain.' He then follows with 'but that is just language'. A student interjects, 'well why does it say in the bible that Jesus ascended into heaven?' The teacher moved on and did not explore the notion of place in religion, missing an opportunity to explore the language of afterlife/paradise/heaven and *heaven* knows what else!

In schools where religion was treated seriously, and where the community served had significant proportions of actively religious people, the teachers (and the school community) clearly considered that they had significant obligations to foster community relations and worked hard to do so. Many considered that learning about the other would improve inter-communal strife. Hence one teacher observes that,

> The profile of RE is very high here, they do lay a lot of weight on our subject purely for the fact that there is a history to the relationships between Muslims and Sikhs particularly and even Hindus as well, in that we had a stabbing and a killing in . . . one of the . . . parks, approximately seven years ago and I think it was felt that we would try to raise the profile across all the . . . community and even bring some of the community environment in for assemblies and things like that because obviously the more they get to know about other religions then the more likely they are to be friendly with them... (Longwood Grammar).

Perhaps to end, we might offer one cautionary, even with respect to our own analysis. In all of this, we should not underestimate the extent to which students are engaged in RE as a function of its not being treated seriously – they are relaxed in it and often the teachers work hard to engage students. During a conversation with students in Northwest, that is to some extent corroborated in our student questionnaire responses, they unequivocally ranked RE very low when compared to subjects such as English, Maths and Physics, but it was this very unimportance that they enjoyed – it was a site that was not to be treated too seriously, where they could 'have a laugh' and relax. If the goal of RE was to relax and have a laugh, then we might observe that it did indeed work. However, we must continue to ask, 'should classes in RE be enjoyable at the expense of the creation of a flat-pack theology, where students are somehow invited to build their own version of religion that embraces their spirituality but pays little enough attention to the linguistic and conceptual demands of the geneaologically rich traditions of religious systems, and the otherness that they embody?'

Appendices

Appendix A: Details on the schools included in this study

Pseudonym	Country	Region (inner city/ suburb/ rural commuter belt/ really rural)	Ethnic/Cultural/ Religious mix of students	Community context (i.e. deprived area? Note do we think this is relevant?	Religious affiliation	School type
Schools\ Bishop Fulton Catholic College	England	South East	Two single-sex schools on one site, ethnic and religious mix with about 60–80% Catholic, around 2,000 students	Inner city, area of deprivation	Roman Catholic	Voluntary aided
Schools\ Brockton Community School	England	South East	Mixed white and Afro-Caribbean, in an area of racial tensions, around 1,500 students	Inner city, area of deprivation	Non-denominational	Comprehensive
Schools\St John Fisher School	England	South East	Largely white, Catholic, over-subscribed, around 2,000 students	Suburban, some deprivation	Roman Catholic	Voluntary aided
Schools\ Armourers' Guild Academy	England	South East	Suburban, around 1,200 students	Suburban, wealthy	Ecumenical Christian	Voluntary controlled

Continued

Pseudonym	Country	Region (inner city/ suburb/ rural commuter belt/ really rural)	Ethnic/Cultural/ Religious mix of students	Community context (i.e. deprived area? Note do we think this is relevant?	Religious affiliation	School type
Schools\ Dundon Grammar	Scotland		Large town, white, some deprivation, around 1,500 students	In a deprived area of a large town	Non-denominational	Comprehensive
Schools\ Dungally College	Northern Ireland		Suburban, around 1,200 students, drawn from large catchment of feeder primaries, engineered mix of roughly 50/50 Protestant and Catholic	Suburban, but with non geographical catchment	Ecumenical Christian	Integrated
Schools\ Linden Girls' School	England	South East	Students almost entirely of Muslim and South Asian background, around 1,200 students	Inner city, area of deprivation	Non-denominational	Comprehensive
Schools\ Kinraddie Academy	Scotland		White, Scottish, around 600 students	Remote rural	Non-denominational	Comprehensive

Schools\Segget Academy	Scotland		White, Scottish, around 600 students	Rural, some outer commuter belt	Non-denominational	Comprehensive
Schools\St Athanasius Grammar	Northern Ireland		White, N. Irish, Catholic, around 600 students, academically selective	Rural	Roman Catholic	Grammar School
Schools\Burns Academy	Scotland	Rural commuter belt for large city	Mostly 'white' Scottish and non-religious	Mixed: within commuting belt for larger urban area, but also an area with council estates	Non-denominational	Comprehensive
Schools\St Ebba's High School	Scotland	Urban, but also rural commuter belt for large city	Mostly 'white' Scottish Catholics	Mixed (not affluent but no overwhelming areas of deprivation)	Roman Catholic	Comprehensive
Schools\Wallace High School	Scotland		Small town, white, some deprivation, around 1,000 students	Small town, large surrounding catchment	Non-denominational	Comprehensive
Schools\St Bede's High School	Scotland		Mostly 'white' Scottish Catholics	Suburban	Roman Catholic	Comprehensive

Continued

Pseudonym	Country	Region (inner city/ suburb/ rural commuter belt/ really rural)	Ethnic/Cultural/ Religious mix of students	Community context (i.e. deprived area? Note do we think this is relevant?	Religious affiliation	School type
Schools\Castle Grammar School	Northern Ireland		Mostly 'white' Northern Irish Protestant, academically selective	Rural	Non-denominational	Grammar school
Schools\Northwest High School	Northern Ireland		Mostly 'white' Northern Irish Protestant	Small town, large surrounding catchment	Non-denominational	Secondary modern
Schools\Holy Cross School	England	North East			Church of England	Voluntary aided
Schools\Northbridge School	England	North East			Non-denominational	Comprehensive
Schools\The Matilda's High School	England	North East			Non-denominational	Comprehensive
Schools\Gorston School	England	Outskirts of London	36% Muslims (non Asian) 46% Sikhs and Hindus (Asian) 18% 'whites' non religious	Large migrant population including asylum seekers	Non-denominational	Comprehensive

Schools\Dickson School	England	South East Rural 'middle England' but within commuting distance of two large cities	Mostly 'white' English who are non religious	Mostly middle class	Non-denominational	Comprehensive
Schools\Cooke's College	England	London	60% to 50% white (who are a mixture of non-religious and religious (C or E) 40% to 50% non-white and of that large minority most are African, Caribbean with bits of some Asian, some Oriental and some Turkish. The non-whites are dominated by the Afro-Caribbean who are mostly Evangelical.	Some students from low income families	Church of England	City academy
Schools\Longwood Grammar School	England	South East	Mostly White English	Suburban/Rural	Non-denominational	Grammar school

Appendix B: Ethnographic schedule

Classroom fieldwork

This appendix indicates the various ways in which the ethnographers gathered information. These schedules were designed to ensure that, as far as possible, similar kinds of information was being collected. In doing so we tried to ensure that we could acquire as rich a sense as possible of the institutions, their culture, leadership, visual climate; indeed their habitus.

Spatial/temporal information

- Layout of classroom
  - Photos of classroom as a reference point (displays, desk layout, presence or absence of religious images, etc.);
  - Get a desk plan from the teacher (to enable us to get to know who the students are and to identify who is speaking);
  - How room/space is used during teaching (i.e. small group work vs facing the front for a lecture);
  - Use of artefacts and teaching tools;
  - Use/Availability of IT.
- Wider school layout (to place classroom in the wider context of the school)
  - How the RE classroom compares to other classrooms;
  - What kinds of resources are available in other parts of the school? (i.e. library);
  - Communal areas (i.e. places where staff or students meet and chat). How are these used, what happens in them, how do teachers/students behave differently in them?
- Community layout (to place the school within the wider context of the community)
  - Where is the school located (map);
  - Urban/rural;
  - Social/ethnic class of neighbourhood;
  - Proximity of places of religious worship (Are these used for fieldtrips or as a source of guest speakers? Do these places have public events that students may attend without any link to the school?).
- Time of day when RE takes place (duration, format – modes of delivery, etc.)
- How much time within the school week do students and teachers devote to RE?

Teacher-student interaction

- Power relations
  - How authority is managed and maintained and how this might be affected by social variables (age, gender, ethnicity, religious background), for example, young teacher having problems controlling class and getting the respect of students, RE in a Catholic school taught by a nun as opposed to a layperson. Does classroom activity follow a predictable routine?
  - How might students undermine the authority of the teacher? (i.e. talking, saying 'you're not Muslims so how can you tell me, who is a Muslim, about Islam,' etc.)
  - Do students 'buy into' what they are being taught and the methods being used? (i.e. are they willing or reluctant participants, are they on task?)
  - The ways in which teachers present themselves to the students (i.e. giving personal info to the students so that they can see what their biases might be, for instance, religious background, marital status, sexuality, etc; clearly expressing their values or just sticking to the curriculum; willing to be open about how they may or may not agree with the curriculum; or taking that attitude that 'you're here to learn and you don't need to know anything about me').
    Note: this will clearly affect student-teacher relations and issues of authority and 'buy in.'
  - Quality of student-teacher relationship (language used to maintain authority over students).
- Discourse
  - 'teacher talk' about management and admin issues;
  - 'teacher talk' that merely provides a description (i.e. this is what happens during a Baptism);
  - 'teacher talk' that looks at conceptual issues (i.e. what is 'sin,' justice?);
  - 'teacher talk' that looks at more abstract issues;
  - teacher's questions to students that deal with administrative issues;
  - teacher's questions that test student's recall;
  - teacher's questions that examine student comprehension (i.e. what is justice?);
  - teacher's questions that examine how students can apply conceptual issues (i.e. can you give me an example of sin);

- teacher's questions that examine student ability to analyse or interpret;
- teacher's questions that examine student ability to synthesize data (i.e. what are common elements when we make comparisons of rites of passage?);
- teacher's questions that invite students to make evaluations or judgements;
- how students respond to such questions, if they answer in a way that is deemed 'acceptable' or correct by the teacher and classmates;
- how these interactions might change when lesson moves to small group work.
- Teaching methods/techniques versus pedagogical intentions;
- Teacher's self perception versus pupils' and other teachers' perspective (competence, rapport);
- Inclusion – description or engagement, language of challenge or compliance, do teachers assume all pupils have same beliefs, or take account of different cultures in the classroom? Where work is differentiated by pupil ability, does the work of the low ability group have the same broad learning aims as the high ability group?

Teachers and students' interaction with curriculum/resources and values

- Content of lesson and methods used to deliver
  - Didactic/reflective;
  - Content driven, topical, discussion, 'personal search';
  - Balance between student needs and exam cramming;
  - Bias;
  - We obviously need to see how this might stick to or deviate from how the head of RE sets the curriculum;
- Teachers' relationship with curriculum and resources
  - Awareness of available resources within school and wider, awareness of role of resources and curriculum guidance;
  - Are links made with other subjects, for example, history, art, social education, and are teachers able to make these links?
  - Teacher willingness to deviate from lesson plan and agreed syllabus/ accommodate contrary views/discuss controversial topics (what might their motivation be for doing this?);

- Control – are they planning own lessons or using what is given to them from others/teaching passively from text book? (if a text is used, which one and why? What ones were rejected?);
- Language used to talk about RE as a subject, and subject matter within it;
- Teachers' views of inspection and examination regime.
- Teachers' relationship with values of curriculum and resources
  - Are teacher values made explicit?
  - Are teachers aware of their own values and how this might influence their teaching?).
- Pupil relationship with curriculum/ resources (e.g. values/ content of curriculum and resources).
  - What values and influences do pupils bring to their learning – for example, external influences (parents, religious communities, media, other students)?

Note: We need to get a feel for the difference between the 'frontstage' (i.e. class room performance of the teacher (or student)) and the 'backstage' (i.e. curriculum planning meetings, how teachers go about making a lesson plan, how they are influenced by the need to get good exam results, what backstage student activities (i.e. gossip) might affect how they act in the classroom).

Non-teaching activities in the classroom

- Direct spiritual interventions, for example, prayer – how are these conducted? Pupil/teacher led? Are all pupils expected to take part?
- Behaviour management;
- Extracurricular activities centred around the RE classroom – are these connected to RE in any way, for example, Scripture Union, or are they unrelated in, for example, a chess club that meets in RE classroom because RE teacher supervises them?
- General student talk/non teaching student-teacher talk – is this different in the RE classroom than in other classes? Why might this be?

Whole school ethos and influence on relationships

- Are aims shared and embedded (in pedagogical practice, in staff-student relationships, in student-student relationships, in behaviour management, in school's public presentation, in management values, in teacher values)?

Student-student interaction

- Do certain students seem to dominate?
- How do students, deal with diversity among themselves (i.e. differences of gender, class, ethnic or religious background and hierarchies)? Where do students gain their understanding of diversity? From the RE classroom, from elsewhere in the school, from outside school?
- What happens in small group or project work?

How does RE teaching compare with that of other subjects?

- Teaching methods and course content;
- Perceived 'usefulness';
- Status as a discipline;
- Characteristics of teachers, for example, promoted/unpromoted, active in wider life of the school, etc.
- Teacher-teacher interaction (outwith classroom)
  - Issues of hierarchy (how is RE syllabus designed and communicated?), that is, do they have group meetings or does the Head of Religious Education matter (note: it would be useful to attend a curriculum planning meeting)
  - How teachers talk about curriculum to other specialists (specialist discourse, buzzwords, current issues, hopes/fears)?
  - How does RE fit in with school management structure (is there a Head of Department? Is it embedded within a 'Humanities' faculty structure? How many teachers are specialists? How many non specialists teach RE?
  - How teachers relate to other subject specialists?
  - How do teachers talk about students?
  - How do teachers talk about school?
  - How are RE teachers viewed within school (status)?
  - Note: it will be interesting to track down new teachers or ones who taught RE in other schools to see how things in this school might differ from others.

Outside/guest speakers and partners involved in delivery and planning of RE, Field trips, etc.

- Who is involved and why?
- How are they identified?

- Frequency?
- What is their role and relationship with school?
- Do students find these valuable or useful?
- Do staff find these speakers' input useful?

Documentation to collect if available

- Minutes of dept planning meetings if available;
- Schemes of work, resources;
- 'Back room' resources, that is, materials given to the school by organizations promoting RE but not used, old textbooks, books in school library, etc.
- Any documentation involving curriculum;
- Documentation given out to students/parents about the RE programme (or anything that might well influence parent/student choice);
- Background info on the teachers (mini CV, which includes years of teaching, where, what types of schools, training (i.e. degrees), school RE results in league tables);
- Background info on students (i.e. looking for sociological variables like gender, class, religious background, are they/their family actively religious (we can get this sort of stuff via a questionnaire)).

Appendix C: Does RE work?: Background info questionnaire for teachers

Thank you for taking the time to fill out this questionnaire. The purpose of this is to give us some background information which will help us with our final analysis. There are some variables, such as type of school, your background as a teacher and your religious background (if any) that we think might affect what happens in the classroom in terms of the way in which you interact with the students and/or deliver material.

Please note: in order to keep our records straight, we will need to know the name of your school. However, all schools will be anonymous when our research material is published or presented. Individual teachers will also be anonymous and will be assigned a fake name. We can either choose one for you or you can choose your own fake name.

If you have any questions about the questionnaire, please do not hesitate in asking me. Your participation in filling out this questionnaire is totally voluntary. You may miss out any questions that you are not happy with.

Name of School:
Type of School:
Local Authority:
Teacher Identifier (please make up a name for yourself):
Position of Teacher:

Educational background

How many years have you been teaching? What subjects and where?
When and where did you get your teaching qualification? In what subject?
When and where did you do your first degree? In what subject?
Where did you go to school?

The school context

How many hours of RE do you teach per week? At what levels?
How does this compare to the rest of your timetable? (i.e. is it a major or minor part? Do you teach other subjects?)
Are you involved in school committees or activities (such as clubs or extra curricular activities)?
Are you involved with any aspect of your schools religious observance (if any)?

The importance of RE

What do you feel is the importance of RE for students in general?
What do you think is the importance of RE in your school?

General background information

Gender:
Age:
Religious affiliation (if any):

Would you say that you are actively religious? And if so, in what way? Has this had any impact or influence on your interactions with students or how you teach RE?

Are you involved in any community activities (outwith school) that involve religious or educational issues?

Appendix D: Interview questions for head teacher

Note: Researchers used this as a basic template and added some school-specific questions.

Intro

- Thanks
- Remind head teacher that he/she does not have to answer any question with which they are uncomfortable
- Ask if they know what the project is about
- Ask for permission to record
- Indicate that the questions will focus on
  - The place of RE within the school
  - Links to the wider community
  - Specific school policies
- Ice-breaker
  - How many years have you been head teacher?
  - Where were you before coming here?
  - How does [name of school] compare to other schools you have taught in?

Place of RE within the school

1. Resources for RE compared to other subjects
   a. Number of staff, staff student ratio, student numbers;
   b. Time for RE classes;
   c. Space (i.e. classroom, equipment, books, etc);
   d. Accocation of RE budget (how are spending decisions made? Who makes them?);
   e. Resources for extra curricular activities (i.e. fieldtrips, guest speakers);

2. Results: How does RE results compare to those in other subjects?
   a. In the school?
   b. Nationally?
   c. How important are exam results for
      i. the school?
      ii. parents?
      iii. students?
   d. Student progression: how many students sit the exams (i.e. GCSE or Scottish?
      i. How many student progress to A-Level/Highers?
      ii. What are the main student destinations after they leave your school (i.e. FE University? Work?)
3. Exam Boards (for English Schools): How was the decision to use your current exam board for RE made? Why this exam board?
4. How is RE regarded as a subject by
   a. Other teachers;
   b. Students;
   c. Parents;
   d. School governers;
   e. Do you think that RE should be a compulsory subject? (why? why not?).
5. Is there anything else you would like to comment on with regard to RE in the school? (i.e. any upcoming changes?)

Links to the wider community

1. What is the wider community?
   a. What is the catchment area?
   b. What is the social profile of student?
      i. Ethnicity
      ii. Class
      iii. Religious background
2. What is your school's involvement with the wider community? (i.e. charity events, fieldtrips, guest speakers?).
   a. How does RE's involvement with the wider community compare to other subjects (i.e. more or less involvement)?

School specific practices/policies

1. Match between the general aims of the school (if these are advertised in any of the school literature) and the aims of the RE curriculum?
2. What is the role of assemblies (i.e. if the school has them)?
3. Structure of the school and decision-making processes
   a. How much leeway do subject heads get?
   b. How much say do parents/school boards get?
   c. How are decisions about the RE curriculum made?
   d. Do students have a feedback mechanism?
4. What are your school policies on:
   a. Maintaining classroom discipline?
      i. Such as three strikes and you are out;
      ii. School uniforms;
      iii. Staff training to deal with discipline;
      iv. Student work diaries.
   b. Dealing with 'problem' students (i.e. underachievers or special needs)?
   c. Dealing with gifted/talented students?
   d. Rewards for good behaviour (i.e. merits)?
   e. Streaming?
   f. Sitting/not sitting RE exams?
   g. Dealing with diversity?
      i. Ethnic difference;
      ii. Provision for people of different faiths.
5. Staff development and sharing of good practice

Is there anything else that you would like to add?

Appendix E: Questions for student focus group

Note: The teachers were asked to select the members of the focus group. Where possible the focus groups were conducted at a time that would not disrupt the students' day (i.e. during their assembly hour so they would not miss any teaching). This takes a full period (i.e. 45 min to 1 hour). Before initiating the focus group discussion, we asked the teacher if there is something specific they would like us to ask the students so they can get feedback.

Introduction

- Thank students for their participation (if students are given merits for their participation, explain this)
- Explain who we are if they do not know this already
- Explain what the project is
- Explain what a focus group entails and why this is important for our research
- Explain that they can use this as a feedback mechanism to their teachers (i.e. if there is a message they would like to pass back about what they like/do not like they can use us to do this)
- Ask permission to tape and explain why it would help if I taped the focus group
- Set the ground rules
  - Only talk one at a time;
  - No wrong answers;
  - Everyone is entitled to their own opinion.
- Ask them if they have any questions
- Remind them that they do not have to answer any questions they are not comfortable with

Religious background

- Is religion important to you? Your family?
- What is your religion? (you do not have to give an answer to this if you do not want to)
- If you/your parents are religious, in what way is it important?
  - To your/their cultural identity;
  - For helping you/them know what is right/wrong;
  - For living your daily lives.
- If you or your family are not religious, do you know someone who is?
  - Why is religion important to this person/these people?

RE as a compulsory subject

- What are your other compulsory subjects?
- Why do you think these other subjects are compulsory?

- How many hours do you get for these subjects compared to RE and what do you think about that (RE too much or too little)?
- Why do you think that RE is compulsory? (i.e. what do you learn from it that is so important that someone has decided that it is compulsory?)
- Do you agree that RE should be compulsory (Why? Why not?)
- Questions about the RE exam (this will be different for each school)
    - Do you all have to sit the RE exam?
    - If you are not sitting the RE exam, how do you feel about lessons that go over exam revision?

Curriculum choices (the shape of the discussion will reflect the particulars of the region/SACRE, etc.)

- World Religions
    - What religions are you learning about?
    - Do you think that it is important to learn about different religions?
    - What religions would you like to learn more about?
- Moral Issues
    - What moral issues are you learning about (e.g. Abortion, euthanasia)?
    - Do you think that it is important to learn about X?
    - Do you learn anything about X in your other subjects?
- Existence of God
    - What do you think about this section of the course?
- What topic have you found the most interesting/important?
- What topic have you found the most boring/a waste of time?
- Is there anything that you would like to learn about in RE that you are not learning?

Teaching techniques

- Intended Learning Objectives (in schools where these are made explicit)
    - For every lesson you have a Learning Objective you are asked to write down, do you find this useful?
- How enjoyable/useful do you find the following teaching techniques (list will vary according to what you have observed in the school)?
    - Video clips;
    - Readings from the text book;

- Writing down answers to questions in your notebooks;
- Group work (such as memory maps);
- Sorting exercises;
- Homework;
- Guest speakers;
- Field trips;
- Online student environment (if the school has one);
- Any other things I missed out?
- How does this compare to other subjects? Is there any thing that other teachers are doing that you would like to see the RE teachers doing?

School practices

- How often do you have assemblies?
  - Why do you think you have them?
  - Do you learn anything useful/interesting from them?
- School activities
  - Do you think that it is important/enjoyable to be involved in school charity work?
  - What do you learn from being involved in school charities?
- School Diary (if they use one)
  - How useful do you find your school diary?
- System of rewards/punishments
  - Do you feel that you get enough reward for good work/behaviour?
  - Do you think that the penalty system works?
- Special help versus Gifted/talented
  - Do any of you get extra help in your classes if you are having problems/ falling behind?
  - Does this work?
  - For those of you who are doing really well in your subjects, are you given anything extra to do?
- School Uniform (for schools that have them)
  - Why do you think that you have to wear a school uniform?

Final questions

- Are any of you thinking about continuing with RE after it is no longer compulsory for you?

- What do you want to do when you leave school?
- If there is something that you really like or would like to change about your RE teaching that you would like to pass onto the teachers, what would that be?
- Do you have any questions you would like to ask us?

Appendix F: Student questionnaire

This was conducted as an online questionnaire.

Category	Questionnaire item	Options
Demographics	Is your school in . . . England, Scotland, or Northern Ireland?	England, Scotland or Northern Ireland
Demographics	Is your school (named schools)	(named schools)
Demographics	Are you a. . . .	boy or girl
Demographics	What is your religious background?	list
Religiosity	Would you describe yourself as religious?	not at all/a little/a lot
Religiosity	Would you describe your family as religious?	not at all/a little/a lot
Religiosity	Do you attend religious classes outside school (e.g. Sunday school or Madrassa, etc.)?	not at all/less than once a week/once a week/ more than once a week
Religiosity	Do you attend religious services outside school (e.g. going to church or temple etc.)?	not at all/less than once a week/once a week/ more than once a week
Aspirations	I plan to go to university	strongly agree/agree/don't know/disagree/strongly disagree
Aspirations	My teachers encourage me to go to university	strongly agree/agree/don't know/disagree/strongly disagree
Aspirations	I want to leave school and get a job as soon as I can	strongly agree/agree/don't know/disagree/strongly disagree
Aspirations	RE will be useful when I am applying for jobs or university	strongly agree/agree/don't know/disagree/strongly disagree
Ethos: school	My school encourages pupils to take on leadership roles	strongly agree/agree/don't know/disagree/strongly disagree

Continued

Category	Questionnaire item	Options
Ethos: school	In my school pupils' views are taken seriously	strongly agree/agree/don't know/disagree/strongly disagree
Ethos: school	My school challenges racist attitudes	strongly agree/agree/don't know/disagree/strongly disagree
Ethos: pupils	My school encourages pupils to carry out volunteer work in the community	strongly agree/agree/don't know/disagree/strongly disagree
Ethos: pupils	My school organizes collections for charities	strongly agree/agree/don't know/disagree/strongly disagree
Ethos: pupils	My school encourages caring for the environment	strongly agree/agree/don't know/disagree/strongly disagree
Ethos: religion	My school has somewhere I could go for prayer or reflection	strongly agree/agree/don't know/disagree/strongly disagree
Ethos: religion	There is someone in my school I could talk to about religious and moral questions	strongly agree/agree/don't know/disagree/strongly disagree
Ethos: religion	The RE teachers normally take Assemblies in my school	strongly agree/agree/don't know/disagree/strongly disagree
Ethos: religion	Religious charities work with pupils in my school	strongly agree/agree/don't know/disagree/strongly disagree
Multiculturalism	How often do you read about the experiences of different cultural or religious groups in?	not at all/a little/a lot
Multiculturalism	Do you think these lessons have helped you to better understand points of view different from your own?	not at all/a little/a lot
Multiculturalism	In your classroom how comfortable are you working with students from different cultural or religious backgrounds?	not at all/a little/a lot
Multiculturalism	In your classroom how comfortable are you in learning about people from different cultural or religious groups?	not at all/a little/a lot

Continued

Category	Questionnaire item	Options
Multiculturalism	Has your school prepared you to work in a job setting where people are of a different religiousbackground?	not at all/a little/a lot
Multiculturalism	Do you believe your school has helped you get along better with members of other religious groups?	not at all/a little/a lot
Multiculturalism	My teachers encourage me to understand people who are different from me?	strongly agree/agree/don't know/disagree/strongly disagree
Multiculturalism	RE helps to encourage people to understand others different from them?	strongly agree/agree/don't know/disagree/strongly disagree
Multiculturalism	RE encourages people to stay with their own kind?	strongly agree/agree/don't know/disagree/strongly disagree
Multiculturalism	Do you believe your school has helped you or will help you in the future to get along better with members of other religious groups?	not at all/a little/a lot
Pedagogy	How often are controversial issues discussed and explored in the classroom?	not at all/a little/a lot
Pedagogy	In your classroom how comfortable are you discussing controversial issues?	very comfortable/comfortable/ not sure/uncomfortable/very uncomfortable
Pedagogy	In RE classes we discuss things a lot more than in other classes	strongly agree/agree/don't know/disagree/strongly disagree
Pedagogy	In RE classes we listen to the teacher talking a lot more than in other classes	strongly agree/agree/don't know/disagree/strongly disagree
Pedagogy	In RE classes we write a lot more than in other classes	strongly agree/agree/don't know/disagree/strongly disagree
Pedagogy	In RE classes we just talk about things all the time	strongly agree/agree/don't know/disagree/strongly disagree
Pedagogy	In RE classes we watch videos all the time	strongly agree/agree/don't know/disagree/strongly disagree

Continued

Category	Questionnaire item	Options
Pedagogy	The language and ideas we need to learn in RE are confusing	strongly agree/agree/don't know/disagree/strongly disagree
Subject status	RE is an important subject in my school	strongly agree/agree/don't know/disagree/strongly disagree
Subject status	RE is as important as subjects like Maths or Science	Much more important/more important/about the same/less important/much less important
Subject status	RE is as important as subjects like English or History	Much more important/more important/about the same/less important/much less important
Subject status	RE is as important as subjects like Citizenship or Personal and Social Health Education	Much more important/more important/about the same/less important/much less important
Subject status	RE classes are interesting	strongly agree/agree/don't know/disagree/strongly disagree
Subject status	RE is one of the easiest subjects to pass	strongly agree/agree/don't know/disagree/strongly disagree
Subject status	Which of these subjects is RE most like?	Maths, English, Science, Citizenship, Personal and Social Education, Modern Languages
Subject status	Which of these subjects is RE least like?	Maths, English, Science, Citizenship, Personal and Social Education, Modern Languages

Appendix G: Does RE work – Analytical framework/template for ethnographic information collected in each school

School Name:

Anonymized Name:

1. Context of School
   a. Community context;
   b. Wider school context;

    c. Layout of classroom;

    d. Whole school ethos and influence on relationships;

    e. Teacher-teacher interaction outside classroom;

    f. Relationship between ethnographer/teacher/student.

2. Context of RE

    a. Name of the subject;

    b. RE teachers' expressed values;

    c. Content of lesson and methods used to deliver;

    d. Comparison of RE teaching to other subjects;

    e. Resources and funds available to RE;

    f. Time allocation and time of day when RE takes place;

    g. Teacher biographical information;

    h. Documentation to collect.

3. Methodology and Teacher Engagement

    a. Planning;

    b. Power relations and teacher engagement;

    c. Discourse;

    d. Teaching methods;

    e. Non-teaching activities in the classroom;

    f. Outside speakers and partners involved in RE, including field trips.

4. Pupils

    a. Student-student interaction;

    b. Pupil feedback on RE learning experiences;

    c. Examples of pupils' RE work;

    d. Pupil relationship with curriculum and resources;

    e. Background information on students.

Bibliography

Aldridge, D. (2011). What is religious education all about? a hermeneutic reappraisal. *Journal of Beliefs and Values, 321,* 33–45.

Allport, G. (1954). *The nature of prejudice.* Reading, MA: Addison-Wesley.

Anderson, B. & Harrison, P. (2010). The promise of non-representational theories. In B. Anderson & P. Harrison (Eds), *Taking place: non-representational theories and Geography.* Ashgate: Farnham.

Anthony, F.-V. (2009). Italy. In H-G Zieberts and U. Reigel (Eds), *How teachers in Europe teach religion: an international empirical study in 16 countries.* Lit Verlag: Berlin.

Apple, M. (1986). *Teachers and texts: a political economy of class and gender relations in education.* London: Routledge.

Armstrong, D. (2009). Religious education and the law in Northern Ireland's controlled schools. *Irish Educational Studies, 28,* 297–313.

Arts and Humanities Research Council/Economic and Social Research Council (2007). *Research Programme Specification* at www.religionandsociety.org.uk/uploads/docs/2009_11/1259236957_Religion_and_Society_-_Programme_Specification_PDF.pdf. Downloaded 20 November 2012.

Arweck, E. & Nesbitt, E. (2011). Religious education in the experience of young people from mixed-faith families. *British Journal of Religious Education, 33,* 31–45.

Ashworth, P. D. (2003) An approach to phenomenological psychology: the contingencies of the lifeworld. *Journal of Phenomenological Psychology,* 34 (6), 145–56.

Ball, S. (1997). Policy sociology and critical social research: a personal review of recent education policy and policy research. *British Educational Research Journal, 23,* 257–74.

Banks, M. & Morphy, H. (1997). *Rethinking visual anthropology.* New Haven: Yale University Press.

Barnes, L. P. (1997). Reforming religious education in Northern Ireland: a critical review. *British Journal of Religious Education, 19,* 73–82.

— (2002). World religions in the Northern Ireland curriculum. *Journal of Beliefs and Values, 23,* 19–32.

— (2004). Religion et éducation en Irlande du Nord. *Carrefours de l'éducation, 17,* 178–95.

— (2008). The 2007 Birmingham agreed syllabus for religious education: a new direction for statutory religious education in England and Wales. *Journal of Beliefs and Values, 29,* 73–81.

Barratt, M. (1994a). *An egg for Babcha: 'bridges to religions' series, The Warwick RE project.* Oxford: Heinemann.

— (1994b). *Lucy's sunday: 'bridges to religions' series, The Warwick RE project.* Oxford: Heinemann.

— (1994c). *Something to share: 'bridges to religions' series, The Warwick RE project.* Oxford: Heinemann.

Barry, B. (2000). *Culture and equality: an egalitarian critique of multiculturalism.* Cambridge: Polity Press.

Battaglia, D. (1997). Displacing the visual: of Trobriand axe-blades and ambiguity in cultural practice. In M. Banks and H. Morphy (Eds), *Rethinking Visual Anthropology.* New Haven: Yale University Press.

Baudrillard, J. (1993). *Symbolic exchange and death.* London: Sage.

Baumfield, V. M. (2002). *Thinking through RE.* Cambridge: Chris Kington.

— (2006). Editorial: textbooks and RE – empowering or restricting? *British Journal of Religious Education, 28,* 223–24.

Baumfield, V. M., Conroy, J. C., Davis, R., & Lundie, D. C. (2012). The Delphi method: gathering expert opinion in religious education. *British Journal of Religious Education, 34,* 5–19.

Baumfield, V. M., Davis, R., & Lundie, D. (2011). *Stories we tell ourselves: practitioner inquiry in RE.* Unpublished paper presented at Association of University Lecturers in RE Annual Conference: Glasgow.

Baumfield, V. M., Hall, E., Higgins, S., & Wall, K. (2009). Catalytic tools: understanding the interaction of enquiry and feedback in teachers' learning. *European Journal of Teacher Education, 32,* 423–35.

Belmonte, A. & Cranston, N. C. (2009). The religious dimension of lay leadership in Catholic schools: preserving Catholic culture in an era of change. *Catholic Education: A Journal of Inquiry and Practice, 12,* 294–319.

Berube, M. R. (1994). *American school reform: progressive, equity and excellence movements, 1883–1993.* Westport: Praeger.

Birmingham ASC. (2007). *The Birmingham agreed syllabus for Religious Education.* Retrieved from www.birmingham-asc.org.uk/agreedsyll.php

Bishops' Conference of Scotland (2011). *This is our faith.* Glasgow: Scottish Education Service.

Black, P. & Wiliam, D. (2006). *Inside the black box.* London: Granada Learning.

Boal, A. (1979). *Theater of the oppressed* (C. A. McBride, M. O. McBride, & E. Fryer, Trans.). London: Pluto Press.

— (2006). *The aesthetics of the oppressed* (A. Jackson, Trans.). London: Routledge.

Boeve, L. (2012). Religious education in a post-secular and post-Christian context. *Journal of Beliefs and Values, 33,* 143–56.

Bourdieu, P. (2005). Habitus. In J. Hillier and E. Rooksby (Eds), *Habitus: a sense of place* (2nd ed.). Aldershot: Ashgate.

Bourdieu, P. & Passeron, J. C. (2000). *Reproduction in education, society and culture* (2nd ed.). London: Sage.

Bourdieu, P. & Wacquant, L. J. D. (1992). *An invitation to reflexive sociology.* Chicago: University of Chicago Press.

Bradford Standing Advisory Council for Religious Education (2011). *Agreed syllabus for religious education 2011–2016.* Bradford: City of Bradford MDC.

Breen, D. (2009). Religious diversity, inter – ethnic relations and the Catholic school: introducing the *responsive* approach to single faith schooling. *British Journal of Religious Education, 31,* 103–15.

British Religion in Numbers Table 2.3 Religion in England and Wales, 2001, by district authority: worksheet. Data from ONS [www.brin.ac.uk/figures/#notes/ accessed 11 October 2012]

Britzman, D. (1998). *Lost subjects, contested objects: towards a psychoanalytic inquiry of learning.* Albany: State University of New York Press.

Brookfield, S. D. & Presskill, S. (2012). *Discussion as a way of teaching: tools and techniques for democratic classrooms.* Oxford: John Wiley and Sons.

Brown, M. W. (2010) The life-world as moral world: vindicating the life-world en route to a phenomenology of the virtues. *Bulletin d'analyse phenomenologique, 3,* 1–25.

Bruce, S. (2002). *God is dead: Secularization in the west.* Oxford: Blackwell.

Bryan, A. (2012). You've got to teach people that racism is wrong and then they won't be racist: curricular representations and young people's understandings of 'race' and racism. *Journal of Curriculum Studies, 44,* 599–629.

Bryan, H. & Revell, L. (2011). Performativity, faith and professional identity: student Religious Education teachers and the ambiguities of objectivity. *British Journal of Educational Studies, 59,* 403–19.

Buie, E. (2012, May 18). A downward spiral if quality officers are cut? *Times Educational Supplement Scotland.* Retrieved from www.tes.co.uk/article.aspx?storycode=6081695

Burns, J. (2012, February 17). Religious education in schools is 'a priority' say MPs. *BBC News.* Retrieved from www.bbc.co.uk/news/education-17068153

Callon, M. & Law, J. (1997). After in the individual in society: lessons on collectivity from science, technology and society. *Canadian Journal of Sociology, 22,* 165–82.

Cameron, D. (2011, February 5). *Speech at Munich security conference.* Retrieved from www.number10.gov.uk/news/speeches-and-transcripts/2011/02/pms-speech-at-munichsecurity-conference-6029

Carr, D. (2007). On the grammar of religious discourse and education. In M. Felderhof et al (Eds), *Inspiring faith in schools: studies in religious education.* London: Ashgate.

Carspecken, P. F. (1996). *Critical ethnography in educational research: a theoretical and practical guide.* London: Routledge.

— (2001). Critical ethnographies from Houston: Distinctive features and directions in Carspecken. In P. Francis & G. Walford (Eds), *Critical Ethnography and Education.* London: Elsevier Science.

Chater, M. & Erricker, C. (2012). *Does religious education have a future?* London: Routledge.

Chun, W. H. K. (2011). The enduring ephemeral, or the future is a memory. *Critical Inquiry, 35*, 148–71.

Clarke, M. & Gregory, K. (2003). *The impact of high stakes testing.* Columbus: Ohio State University Press.

Cochran-Smith, M. & Lytle, S. L. (2009). *Inquiry as stance: practitioner research in the next generation.* New York: Teachers College Press.

Coll, R. (2007). Student teachers' perception of their role and responsibilities as Catholic educators. *European Journal of Teacher Education, 30*, 445–65.

Collinson, C. & Miller, C. (1981). *Believers.* London: Edward Arnold.

Conquergood, D. (1991). Rethinking ethnography: towards a critical cultural politics. *Communication Monographs, 58*, 179–94.

Conroy, J. C. (Ed.) (1999). *Catholic education inside-out: outside/in.* Dublin: Veritas.

— (2002). A very Scottish affair: Catholic Education and the state. *Oxford Review of Education, 27*, 543–58.

— (2004). *Betwixt and between: the liminal imagination, education and democracy.* New York: Peter Lang.

— (2008). Sectarianism and Scottish Education. In T. Bryce and W. Humes (Eds), *Scottish education.* Edinburgh University Press, Edinburgh.

— (2009). The enstranged self: Recovering some grounds for pluralism in education. *Journal of Moral Education, 38*, 145–64.

Conroy, J. C. & Davis, R. (2008). Citizenship, education and the claims of religious literacy. In M. Peters et al (Eds), *Global citizenship education: philosophy, theory and pedagogy.* Rotterdam: Sense.

— (2010). Religious Education. In R. Bailey, R. Barrow, D. Carr, & C. McCarthy (Eds), *The SAGE handbook of philosophy of education* (pp. 451–66). London: SAGE.

Conroy, J.C. & Lundie, D. (2013). Does religious education work? On nested identities. In L.Woodhead (Ed.), *New Methods in the Study of Religion.* Oxford: Oxford University Press.

Conroy, J. C., Davis, R. A., & Boland, M. (1998). *Values interventions and the development of moral reasoning in Primary 7.* Glasgow, UK: St. Andrew's College/ Gordon Cook Foundation.

Conroy, J. C., Lundie, D., & Baumfield, V. (2012). Failures of meaning in religious education. *Journal of Beliefs and Values, 33* (3), 307–21.

Conroy, J. C., Lundie, D., & Boland, M. (2011). Theatre and meaning-making in the classroom. *AHRC/ESRC Religion & Society Education Conference*, Warwick.

Conroy, J. C. & McGrath, M. (2007). Secularisation and catholic education in Scotland. In G. R. Grace & J. O'Keefe (Eds), *International handbook of Catholic education: challenges for school systems in the 21st century.* Dordrecht: Springer.

Convey, J. J. (2012). Perceptions of Catholic identity: views of Catholic school administrators and teachers. *Catholic Education: A Journal of Inquiry and Practice, 16*, 187–214.

Cooling, T. (1994). *Concept cracking: exploring Christian beliefs in school.* Stapleford: Stapleford Project Books.

Cooney, M. (2012). The way, the truth and the life in Catholic Religious Education: the story of an educational innovation. *International Studies in Catholic Education, 4,* 136–151.

Copley, T. (2008). *Teaching religion: sixty years of religious education in England and Wales.* Exeter: University of Exeter Press.

Cormack, R. J., Gallagher, A. M., & Osborne, R. D. (1991). Educational affiliation and educational attainment in Northern Ireland: the financing of schools in Northern Ireland. *Annex E, sixteenth report of the standing advisory commission on human rights, house of commons papers* (488). London: HMSO.

Cornwall County Council (2011). Cornwall Agreed Syllabus, at www.cornwall.gov.uk/default.aspx?page=7813 downloaded 20 June 2012.

Dahlberg, K., Dahlberg, H., & Nystrom, M. (2008) (Eds), *Reflective lifeworld research* (2nd ed.). Lund, Sweden: Studentlitteratur.

Darling, J. (1980). Curriculum retardation and its treatment: The case of religious education in Scotland. *British Journal of Religious Education, 3,* 13–17.

David, R. G. (2000). Imaging the past: the use of archive pictures in secondary school History textbooks. *Curriculum Journal, 11,* 225–46.

Dawkins, R. (2006). *The God delusion.* London: Bantam Press.

DCSF (2010). Religious education in English schools: Non-statutory guidance, www.gov.uk/government/uploads/system/uploads/attachment_data/file/190260/DCSF-00114-2010.pdf downloaded 20 October 2012.

Department for Children, Education, Lifelong Learning and Skills (DCELLS) (2008). *National exemplar framework for Religious Education for 3 to 19-year-olds in Wales.* Cardiff: DCELLS.

Department for Children, Schools and Families (DCSF) (2007). *Faith in the system: the role of schools with a religious character in English education and society.* Nottingham: DCSF Publications.

— (2009). *Religious education in English schools: non-statutory guidance 2009.* Nottingham: DCSF publications.

Department for Education (DfE) (1994). *Circular 1/94: religious education and collective worship.* London: DfE Publications.

Department for Education Northern Ireland (2007). *Core syllabus for religious education* at www.deni.gov.uk/re_core_syllabus_pdf.pdf downloaded 26th July 2012.

Dewey, J. (1938/1998). *Education and experience.* Indiana: Kappa, Delta, Pi.

Donaldson, G. (2011). *Teaching Scotland's future: report of a review of teacher education in Scotland.* Edinburgh: Scottish Government.

Dorset Agreed Syllabus Working Party (2005). *Research: asking the big questions.* Retrieved from www.dorsetforyou.com/educ/sacre.

Eagleton, T. (2012). *The event of literature.* New Haven and London: Yale University Press.

Ecclestone, K. & Hayes, D. (2008). *The dangerous rise of therapeutic education.* London: Routledge.

Education Scotland (no date). *A curriculum for excellence: religious and Moral Education* at http://www.educationscotland.gov.uk/learningteachingandassessment/curriculumareas/rme/nondenominational/index.asp downloaded 26th November 2012.

Edwards, R. (2011). Translating the prescribed into the enacted curriculum in college and school. *Educational Philosophy and Theory, 43*, 38–54.

Egan, J. (1988). *Opting out: Catholic schools today.* Leominster: Fowler Wright books

Egan, K. (2003). *Getting it wrong from the beginning: our progressivist inheritance from Herbert Spencer, John Dewey and Jean Piaget.* New Haven, CT and London: Yale University Press.

Eke, R., Lee, J., & Clough, N. (2005). Whole-class interactive teaching and learning in religious education: transcripts from four primary classrooms. *British Journal of Religious Education, 27*, 159–72.

Engebretson, K. (2002). Writing church-sponsored religious education textbooks. *British Journal of Religious Education, 25*, 33–46.

Erickson, F. (1984). What makes school ethnography 'ethnographic'? *Anthropology and Education Quarterly, 15*, 51–66.

— (1990). Qualitative methods. In R. L. Linn & F. Erickson (Eds), *Research in learning and teaching: volume two.* New York: MacMillan Publishing Company.

Erricker, C. (2010). Religious education: a conceptual and interdisciplinary approach for secondary level, Abingdon: Routledge.

Esfeld, M. (2003). What are social practices? Indaga. *Revista internacional de Ciencias Sociales y Humanas, 1*, 19–43.

Ewing. K. P. (2006). Revealing and concealing: interpersonal dynamics and the negotiation of identity in the interview. *Ethos, 34*, 89–122.

Fancourt, N. (2005). Challenges for self-assessment in Religious Education. *British Journal of Religious Education, 27*(2), 115–25.

Felderhof, M. (2004). The new national framework for RE in England and Wales: A critique. *The Journal of Beliefs and Values, 25*(2), 241–8.

— (2007). Religious education, atheism and deception. In M. Felderhof, P. Thompson, & D. Torevell (Eds), *Inspiring Faith in Schools: Studies in Religious Education.* Hampshire: Ashgate.

— (2010). National and local RE: A further contributions to discussions, the QCA and RE: A tour de force. *Resource, 32*(2), 10–12.

Fenwick, T. & Edwards, R. (2010). *Actor-network theory in education.* London: Routledge.

Findlay, L. (2009). Debating phenomenological research methods. *Phenomenology & Practice, 3*, 6–25.

Franchi, L. (2011). Healing the wounds: St. Augustine, catechesis, and religious education today. *Religious Education, 106*, 299–311.

Francis, L. J. (2002). Catholic schools and Catholic values? a study of moral and religious values among 13–15 year old students attending non-denominational and Catholic schools in England and Wales. *International Journal of Education and Religion, 3*, 69–84.

— (2005). Independent Christian schools and pupils values: an empirical investigation among 13–15-year-old-boys. *British Journal of Religious Education, 27,* 127–41.

Francis, L. J., Ap Sion, T., & Penny, G. (2012). *Young people's attitudes to religious diversity in Wales.* Lampeter: University of Wales, St. Mary's. www.st-marys centre. org.uk/docs/Young%20people's%20attitudes%20to%20religious%20diversity.pdf. downloaded 10 November 2012.

Francis, L. J. & Robbins, M. (2005). *Urban hope and spiritual health: the adolescent voice.* Peterborough: Epworth.

Franken, L. & Loobuyck, P. (2011). *Religious education in a plural, secularised society: a paradigm shift.* Munster: Waxmann Verlag.

Freathy, R. (2008a). The triumph of religious education for citizenship in English schools, 1935–1949. *History of Education, 37,* 295–316.

— (2008b). Three perspectives on religious education and education for citizenship in English schools, 1933–1944: Cyril Norwood, Ernest Simon and William Temple. *British Journal of Religious Education, 30,* 103–12.

Gallagher, T. (2004). *Education in divided societies.* London: Palgrave/Macmillan.

— (2005). Faith schools and Northern Ireland: a review of research. In R. Gardner, J. Cairns, & D. Lawton (Eds), *Faith schools: consensus or conflict?* Oxford: Routledge Falmer.

Gallagher, T. & Lundy, L. (2006). Religious education and the law in Northern Ireland. In J. L. M. López-Muñiz, J. de Groof, & G. Lauwers (Eds), *Religious Education in public schools: study of comparative law.* Dordrecht: Springer.

Gardner, R., Cairns, J., & Lawton, D. (2005). *Faith schools: consensus or conflict?* Oxford: Routledge Falmer.

Gearon, L. (2012). European Religious Education and European civil religion. *British Journal of Educational Studies, 60,* 151–69.

Geary, P. J. (1994). *Living with the dead in the middle ages.* Ithaca: Cornell University Press.

Geddes, G. & Griffiths, J. (2003). *Revise for Religious Studies GCSE: AQA specification A.* Oxford: Heinemann.

Geerinck, I., Masschelein, J., & Simons, M. (2010). Teaching and knowledge: a necessary combination? An elaboration of forms of teachers' reflexivity. *Studies in Philosophy and Education, 29,* 379–93.

Girard, R. (2004). *I see Satan fall like lightning* (J. G. Williams, Trans.). Maryknoll, NY: Orbis Books.

Glaser, B. G. (1978) *Theoretical sensitivity, advances in the methodology of grounded theory.* Mill Valley, CA: Sociology Press.

Glaser, B. G. & Strauss, A. L. (1967). *The discovery of grounded theory: strategies for qualitative research.* Chicago, IL: Aldine.

Goldman, R. (1968). *Religious thinking from childhood to adolescence.* London: Routledge and Kegan Paul.

Goodwin, M. & Goodwin, C. (2000). Emotion within situated activity. In A. Durranti, *Linguistic anthropology: a reader*. Cambridge: CUP.

Green, E. & Cooling, T. (2009). *Mapping the field: a review of the current research evidence on the impact of schools with a Christian ethos*. London: Theos.

Greer, J. E. (1972). *A questioning generation*. Belfast: Church of Ireland Board of Education.

Greer, J. & Francis, L. J. (1998). The religious profile of pupils in Northern Ireland. *Journal of Empirical Theology*, 3, 35–50.

Grimmitt, M. (1987). *Religious Education and human development*. Great Havering: McCrimmon Publishing.

— (2000a). Constructivist pedagogies of Religious Education project: re-thinking knowledge, teaching and learning in Religious Education. In M. Grimmitt (ed.) *Pedagogies of Religious Education*. Great Wakering: McCrimmon. (pp. 189–207).

— (2000b). *Pedagogies of religious education: case studies in the development of good pedagogic practice*. Great Wakering, Essex: McCrimmon.

Guardian, The. (2005, September 19). Britain sleepwalking to segregation. *The Guardian*. Retrieved from www.guardian.co.uk/world/2005/sep/19/race. socialexclusion accessed 19 May 2011.

Hand, M. (2011). *Is Religious Education possible? A philosophical investigation*. London: Continuum.

Harrison, M. & Klippax, S. (1996). *Thinking about God*. London: Collins Educational.

Hayward, M. (2006). Curriculum Christianity. *British Journal of Religious Education*, 28, 153–71.

Her Majesty's Inspectorate of Education (HMIE) (2001). *Standards and quality in secondary schools: religious and moral education 1995–2000*. Edinburgh: Astron.

Hervieu-Léger, D. (2000). *Religion as a chain of memory*. Cambridge: Polity Press.

Holmes, J. & Stubbe, M. (2003). *Power and politeness in the workplace: a sociolinguistic analysis of talk at work*. Edinburgh: Pearson Education.

Hornberger, T. (1982). *A curriculum to change attitudes towards the Amish*. Pennsylvania: University of Pennsylvania.

Hull, J. M. (1984). *Studies in religion and education*. Lewes: Falmer.

— (1988). Religious education in the education reform bill. *British Journal of Religious Education*, 11, 1–3.

— (1989). The content of religious education and the 1988 Education Reform Act. *British Journal of Religious Education*, 11, 59–61.

Hulme, M., Baumfield, V., & Payne, F. (2009). Building capacity through teacher enquiry: the Scottish Schools of Ambition. *Journal of Education for Teaching: International Research and Pedagogy*, 35, 409–24.

Huntigton, S. (1996). *The clash of civilizations and the re-making of world order*. New York: Simon & Schuster.

Hyde, B. (2008). Weaving the threads of meaning: a characteristic of children's spirituality and its implications for religious education. *British Journal of Religious Education, 30,* 235–45.

Hymes, D. (1996). *Ethnography, linguistics, narrative inequality: toward an understanding of voice.* London: Taylor & Francis.

I'Anson, J. (2004). Mapping the subject: student teachers. Location and the understanding of religion. *British Journal of Religious Education, 26,* 45–60.

Issitt, J. (2004). Reflections on the study of textbooks. *History of Education, 33,* 683–89.

Jackson, R. (1997). *Religious education: an interpretive approach.* London: Hodder & Stoughton.

— (1999). The Warwick RE project: an interpretive approach to religious education. *Religious Education, 94,* 201–16.

— (2004). *Rethinking religious education and plurality: issues in diversity and pedagogy.* London: Psychology Press.

Jackson, R., Barratt, M., & Everington, J. (1994). *Bridges to religions: teacher's resource book.* Oxford: Heinemann.

Jackson, R., Ipgrave, J., Hayward, M., Hopkins, P., Fancourt, N., Robbins, M., Francis, L., & McKenna, U. (2010). *Materials used to teach about world religions in schools in England: research report.* Warwick: University of Warwick.

Jenkins, J. (1992). *Examining religions: contemporary moral issues.* London: Heinemann.

Judge, H. (2002). *Faith-based schools and the state: Catholics in America, France and England.* Oxford: Symposium.

Kant, I. (2008). *The critique of judgement* (J. C. Meredith, Trans.). Retrieved from http://ebooks.adelaide.edu.au/k/kant/immanuel/k16j/

Kassam, K. A. (2010). Pluralism, resilience and the ecology of survival: case studies from the Pamir mountains of Afghanistan. *Ecology and Society, 15,* 8.

Kerry, T. (1984). *Teaching religious education.* Cheltenham: Nelson Thornes.

Laats, A. (2010). Forging a fundamentalist 'one best system': struggles over curriculum and educational philosophy for Christian day schools, 1970–1989. *History of Education Quarterly, 50,* 55–83.

Laidlaw, J. (1972). The millar report. *Learning for Living, 12,* 7–8.

Latour, B. (2005). *Reassembling the social: an introduction to actor-network theory.* Oxford: Oxford University Press.

Learning and Teaching Scotland (LTS) (2010a). *What is a curriculum for excellence?* Retrieved from www.ltscotland.org.uk/understandingthecurriculum/ whatiscurriculumfor excellence/index.asp.

— (2010b). *Religious education in Roman Catholic schools.* Retrieved from www.ltscotland. org.uk/learningteachingandassessment/curriculumareas/rme/rerc/index.asp.

— (2011). *The purpose of the curriculum: what is curriculum for excellence.* Retrieved from www.ltscotland.org.uk/understandingthecurriculum/ whatiscurriculumforexcellence/thepurposeofthecurriculum/index.asp

Lefstein, A. & Snell, J. (2009). Linguistic ethnography in action: initial, illustrative analysis of a literacy lesson. Paper presented at *Ethnography, Language and Communication Seminar in the North*, University of Glasgow, Scotland. www.google.de/url?sa=t&rct=j&q=&esrc=s&source=web&cd=7&ved=0CGQQFjAG&url=http%3A%2F%2Fwww.esrc.ac.uk%2Fmy-esrc%2Fgrants%2FRES-061-25-0363%2Foutputs%2FDownload%2Fee60e4e2-3276-4a1e-92ef-1b7dc24c59b6&ei=mIK_UIrQHcrOsgbP4IDYCw&usg=AFQjCNF6DamIaXBeW4IZmcoLzA1G1Iptpg. Downloaded 1 December 2012.

Leigh, I. (2012). Objective, critical and pluralistic? Religious education and human rights in the European public sphere. In L. Zucca et al. (Eds), *Law, state and religion in the New Europe: debates and dilemmas.* Cambridge: CUP.

Lijphart, A. (1975). *The politics of accommodation: pluralism and democracy in the Netherlands.* Ewing, NJ: University of California Press.

Linstone, H. A. & Murray, T. (1975). *The Delphi method: techniques and applications.* Addison Wesley.

Lloyd, I. (2007). Confession and reason. In M. Felderhof et al (Eds), *Inspiring faith in schools: studies in Religious Education.* London: Ashgate.

Lundie, D. (2011). *The Other in the curriculum: ethnographic case studies on the spiritual, moral, social and cultural dimensions of religious education in sites of value commitment and contestation in the UK.* Unpublished doctoral dissertation, University of Glasgow, UK.

Lundie, D. & Conroy, J. (2012). Seeing and seeing through: forum theatre approaches to ethnographic evidence. *Journal of Beliefs and Values, 33* (3) 329–42.

MacBeath, J. & Mortimore, P. (2001). *Improving school effectiveness.* Buckingham: Open University Press.

Macintyre, T. & Hamilton, S. (2010). Mathematics learners and mathematics textbooks: a question of identity? Whose curriculum? Whose mathematics? *Curriculum Journal, 21*, 3–23.

Maclure, M. (2003). *Discourse in educational and social research.* Buckingham: Open University Press.

Mayled, J. (2002). *Discovery: philosophy and ethics for OCR GCSE Religious Studies.* London: Nelson Thorne.

Mayled, J. & Aluwahlia, L. (2002). *Discovery: Philosophy & ethics for OCR GCSE Religious Studies,* Cheltenham: Nelson Thornes.

Mayled, J. & Anderson, J. (2010). *GCSE religious studies: philosophy and applied ethics revision guide for OCR B.* Retrieved from www.amazon.co.uk/GCSE-Religious-Studies-Philosophy-Revision/dp/1444110713/ref=pd_bxgy_b_img_b

McAdam, N. (2011, April 1). Robinson outlines 'future' of education in Northern Ireland. *Belfast Telegraph.* Retrieved from www.belfasttelegraph.co.uk/news/education/robinson-outlines-future-of-education-in-northern-ireland-15133166.html

McArdle, K. & Coutts, N. (2010). Taking teachers' continuous professional development (CPD) beyond reflection: adding shared sense-making and collaborative engagement for professional renewal. *Studies in Continuing Education, 32*, 201–15.

McGovern, D. (2010). *Hospitality to the other in faith-based schools* (Doctoral Dissertation). Retrieved from http://eleanor.lib.gla.ac.uk/search

McKinney, S. & Hill, R. (2010). Gospel, poverty and Catholic schools. *International Studies in Catholic Education, 2*, 163–75.

Mercier, C. (1996). *Muslims: 'interpreting religions' series, The Warwick RE project.* Oxford: Heinemann.

Milbank, J. (1993). *Theology and social theory: Beyond secular reason.* Oxford: Blackwell.

Ministry of Education (1918). *The Education Scotland Act, 1918.* London: HMSO.

— (1944). *The Education Act, 1944.* London: HMSO.

— (1988). *The Education Reform Act, 1988.* London: HMSO.

Mitchell, C. (2006). *Religion, identity and politics in Northern Ireland.* Aldershot: Ashgate.

Moulin, D. (2011). Giving voice to 'the silent minority': the experience of religious students in secondary school religious education lessons. *British Journal of Religious Education, 33*, 313–26.

Narisetti, I. (2009). *How religion abuses children's rights.* Amherst, NY: Prometheus Books.

National Association of Teachers of Religious Education (NATRE) (2011). *Survey of teachers: The impact of the English Baccalaureate on RE in secondary schools.* London: NATRE.

— (2012). *An analysis of a survey of teachers on GCSE change and RE in light of the EBacc changes.* London: NATRE.

Newby, M. (2005). A curriculum for 2005. *Journal of Education and Teaching, 31*, 297–300.

NICC (n.d.) www.nicurriculum.org.uk/key_stages_1_and_2/areas_of_learning/religious_education/

Nicholls, J. (2005). The philosophical underpinnings of school textbook research. *Paradigm, 3*, 24–35.

Nichols, S. & Berliner, D. (2007). *Collateral damage: how high-stakes testing corrupts America's schools.* Cambridge, MA: Harvard University Press.

Nixon, G. (2010). *Religious education in Scotland.* Retrieved from www.mmiweb.org.uk/eftre/reeurope/scotland_2011.html

ODIHR Advisory Council of Experts on Freedom of Religion or Belief (2007). *Toledo guiding principles on teaching about religions and beliefs in public schools.* Warsaw: OSCE / ODIHR.

OECD. (2010). *The high cost of low educational performance: the long run economic impact of improving PISA outcomes.* Paris: OECD.

Office for National Statistics Census (ONS Census) (2001). *2001 Census.* Retrieved from www.statistics.gov.uk/

Ofsted (2010). *Transforming religious education: religious education in schools 2006–09.* Manchester: Ofsted.

O'Grady, K. (2010). Researching religious education pedagogy through an action research community of practice. *British Journal of Religious Education, 32*, 119–31

Parliament (1996). Hansard. 5 Jul Column 1691. UK Government.

Pettigrew, T. F. & Tropp, L. R. (2006). A meta-analytic study of intergroup contact theory. *Journal of Personality and Social Psychology, 90,* 751–83.

Pinar, W. (2006). *Race, religion and a culture of reparation: teacher education for a multicultural society.* New York: Palgrave.

Pinker, S. (2008). *The stuff of thought: language as a window into human nature.* Harmondsworth: Penguin.

Pope, A. (1899). *An Essay on Man.* E. E. Morris (introduction and notes). London: MacMillan.

Qualifications and Curriculum Authority (QCA) (2004). *Religious education: the non-statutory national framework.* Norwich: QCA Publications.

Rampton, B. (2007). Neo-hymesian linguistic ethnography in the United Kingdom. *Journal of Sociolinguistics, 11,* 584–607.

RE Council (1989). *Advisory booklet Handbook for agreed syllabus conferences, sacres and schools.* London: REC.

— (n.d.). Guidance on Selecting Resources at http://religiouseducationcouncil.org.uk/educators/a-practice-code-for-teachers-of-re, dowloaded 24 May 2013.

Richards, J. C. (1993). Beyond the text book: the role of commercial materials in language teaching. *RELC Journal, 24,* 1–14.

Richardson, N. & Gallagher, T. (Eds) (2011). *Education for Diversity and Mutual Understanding.* Bern: Peter Lang.

Ritchie, D. (2001). *Panel report: Oldham independent review.* England: Oldham Independent Review.

Rose, G. (1992). *The broken middle: out of our ancient society.* Oxford: Blackwell.

Rymarz, R. & Engbretson, K. (2005). Putting textbooks to work: empowering religious education in teachers. *British Journal of Religious Education, 27,* 53–63.

Sackman, H. (1974). *Delphi assessment: expert opinion, forecasting and group procedure.* Santa Monica, CA: Rand Corporation.

Schagen, I. & Schagen, S. (2002, September). *Using national value-added datasets to explore the effects of school diversity.* Paper presented at the Annual Conference of the British Educational Research Association, University of Exeter, England. Retrieved from www.leeds.ac.uk/educol/documents/00002325.htm

Scheele, D. S. (1975). Reality construction as a product of Delphi interaction. In H. A. Linstone & M. Turoff (Eds), *The Delphi method: techniques and applications.* Reading, MA: Addison-Wesley Publishing Company.

Schihalejev, O. (2009). Dialogue in religious education lessons: possibilities and hindrances in the Estonian context. *British Journal of Religious Education, 31,* 277–88.

Schweitzer, F., Riegel, U., & Ziebertz, H.-G. (2009). Europe in comparative perspective. In H.-G. Ziebertz & U. Reigel (Eds), *How teachers in Europe teach religion: an international empirical study in 16 countries.* Lit Verlag: Berlin.

Scollon R. & Scollon S. W. (2007). Nexus analysis: refocusing ethnography on action. *Journal of Sociolinguistics, 11*, 608–25.

Scottish Central Committee on Religious Education (SCCORE) (1978). *Bulletin 1: a curricular approach to religious education*. Edinburgh: Scottish Education Department.

Scottish Office Education Department (SOED) (1972). *Moral and religious education in Scottish schools: report of a committee appointed by the secretary of state*. Edinburgh: Scottish Office.

— (2004). *Religious education 5–14 Roman Catholic school*. Edinburgh: SOED.

Scottish Qualifications Agency [SQA] (2012). *Annual report and accounts*. Retrieved from www.sqa.org.uk/sqa/files_ccc/Annual_Report_and_Accounts_2011–12.pdf

Sharpley, R. & Stone, P. R. (2011). Socio-cultural impacts of events: meanings, authorized transgression, and social capital. In S. Page & J. Connell (Eds), *The Routledge handbook of events*. London: Routledge.

Sikka, S. (2010). Liberalism, multiculturalism, and the case for public religion. *Politics and Religion, 3*, 580–609.

Skulmoski, G. J., Hartman F. T., & Krahn, J. (2007). The Delphi method for graduate research. *Journal of Information Technology Education, 6*, 1–21.

Smart, N. & Horder, D. (Eds) (1978). *New movements in religious education*. Lewes: Falmer.

Spradley, J. P. (1979). *The ethnographic interview*. London: Harcourt Brace Jovanovich

Stenhouse, L. (1975). *An introduction to curriculum research and development*. Oxford: Heinemann.

Stern, L. J. (2006). *Teaching religious education: researchers in the classroom*. London: Continuum.

— (2007). *Schools and religions: Imagining the real*. London: Continuum.

— (2010). Research as pedagogy: building learning communities and religious understanding in RE. *British Journal of Religious Education, 32*, 133–46.

Strhan, A. (2010). A religious education otherwise? An examination and proposed interruption of current British practice. *Journal of Philosophy of Education, 44*, 23–44.

Sturm, J., Groenendijk, L., Kruithof, B., & Rens, J. (1999). Educational pluralism: a historical study of so-called 'pillarization' in the Netherlands, including a comparison with developments in South African education. *Comparative Education, 34*, 281–97.

Swayne, L. (2010). Heteronomous citizenship: civic virtue and the chains of autonomy. *Educational Philosophy and Theory, 42*, 73–93.

Thompson, P. (2004). Whose confession? Which tradition? *British Journal of Religious Education, 26*, 61–72.

Trondman, M. (2008). Bypass surgery: rerouting theory to ethnographic study. In G. Walford (Ed.), *How to do educational ethnography*. London: Tufnell Press.

Vermeer, P. (2012). Meta-concepts, thinking skills and religious education. *British Journal of Religious Education, 34,* 334–47.

Voegelin, E. (1952 and 1965) *The new science of politics: an introduction.* Chicago: University of Chicago Press.

Walbank, N. (2012). What makes a school Catholic? *British Journal of Religious Education, 34,* 169–81.

Watson, J. (2004). Educating for citizenship: the emerging relationship between religious education and citizenship education. *British Journal of Religious Education, 26,* 259–71.

Watton, V. (2005). *Religion and life.* London: Hodder Murray.

Wayne, E., Everington, J., Kadodwala, D., & Nesbitt, E. (1996). *Hindus, 'interpreting religions' series: the Warwick RE project.* Oxford: Heinemann.

Wells, A. S. (2009). *Both sides now: the story of school desegregation's graduates (The George Gund Foundation Imprint in African American Studies).* United States: University of California Press.

Wenger, E. (1998). *Communities of practice: learning, meaning and identity.* Cambridge: Cambridge University Press.

Wengraf, T. (2001). *Qualitative research interviewing: biographic narrative and semi-structured methods.* London: Sage.

Withey, D. A. (1975). Education and the cult of relevance. *British Journal of Educational Studies, 28,* 168–80.

Wright, A. (1993). *Religious education in the secondary school: prospects for religious literacy.* London: David Fulton.

— (2004). *Religion, education and post-modernity.* London: Routledge.

Index

Agreed Syllabus 52, 61, 65–71, 81, 119, 203, 234
Ahluwalia, L. 149
AHRC/ESRC Religion & Society Programme 1
Aldridge, D. 108–9
Allport, G. 207
ambitions 165, 196–7
Anderson, B. 166
Anderson, J. 161
Anthony, F.-V. 36
anthropology 1, 128, 251, 256, 258
Armstrong, D 72
Ashworth, P. D. 15
assessment 2–3, 24, 50–2
    Assessment is For Learning (AiFL) 51
    CCEA Exam Board 76
    Edexcel Examinations Board 70, 149
    exam boards 71, 76, 148
    exams 4, 123–4, 126, 129, 135, 137, 147–8, 160–1, 179–84, 196, 199
    GCSEs 57, 70–1, 76, 88, 113, 125–6, 128, 149–52, 156, 161–3, 183, 198
    OCR Exam Board 149, 161, 163
    QCDA Exemplification Materials 68
    SQA Intermediate 2, 54
attainment targets 74

Bahá'í 67
Ball, S. 63, 219
Banks, M. 154
Barnes, P. 68, 72, 74, 75
Barratt, M. 10
Barry, B. 102
Battaglia, D. 143
Baudrillard, J. 131
Baumfield, V. 5, 12, 58, 80, 86, 88, 96, 108, 135, 141, 169, 175, 178, 202, 206
Belmonte, A. 104
Berliner, D. 224
Berube, M. R. 191

Bible 46, 74, 77, 89, 94, 121, 127, 154, 156–7, 163, 165–7, 226
Black, P. 51
Blair Faith Foundation 184
Boal, A. 27
Boeve, L. 93
Bourdieu, P. 16, 139, 200
Breen, D. 207
Britzman, D. 107
Brookfield, S. 98
Brown, M. W. 15
Bruce, S. 124
Bryan, A. 104
Bryan, H. 96
Buddhism 38, 50, 67, 70–1, 122, 124, 156
Buie, E. 187
Burns, J. 117, 198

Callon, M. 142
Cameron, D. 129
Campbell, M. 149
Carr, D. 113
Carspecken, P. F. 15, 31
Catholic 47–51, 53, 56, 59, 68–74, 76, 78, 81–2, 92–4, 104–7, 109–10, 122–3, 133, 157, 160, 166, 190, 192, 194–6, 199, 201–3, 205–7, 209–16
    Church in Scotland 50, 77, 80
Chater, M. 5, 10, 54, 69, 221
Christianity 47, 52, 54, 58, 66–8, 70, 72–7, 80–2, 92, 100, 118, 124, 126, 128, 131–3, 136–8, 148, 151, 153–6, 166–7, 192, 194–5, 203, 206, 213, 221
Chun, W. H. K. 99
Church of England/Anglican 19, 66, 68, 71, 185, 192
Church of Ireland 74
Church of Scotland 134
citizenship 60, 79, 91, 103, 117–24, 132–3, 151, 185–6, 198, 210–11, 213, 216–17
Clarke, M. 224

Cochran-Smith, M. 174
Coll, R. 104
Collinson, C. 149
community 93, 125–6
Conquergood, D. 91
Conroy, J. 12, 14–15, 38, 59, 77, 79, 85, 104, 111, 118, 129, 138, 142, 152, 160, 190, 208, 210, 215
Contact Theory 207
Convey, J. J. 104
Cooling, T. 176, 198
Cooney, M. 92
Copley, T. 132
Cormack, R. J. 190
Coutts, N. 95
Cranston, N. C. 104
critical realism 108
culture 139, 150, 225
    educational 14, 19, 85, 95, 97, 99, 103, 139, 143, 181, 221, 232, 252
    political, 35–61, 88, 100, 211, 214, 262
    popular 133, 150, 159
    religious 117, 183–4, 200, 202, 252
Curriculum for Excellence 22, 42–3, 51, 80, 118
curriculum guidelines 5–14, 78–80
curriculum resources 119
curriculum shape 4, 59

Dahlberg, K. 15
Darling, J. 76, 79
David, R. G. 167
Davis, R. 36, 85, 190–1
Dawkins, R. 17
DCELLS 64
DCSF 42, 69, 71, 117, 123–5, 153
Delphi method 11–13, 16, 86–8
    analysis of 13
    rationale 12
Delphi seminar 5–6, 20, 29, 49, 58, 65, 82, 96, 108, 118–21, 134, 137, 169–72, 184, 206, 209, 213, 220
Department of Education: Northern Ireland 42, 52
Dewey, J. 39
DFES Circular 1/94 67
DFES Circular 3/89 66
diversity 3, 63, 101, 125, 129, 151, 191–2, 206–7

Donaldson, G. 175
Duns Scotus, J. 1

Eagleton, T. 55, 57
Ecclestone, K. 5, 128
Education (Scotland) Act 1918 78
Education Act 1870 66
Education Act 1944 65
Education Act in Northern Ireland 1947 74
Education and Skills Authority 73
Education Reform Act 1988 44, 65, 68, 74
Education Reform Order (Northern Ireland) 1989 74
Edwards, R. 142, 144
Egan, J. 10, 124
Egan, K. 101
Eke, R. 10
Engbretson, K. 147–8
epistemic 4, 31, 35, 37, 39, 46, 49, 55, 58, 65, 67, 69, 72, 118, 121, 124, 128, 138, 209, 212, 221
Erickson, F. 86–7
Erricker, C. 5, 10, 54, 69, 221
Esfeld, M. 57
ethnicity 18, 20, 25, 101–2, 202, 232–3, 236, 240–1
ethnography 207, 209
    analysis 26, 30–33
    challenges 16
    contextual themes 30
    encounter types 15–16
    feature of project 10
    fieldwork 17–20, 22
    focus of 20
    gathering data 20, 23–6
    hypothesis-oriented phase 31
    Kappa coefficient 32–3
    language-centred themes 31
    mapping of data 13
    as a method 9–10, 15
    models of 15
    multimodal 14, 87
    notes 152
    NVivo 8 database 29, 32
    pilot phase 30–2
    profiling 112
    pupil pursuit 23
    questionnaire 29–36, 173, 190–201

stages 15
template of project 12
themes 194
ethos 28, 30–2, 43, 92–3, 107, 124–5, 189, 199–206
evangelical 47, 81, 92, 110, 138, 156, 212
Ewing, K. P. 102
expectations for religious education 41–4

Fancourt, N. 51
Felderhof, M. 69, 139
Fenwick, T. 142
Festivals of Light 122
Findlay, L. 15
Forum Theatre 27, 30, 49, 178, 181, 184–5, 190
Franchi, L. 95
Francis, L. J. 10, 201, 203
Franken, L. 88
Freathy, R. 88, 216
Free Churches 61, 68

Gallagher, T. 73, 76, 191
Gardner, R. 190–1
Gearon, L. 92
Geary, P. J. 38
Geddes, G. 149
    Revise for Religious Studies GCSE 149
Geerinck, I. 95
Girard, R. 139
Glaser, B. G. 32
goals of religious education 36
Goldman, R. 154, 221
Goodwin, C. 87
Goodwin, M. 87
Gove, Michael 53
Green, E. 198
Greer, J. E 10, 206
Gregory, K. 224
Griffiths, J. 149
Grimmitt, M. 36, 45, 175, 178
Guardian 129

Hamilton, S. 151–2
Hand, M. 46
Hansard 53
Harrison. M.
    Thinking about God 149
Harrison, P. 166

Hayes, D. 5, 128
Hayward, M. 154
Head of Department 17, 39, 48, 53–4, 57, 88, 96–101, 105–6, 111, 121, 130, 143, 145–7, 156, 180, 183–6, 202, 213
head teacher 18, 23–4, 49, 54, 89–90, 92, 94, 105, 109, 125–6, 183, 185–6, 211
hermeneutics 86, 109
Hervieu-Léger, D. 39
Hill, R. 92
Hinduism 61, 67, 70, 130, 151, 158, 192
HMI 23, 78–9
Holmes, J. 87
homosexuality 47
Hopkins, G. M., inscape 1
Horder, D. 221
Hornberger, T. 207
Hull, J. 45, 66–7, 70, 221
Hulme, M. 196
humanism 67
Huntington, S. P. 219
Hyde, B. 10
Hymes, D. 15, 31

I'Anson, J. 176
inscape 1–3, 189
Inter-Faith Forum 75
Islam 44, 50, 52, 67, 70, 75, 98, 122, 126, 133, 136, 148, 153, 156, 160, 163, 195
Issitt, J. 141, 150

Jackson, R. 10, 95, 119, 123, 146, 153, 161, 176
Jainism 67
Judaism 67, 70, 75, 98, 133, 151, 156, 192
Judge, H. 59

Kant, I. 139
Kassam, K. A. 129
Kerry, T. 21, 124
Kippax, S.,
    Thinking about God 149
Koran/Qur'an 127, 135–6, 154–5, 157–8

Laats, A. 107
Laidlaw, J. 77
language 6, 30, 35, 37, 39–40, 43, 48, 54, 56, 64, 80, 82, 103, 106, 108, 126, 131, 133, 139, 157, 213, 224–6

Latour, B. 142–4, 150–1
Law, J. 142
Lefstein, A. 144
Leigh, I. 95
Lijphart. A. 191
Linstone, H. A. 11
literacy 31, 36, 43, 103, 209, 219, 222–5, 254, 260, 264
Lloyd, I. 114
Local Education Authority 66, 73, 79
Loobuyek, P. 88
LTS 80, 118
Lundie, D. 12, 14–15, 59, 135, 202, 210
Lundy, L. 73
Lytle, S. L. 174

McAdam, N. 124
McArdle, K. 95
McGovern, D. 208
Macintyre, T. 151–2
McKinney, S. 92
Maclure, M. 86
Marginalization 161
Mayled, J. 161
    Discovery 149
media (news, newspaper, TV) 39, 99–100, 132–3, 141, 153, 162, 163, 235
    newspaper 162
    portrayals of religion 132
Mercier, C. 10
Methodist Church 74
Milbank, J. 155
Mitchell, C. 72
moral 38, 40, 42–3, 46, 50–1, 53, 58, 71, 74, 77, 79–80, 85, 91, 95, 101, 107, 118–20, 125, 129–30, 132, 137, 143, 151, 153, 162, 169–70, 174, 181, 184, 201–2, 204–5
moral claims 120
moral development 43, 118, 129, 153
Morphy, H. 154
Moulin, D. 99
multicultural education 4, 9, 82, 101–4, 106–7, 113, 118, 123–4, 202, 224–5
    in Northern Ireland 75–6
    in Scotland 76–7
multiculturalism 4, 31, 43, 118–25, 129, 139–40, 183, 191, 206–8, 212, 224–5
multi-faith approach 67, 75, 82, 154

Muslim 12, 18–19, 44–5, 47, 61, 68, 81, 98, 128, 130, 135–6, 148, 152–4, 157–8, 160, 192

Narisetti, I. 139
National Association of Teachers of Religious Education 170, 175
national curriculum 67–9, 80, 152
National Exemplar Framework for Religious Education- Wales 72
National Framework 67–71, 118
nested identity 58–60, 169, 190–1
Newby, M. 152
Nicholls, J. 165
Nichols, S. 224
Non-Statutory National Framework for England 41, 58, 63, 66–8, 71, 82, 118
normative (normativity) 1, 10, 57, 69, 83, 91, 103, 149, 179, 187, 219
Northern Ireland Core Syllabus 1993 76

ODIHR 54
OECD 198
Ofsted 23, 119, 123, 137, 161, 181, 196
O'Grady, K. 175, 179
O'Hagan, F. 190–1
Open College Network 161
otherness 58, 123–4, 131, 134, 140, 212, 226

pedagogy 4, 101–5, 120, 122–3, 126, 129–33, 137–40, 158, 163, 171–2, 184, 196, 211–15, 222
    role of teacher 95–100, 111–12
Pentecostal 126
personalism 5
Pettigrew, T. F. 207
philosophy 12, 28, 54, 57, 71, 88, 95–7, 111–14, 126, 128, 139, 148, 161, 170, 174, 197
Pinar, W. 224
Pinker, S. 225
pluralism 43, 61, 111–12, 117–29, 137, 139–40, 206
policy 2, 5, 52–5
    as enacted in classroom 19
    legislative differences across the UK 4
    literature of 11
    multiculturalism in 118–19

objectives 30
professionals who shape 11–12
relation between policy and
    practice 105, 143, 171
in Scotland 76
Pope, A. 35, 41
Presbyterian Church 74, 77, 79, 131, 192
Presskill, S. 98
Protestant 18, 72–4, 76, 166, 191
PSHE (Personal, Social and Health
    Education) 42, 185–6, 198, 210–11,
    216

QCA 58, 64, 67, 69, 117, 148

racism 44, 101–2, 106, 125, 190, 202, 216,
    224
RE Council 67
reincarnation 47
research design 3, 26
resources 2, 3, 9, 12, 14, 19, 23, 25, 28,
    31, 53, 71, 76, 78, 92, 99, 101, 119,
    142, 144–53, 158, 161, 163–6, 179,
    197, 209, 220, 223, 232–7, 239,
    249, 262
Revell, L. 96
Richards, J. C. 147
Richardson, N. 76
Ritchie, D. 191
Rose, G. 172
Rymarz, R. 147

Sackman, H. 12
SACREs 11, 52, 54, 58, 61, 66, 68, 80, 119
SCAA model syllabuses 67
Schagen, I. 198
Schagen, S. 198
Scheele, D. S. 172
Schihalejev, O. 214
schools,
    selection of 17
Schweitzer, F. 36
Scottish Central Committee on Religious
    Education 77
Scottish *Curriculum for Excellence* 42–3,
    51
Sharpley, R. 92
Sikhism 61, 67–8, 70, 160, 192, 226
Sikka, S. 102

Skulmoski, G. J. 11
Smart, N. 221
Snell, J. 144
social constructivism 222–3
social practice of religion 10, 37–8, 57–9,
    74, 79, 117–18, 123, 129–30, 136, 159,
    169, 176, 193–6, 199–200
Spradley, J. P. 14
Standing Advisory Council on Religious
    Education 11, 66, 202
Stenhouse, L. 178
Stern, L. J. 107, 119, 129, 175, 178, 179
Stone, P. R. 92
strangeness 3–4, 41, 45–6, 51–2, 55,
    57, 59, 61, 68, 80, 121, 123, 129, 133,
    135, 139
Strauss, A. L. 32
Strhan, A. 108
Stubbe, M. 87
student questionnaire 191–217
student voice 5, 25, 38, 40, 47, 56, 89, 97,
    99, 113–14, 122, 126–7, 131–5, 137–8,
    155–6, 160, 165, 177, 182, 197–8,
    225–6
Sturm, J. 191
sublimated dissonance 37
Swayne, L. 104

taxonomy 112–13
teachers,
    access to data and research design 22
    identity of 102
    role of the teacher 4, 111–12, 129–31,
        136–40, 163, 176–9
    voice 47, 50, 104–5, 107, 113, 126–7,
        131–4, 136–7, 147, 152–3, 155–7,
        162–3, 173–4, 178, 194, 198, 200, 205,
        225–6
textbooks 4, 141–67
    authorship 160
    and other devices 142–3, 163
    panoramas 154, 165
    relationship with exams 147–50, 160–1,
        165
    relationship with teacher 143, 146–9,
        152, 160–5
theology 1, 124, 149, 170, 171, 226
This is Our Faith 50
Thompson, P. 151

transcendent 38–40, 50, 61, 109, 111, 135, 139, 162
Tropp, L. R. 207
truth as taxonomy 112
truth claims in the classroom 4, 43, 71, 86, 108–14, 126

University of Glasgow 27, 29

value/s 5, 30–2, 37, 42–4, 54, 58, 85, 89, 92–5, 98, 101, 104–7, 110–11, 118, 125, 129, 131–2, 134, 136–40, 162, 181, 196, 201, 204, 213, 216, 222
Vermeer, P. 89
Voegelin, E. 39, 61

Walbank, N. 104
Warwick Religious Education Research Unit 10, 25, 175–6
Watson, J. 216
Watton, V.,
    Religion and Life 149
Wayne, E. 10
Wells, A. 191
Wenger, E. 186
Wengraf, T. 33
Wiliam, D. 51
Withey, D. A. 101
Wright, A. 10, 36, 108, 176

Zoroastrianism 67

CPSIA information can be obtained
at www.ICGtesting.com
Printed in the USA
LVHW080016040119
602644LV00007B/133/P

9 781474 23465